00312

S0-BEC-272

ABOUT THE PUBLISHER
The New York Institute of Finance

... more than just books.

NYIF offers practical, applied education and training in a wide range of financial topics:

* *Classroom training:* evenings, mornings, noon-hour
* *Seminars:* one- and two-day professional and introductory programs
* *Customized training:* need-specific, on your site or ours, in New York City, throughout the United States, anywhere in the world
* *Exam preparation:* NASD licensing (including Series 7), CFA prep, state life and health insurance licensing

Subjects of books and training programs include the following:
* *Account Executive Training*
* *Brokerage Operations*
* *Futures Trading*
* *International Corporate Finance*
* *Options as a Strategic Investment*
* *Securities Transfer*
* *Technical Analysis*

*When Wall Street professionals think **training**, they think **NYIF**.*

Please write or call for our catalog:

 **New York Institute
of Finance**
70 Pine Street
New York, NY 10270–0003
212 / 344–2900

Simon & Schuster, Inc.   A Gulf+Western Company
"Where Wall Street Goes to School"[tm]

THE NEW YORK
INSTITUTE OF FINANCE
GUIDE TO
INVESTING

New York Institute of Finance

Library of Congress Cataloging-in-Publication

New York Institute of Finance guide to investing.

Bibliography.
Includes index.
1. Investments—United States. 2. Securities—
United States. 3. Brokers—United States. I. New
York Institute of Finance.

HG4921.N53   1987   332.6'78   87–11323
ISBN 0–13–620436–8

This publication is designed to provide accurate and authoritative information in regard to the subject matter covered. It is sold with the understanding that the publisher is not engaged in rendering legal, accounting, or other professional service. If legal advice or other expert assistance is required, the services of a competent professional person should be sought.

From a Declaration of Principles Jointly Adopted
by a Committee of the American Bar Association and
a Committee of Publishers and Associations

© 1987 by NYIF Corp.
A Division of Simon & Schuster, Inc.
70 Pine Street, New York, NY 10270

All rights reserved.
No part of this book may be reproduced
in any form or by any means without permission
in writing from the publisher.

Printed in the United States of America

10 9 8 7 6 5 4 3 2

New York Institute of Finance
(NYIF Corp.)
70 Pine Street
New York, New York 10270

Contents

3

There's More Than One Way to Invest, 37

4

There's More Than One Market, 71

5

General Investment Goals and Guidelines, 89

6

Determining Your Investment Goals, 107

7

Opening an Account, 123

8

Entering an Order, 135

9

Security Analysis, 143

10

A Case Study in Securities Analysis, 163

11
Technical Analysis, 213

12
Your Rights as an Investor, 241

Introduction

For most people, the word "investing" means the same as the "stock market" or "Wall Street." On the evening news, you hear that the "market" is up, down, or unchanged. In newspaper and magazine articles, you read about "Wall Street" trends and developments. Advisory services try to convince you of their success in predicting "stock market" trends.

If you are about to invest for the first time, you might have two impressions: (1) that the stock market is the only game in town and (2) that Wall Street is the only place it's played.

But neither impression is correct.

First, the stock market is only one area of investment. While many people choose to put their money into stocks, many others invest in bonds, U.S. government securities, municipal bonds, mutual funds, options, and even commodities. In fact, despite the size and activity of the stock market, it is dwarfed by other securities markets. For example, on an active trading day, about 20 million shares of stock are traded in the United States—a volume measured in billions of dollars. Yet it represents only a small fraction of the daily dollar volume of the government securities market.

Second, Wall Street is *not* the only investment arena. The securities markets extend far beyond southern Manhattan. In addition to the New York Stock Exchange and the American Stock Exchange in New York, there are a number of regional exchanges throughout the United States. Millions of trades take place every day on the floors of these exchanges. Operating side by side with the exchanges is the over-the-counter (OTC) market, in which transactions are negotiated over the phone and information communicated via computerized networks.

That's just the U.S. market. Overseas markets include the London Stock Exchange, the Tokyo Stock Exchange, and many others. With nearly instantaneous, worldwide data transmission an everyday occurrence, international stock trading is becoming increasingly commonplace.

The New York Institute of Finance Guide to Investing takes you through the world of investments, acquainting you with the brokerage firms, the investment products and services, the markets, and the methods of investment analysis.

- Chapter 1 explains the services offered by brokerage firms and what you may expect from them.
- Chapters 2 and 3 describe the various types of products available to investors.
- Chapter 4 is a tour through the exchange and over-the-counter markets.
- Chapters 5 and 6 help you to define your investment goals—what you need or want to do with your disposable money. They also enable you to determine *whether* you should be investing in securities.
- Chapters 7 and 8 show you how to open an account with the brokerage firm of your choice and how to enter an order. They also explain what you should expect from the firm and how to avoid problems.

- Chapters 9 through 11 explain the various methods used by investors—both individual and institutional—to select profitable investments.
- Finally, Chapter 12 outlines your rights as an investor—the steps to take if you feel you have been wronged.

At the end of the book, a listing of regulatory agencies' addresses and phone numbers, an extensive glossary, and an index make this a book that you will use for a long time.

If you are about to make an investment decision for the first time—or if you have been wanting to know more about investing—this *Guide* will answer your questions and help you to make intelligent, informed decisions.

1

The Brokerage Firm and You

What the Brokerage Firm Does for the Investor

You can buy and sell many things—even "big ticket" items such as cars—without the professional advice of a salesperson, lawyer, or accountant. Although it is not advisable to do so, people sometimes even buy or sell real estate without the aid of an agent or lawyer. People are free to buy and sell almost anything without involving professional salespeople, but legal problems may arise.

So it is with securities: You may buy and sell stocks and bonds without a lawyer or salesperson (that is, a broker or "stockbroker")—there's no law against doing so—but you run into many difficulties if you try. For instance, if you were to buy a stock without going through a brokerage firm you would have to deal with these questions:

- How do you get in touch with someone who owns the stock in the quantity you want to buy and who is willing to sell at or below the price you want to pay?

- How do you execute the transaction? Do you arrange for a meeting with the seller, at which time you exchange your payment check for the stock certificates? If a meeting is not possible, do you mail a check to the seller, who waits for it to clear before sending you the stock?
- How do you verify that the stock certificate is bona fide or that the seller is the rightful owner?
- Where do you keep your stock so it is safe from fire and theft?
- If the certificate is lost or destroyed, how do you prove that *you* are the rightful owner?

When you were ready to sell the stock, you would have to go through a similarly troublesome procedure. Obviously, if every investor had to conduct transactions in this way, the stock market could not be as large or active as it is.

Order Execution and Clearance

A brokerage firm handles all these matters for you. In fact, most investors are totally unaware of such services except when an occasional error is made. For the most part, once you have an account with a brokerage company, all you have to do is call your stockbroker and explain what transaction you want to make. Usually within minutes, the broker returns your call, confirming execution of your order. You buy or sell stock, but all you are aware of is that brief conversation with the salesperson. Your part in the actual trade is as easy as that. (Of course, the decision to buy or sell is not so easy. Questions about whether the market is going up or down, where it is headed tomorrow or next week, which stock to purchase, what price is "right," and when to sell are dealt with in later chapters.)

When you place an order with the stockbroker, you generally don't see how much behind-the-scenes activity takes place. As the broker receives your order, an order ticket is filled out. After you hang up, the order is passed to the firm's order room, whose staff executes it. From that point, a series of clearing operations takes place, whereby the stock is paid for and the new owner's name recorded. The actual stock certificates are sent to the new owner or held by the brokerage firm. All the paperwork is handled in compliance with federal and other regulations, out of the customer's sight. By providing order execution, clearing, and other services, brokerage firms enable millions of investors to participate in the stock market every day. Because investors can buy or sell so readily, stocks are considered *liquid* investments, that is, stock owners can convert their stocks into cash quickly and easily by selling them in this very active marketplace.

Roles of the Brokerage Firm

For the services provided to investors, the brokerage firm charges a *commission*, which is usually a percentage of the total dollar amount of the transaction. For example, let's say that you've told your stockbroker to buy 100 shares of ABC stock, and the order is executed at $17 per share. You have just spent $1,700, that is $17 times 100 shares. The brokerage firm might charge you a 2.5% commission for execution and clearing; that comes out to $42.50 ($1,700 times .025). The total cost of the purchase and commission is $1,742.50 ($1,700 purchase price plus $42.50 commission).

From the brokerage firm's point of view, individual investors like yourself represent *retail* clientele, as opposed to their "institutional" customers. Investors' commissions—or *retail* commissions—represent only part of a brokerage firm's revenues. Other earnings come from the purchase and sale of stocks and other securities in behalf of the firm itself. When a firm executes a trade in behalf of a customer (retail *or* institutional), it is said to be acting as a *broker* or *agent*: the two words mean the same thing. When the firm buys and sells for its own account, it is acting as a *dealer* or as *principal*: again, these two terms are synonymous. Most firms, large and small, act in both capacities; so you might hear them referred to as *broker/dealers*.

In both roles the broker/dealer is said to be acting in the *secondary market*, the market you hear about on the nightly newscast and read about in the daily newspaper. Stocks (and other securities) trade hands in this secondary market every day.

What, then, is the primary market? This market is where stocks (and bonds) first become available to the public. When a corporation wishes to raise money, one way to do so is to *issue* stocks or bonds in what is known as an underwriting. In an *underwriting*, the brokerage firm buys the new stock or bond issue and resells it at a higher price to investors, thereby earning a profit. In this process (whereby capital is raised for American businesses), the brokerage firm is said to be acting as an *investment banker*. Underwritings are usually handled by groups of firms, rather than just a single firm, who all act as investment bankers. In this way, the underwriters dilute the risk and facilitate the sale (or *distribution*) of the issue. Once the issue is sold (distributed), it is traded in the secondary market.

These roles—agent, principal, and investment banker—are assumed by the brokerage firm. Perhaps you can see where you fit in as an individual investor, or a potential investor. Your investment dollars, along with those of millions of other investors, become part of the American investment marketplace, or *capital market*. Your dollars help to finance business if you invest in corporate securities, and government if you buy U.S. Treasury or state authority bonds. In the process, you stand to gain if the value of your investment rises, and the brokerage firms can gain by earning commissions on your trades and profits on their own.

What the Stockbroker Does for You

At one time, the term *stockbroker* was perfectly appropriate for describing the sales representative of a brokerage house. The representative acted as a broker for the firm's customers and dealt for the most part in stocks only. Earnings came from the commissions that the firm shared with the representative. The stockbroker was therefore also called the "customer's man."

Nowadays that same person may be called a *registered representative* (because registration with the National Association of Securities Dealers is required), an *account executive* (AE), a *financial counselor*, or a *financial advisor* or *consultant*—the titles vary from firm to firm. All the titles, however, reflect a greater responsibility than just brokering stock. Sales representatives are now more like financial advisors than ever before: Their role is not merely to execute orders in behalf of their clients, but to become sufficiently familiar with their clients' financial situations to plan for them, or at least to make intelligent, informed recommendations.

To function as representatives in the securities industry, salespeople must possess a working knowledge of a broad array of investment products. They must also be sensitive to the requirements of all regulatory bodies, such as the Securities and Exchange Commission (SEC), the National Association of Securities Dealers (NASD), or the exchanges—to name just a few. Everything they do as registered representatives (or account executives) is subject to stringent regulations.

To assure a minimum level of competence among these financial professionals, the SEC requires all would-be representatives to take a vigorous examination, prepared by the New York Stock Exchange and administered by the NASD. Passing the examination entitles reps to deal with customers, but it is only the beginning of the learning process. Once in practice, they must continually learn what they can about investment products, old or new, and about their clients' needs and objectives.

The account executive's job is not easy. Earning a living means doing all the things that other successful salespeople do: constant prospecting, asking for referrals, servicing accounts, and so on. Yet all this must be done in an environment that is laced with regulation upon regulation. A false step, however unintended, can incur penalties from fines to loss of job or even imprisonment.

Another aspect of the AE's job makes it more difficult than those of most other financial professionals: When you engage the services of a lawyer or accountant, you don't necessarily have to understand why you must sign a document placed before you or how your tax return was calculated. The AE who recommends an investment to you, however, is responsible to be certain that you understand the nature of the investment, its risk, and its potential return. You have to "own" the investment decision because *you* initiate the order, not the broker. If you enter into an investment that is unsuitable for you, and the AE lets you do so, the sales representative and/or the firm can be held responsible for any losses you incur. As a result, part of the AE's task is to educate you, the client. Your responsibility of course, is to learn the language and business of the securities industry. This book will help you get started on that learning process.

Full-Service and Discount Firms: You Pay for What You Get

For most of the U.S. stock market's history, commission rates were fixed. No brokerage house was permitted to charge less than industry-wide minimums. Then came May Day, or May 1, 1975. On that day, commission rates became *negotiable*. That is, brokerage firms could charge as low or as high a commission rate as the competition or profit margins allowed. With negotiated commission rates, firms could charge a higher or lower commission rate, depending on the services they rendered to the investor. In this regard, brokerage firms are broadly classified as either full-service or discount brokerages. The following describes the basic differences in the services provided by each.

Full-Service Firms

A *full-service firm*, as its name implies, provides its clients with considerable assistance, generally in the form of the following five types of service:

1. *Investment research*. Analysts are employed by the firm to watch the markets, seek out good investments, and furnish

research reports to the sales staff, who use the information in making recommendations to their clients.

2. *Asset management*. A number of brokerage companies offer cash management accounts, which serve as savings accounts, checking accounts, and investment accounts—all in one. As an example of this type of cash management, suppose you sold some stock but are not sure where to place the sales proceeds. You can "park" the money in the firm's money market account and earn moderate interest income while you make up your mind.

3. *Investment advice*. The research department's analysts make recommendations in general, but only your account executive can give you advice to suit *your* individual financial goals and personality. The full-service AE, in touch with a number of investment products and markets, is responsible to give you the best advice possible for your situation and objectives.

4. *Order execution*. As you will see in Chapter 8, the brokerage firm is set up to execute your order for the best available price in the appropriate market. Most orders can be executed in minutes.

5. *Clearing*. Every order execution has a long paperwork "trail," most of which is necessary for legal reasons.

Full-service firms fall into several categories. *Wire houses* are very large, diversified firms, whose names are generally familiar even to noninvestors: Merrill Lynch, E.F. Hutton, Dean Witter Reynolds, Shearson/American Express, Prudential Bache, and Smith Barney. As large as these firms are, they still try to expand their retail business (that is, open accounts for individual investors). They are the department stores of the investment world, offering the investor a wide range of investment products and the means to keep checking, savings, and investment monies all in one account.

In contrast to wire houses, *specialized firms* deal in only one type of product, for example, U.S. government or municipal bonds. Perhaps the best known specialized firm is Lebenthal &

Co., specialists in municipal bonds. Other specialty firms are not as familiar to the general public.

Another type of firm is the New-York-based house, whose clients are well-heeled and very sophisticated in investment matters. Firms such as Morgan Stanley, Donaldson Lufkin, and Bear Sterns are sometimes referred to as *carriage trade houses* (a reference to the "limousines" of the past). These companies offer especially well-developed research reports, savvy representatives, and extremely personalized service. In addition, as one of their clients you would have the opportunity to purchase new issues of stocks and bonds (the primary market).

This type of firm is not nearly as interested as the wire house in the typical investor's account. The clientele of carriage trade houses is upscale, and you generally need a reference from one of the firm's own clients to open an account. Besides, these houses do not usually provide the range of overall financial services you can get elsewhere.

Firms such as Gruntal, Butcher and Singer, Mosely, Thomson McKinon, and Advest offer characteristics of both the wire houses and the carriage trade houses. These firms provide all or most of the products and services of the large wire houses, but cater to the small and medium-sized investor in a more personalized way. For want of a better term, we call them *boutique firms*.

Regional houses also seek retail accounts. They are not as large as the wire houses, but they offer personalized service that makes doing business a pleasure. Although their research staffs are limited in size, they often "discover" local companies that are good investments. If you don't need the national contacts or the cash management accounts offered by the wire house, the regional firm is a likely candidate for your investment dollars.

Discount Firms

A *discount firm* differs from a full-service house in that it basically furnishes only two services: *order execution* and *clearance*. You do your own research and security analysis, picking your investments without the help of the firm. Typically, your account executive is a voice at the other end of a toll-free phone line. (The alternative to a toll-free line is a branch office, the cost of which only increases commission rates.) The representative (who probably works on salary instead of for commissions) takes your order and confirms its execution. The back office takes care of clearing the transaction. Some firms offer a newsletter and possibly a money market fund account, where your money can earn interest between investments. The advantage of accepting these reduced services is a substantial saving in commission dollars. Generally, discounters' rates are about a quarter to two-thirds lower than full-service firms.

Discount commissions generally take two forms (see Figure 1-1):

Figure 1-1. *Comparison of Full-Service and a Discount Firm's Commissions on Various Types of Investment Products.*

Stocks (See Chapter 2)

Number of Shares	Price per Share	Discount Broker	Full-Service Broker	Difference
100	50	$ 44	$ 98	$ 54 or 55%
300	20	$ 74	$150	$ 76 or 51%
500	30	$108	$280	$172 or 61%
1000	25	$137	$442	$305 or 69%
5000	8	$170*	$860	$690 or 80%

Options (Explained in Chapter 3)

Number of Contracts	Price per Contract	Discount Broker	Full-Service Broker	Difference
3	5	$48	$ 70	$ 22 or 31%
5	7	$70	$110	$ 40 or 36%
10	4	$75	$156	$ 81 or 52%
15	2	$65	$179	$114 or 64%
25	1¾	$79	$260	$181 or 70%

*Over the counter. Listed stocks are minimum 5¢ per share. ("Over the counter" and "listed" are explained in Chapter 4.)
(All transactions usually subject to a minimum commission.)

1. *A percentage of the share's price.* For example, if you sold 100 ABC stock at $20.50, you would pay a commission that represents a percentage of the total sale price: 100 ABC at $20.50 equals $2,050, times a commission rate of 1.1%, equals a commission of $22.55.

2. *A dollar amount based on the number of shares traded.* For example, if you bought 100 shares of ABC (at any price), you pay a fixed amount per share, such as 20 cents. In this case, the commission would be $20 (100 shares times 20 cents).

Full-Service or Discount Broker?

In deciding whether to go with a full-service house or a discounter, the chief consideration is obvious: *How much help do you need in making your investment decisions?* If you are confident of your own research and analysis, then a discounter is probably appropriate. If, on the other hand, you need assistance in these areas, as well as the personalized counseling of a representative, then full-service might be the better choice.

A "dollar-wise" argument may make the choice clearer. If you save commission dollars on a purchase executed by a discounter, the return on your investment would not have to be as great as if the order had been placed with a full-service house. For example, compare a purchase made through both types of firms:

	Commission	
	Full-Service	*Discounter*
Purchase	*(2.5%)*	*(1.1%)*
100 shares of ABC at $30: $3,000	$75	$33

If you add the cost of the commission to the price of the stocks, here's what you actually pay:

	Full-Service	*Discounter*
Price: $3,000 divided by 100 shares	$30.00	$30.00
Commission divided by 100 shares	$ 0.75	$ 0.33
Total	$30.75	$30.33

The stock purchased through the full-service house must rise $0.75 in value before you start to gain. The discounter-purchased stock needs to rise only $0.33. Given that information, the question you must answer is whether you can pick a stock whose value *will* appreciate sufficiently without professionally conducted research and investment advice.

Your Relationship with Your Account Executive

If you opt for a full-service house, the next step is to develop a relationship with a suitable account executive. (A discount firm will simply assign an AE to your account.) Finding an AE who meets your personal and financial needs requires an active search, because the AE/client relationship must meet the needs of both parties. For example, suppose you intend to periodically purchase stock for several thousand dollars and to hold it long term (for five years or more). Suppose also that your risk tolerance is low (that is, you prefer low-risk investments). If you were to open an account with an AE whose clients buy and sell more actively and who deal in relatively high-risk investments, your account might not get the attention it requires. To avoid this kind of situation, you should discuss your finances and aims openly and make certain that you understand what kind of account the AE is accustomed to handling. (Chapter 7 describes in detail how to search for a brokerage firm and account executive that are right for you.)

How Much Does the AE Need to Know?

The need for compatibility between client and AE raises the question of how much the AE needs to know about you personally, about your financial status, and about your financial goals. Questions your prospective AE would ask include:

- How much money do you earn a year?
- Do you have any savings?
- How much do you owe?
- Have you ever purchased stocks or bonds before?

You are not asked such questions every day; the answers are generally—and rightly—considered to be solely your business. Giving out this type of information can make a person uncomfortable or embarrassed, but the account executive is going to ask this much and more about your financial situation.

Does the AE really need all this information? Yes, to give you sound advice, the AE should be completely informed about your financial situation and objectives. Without a clear picture of your finances—your income, savings, other investments, and so on—an AE can only guess at what investments best suit your goals and how able you are to absorb possible financial loss.

At worst, customers who represent themselves as being "better off" than they really are can find themselves over their heads in investments that require more disposable cash than they have. At best, the AE may recommend investments that simply don't do what these customers want. It only makes sense to give your AE all the information required *(full disclosure)*.

The burden of full disclosure rests on the account executive or sales representative as well as on you. Rule 405 of the New York Stock Exchange is known as the "know your customer" rule. This rule obliges the account executive to get the information needed to provide proper service. (We explain this information in more detail in Chapter 7.) Full disclosure is so important that if you refuse to supply some or all of the information required, the brokerage firm may lawfully refuse to open an account for you.

This time-tested analogy explains the need for full financial disclosure: When you go to a doctor for an ailment, you serve your best interest by telling the doctor as much as you can about the problem. If you refuse to do so, the doctor may—and probably should—refuse to treat you. Information from you is needed to choose the proper treatment. The doctor who does not insist on full disclosure can easily do you more harm than good by treating you. Your relationship with the account executive is a professional one, as it is with a doctor, lawyer, or accountant. In fact, if an AE is ready to take your order before getting a complete accounting from you, you should consider whether his or her aim is to render a long-term professional service—or just to make a commission.

Does full disclosure give the AE the right to know whether you have accounts with other brokerage firms? You are not legally bound to tell the AE, but generally, both you and the AE can benefit by sharing this knowledge. If you feel that other account executives are especially suited to handling parts of your investment program, say so. By being open, you give all the AEs involved a greater insight into your financial situation. They can thus make recommendations that better suit your objectives and waste less of everyone's time. In the worst case, if you do not inform your AEs about your other accounts, one advisor who doesn't know about the other's activities may unknowingly counteract them. So be fully candid with everyone. No feelings should be hurt if you are dealing with professionals.

Even when dealing with a discounter, you must still fill out certain disclosure forms, and the AE is subject to the "know your customer" rule. Should you place an order that seems inconsistent with the information on the disclousre forms, the discount broker is obliged to make certain that you are not undertaking an investment position that is beyond your financial capabilities. Because the discount AE is serving more like a stockbroker and less as a financial advisor, however, more of the burden of prudence and discretion falls on your shoulders.

What to Expect From the AE

Full-Service Firm. When you pay for full service, you should get it. Some investors, however, abuse their right to consultation with the AE—they call to chat or to get information that is readily available in the financial news. If you call the AE without a sound business reason you only waste everyone's time and create a nuisance.

On the other hand, when you *are* calling for a legitimate purpose, the AE is obligated to take your call or return it. If your messages are not returned or your requests for information are ignored, don't stand for such treatment. Insist on proper service and, if you don't get it, take your business elsewhere. An effective client/AE relationship must work both ways.

When the relationship becomes unsatisfactory for either

party, often the cause is a lack of communication. For example, if you make a purchase of stock but do not have the financial means to make any other transactions for six months, make that fact known to the AE. You will spare yourself the awkward experience of having continually to reject the AE's recommendations during that period. The AE in turn, will not waste time making recommendations to you, and will not have to wonder what recommendation if any, *will* be acceptable to you. Your openness can prevent such difficulties.

Another element of a healthy relationship is mutual consideration: The AE should be sensitive to your need to feel comfortable with your investments, and you have to be considerate of the AE's need to use time efficiently. It's no secret that the time salespeople spend on nonsales-related activities is time taken away from selling activities. Time is an extremely precious thing to anyone who sells for a living and the AE, whose commissions and professional evaluation depend on sales generated, is no exception. In fact, the AE who habitually stays on the phone with you, talking about nonbusiness matters, is probably not doing what an AE is supposed to be doing—solving other clients' problems, reviewing research, and, above all, selling. If you expect considerate treatment from AEs, remember what time means to them.

You can handle some routine matters without having to go through the AE by working with the *sales assistant* (SA) at the brokerage firm. This person is sometimes the AE's personal assistant, but more likely the AE shares the services of a pool of such assistants. These people can be extremely helpful. For example, if you are waiting on an overdue check, want to make an address change, or have some other routine administrative matter, ask to speak with the assistant. In fact, get to know the SA's name; you can get many things done through this "office specialist." (By law, an assistant may *not* discuss an investment with you, much less express an opinion about a stock or the market. Generally, assistants are not registered and therefore are not permitted to advise clients. Even if an SA is registered, the brokerage firms usually prohibit everyone but their registered salespeople from making recommendations or rendering financial advice. So don't put the assistant on the spot by expecting such advice.)

On the other hand, obviously it is in the interest of your account executive to stay in touch with you and with your investments. Professional representatives gladly spend time with their clients to discuss a particular purchase or sale, a change in investment goals, or any question concerning their clients' financial situation. Investment advice is the primary service offered by the representative of the full-service firm. By all means, take full advantage of that service—but not of the AE. Before dialing the AE, ask yourself two questions:

1. Is the purpose of the call to obtain investment advice?
2. If the answer to the first question is no, can or should a sales assistant help me?

If using this kind of discretion makes you feel that you aren't "getting your money's worth," remember that you are actually making the best use of your time and the AE's. In the long run, the time you do spend in consultation with the AE will be far more fruitful and your relationship more beneficial for you both.

Discount Firm. With a discounter, don't forget that what you are paying for is only to have your order executed and the transaction cleared. You are not paying for research, asset management, or investment advice. You may therefore reasonably expect the AE to:

- take your order accurately and courteously,
- enter the order for execution, and
- confirm the execution to you by phone.

In addition, if a mistake is made, the AE should work with you to correct it promptly and satisfactorily.

What If It Doesn't Work Out?

Don't be surprised if you change AEs several times before staying with one. New investors often try a number of AEs and/or brokerage firms before finding the person and company that meet their needs. At some time you will probably break off with one account executive and start an account with another. How to do this and what to do if you feel you've been wronged are explained in Chapter 12.

Your Comfort Level

When dealing with a brokerage firm and its account executive, your comfort level is important. You must understand the language and phrasing that the AE uses in making proposals, and you must know what to expect when you speak with an AE or place an order. The rest of the book attempts to make you more knowledgeable about the mechanics of investing, and in so doing, to make you more comfortable when you pick up a phone and call *your* account executive.

2

What Is a Stock?

Everyone has heard of stocks and the stock market.

But what exactly *is* a stock? A stock represents a "share" of the ownership of a business. A stockholder or shareholder—an owner of stock—actually owns a percentage of the company. The more stock people own, the larger their share in the ownership. For example, a person who owns 5% or more of a company's stock is said to be a *major stockholder*.

In another sense, the term *share* may refer to a stock certificate; that is, a piece of paper (see Figure 2-1). Someone owning thirty shares of a company is issued one certificate representing thirty shares.

The rise and fall of a stock's price (value) is determined by the company's success or failure. If the company's management earns a profit, then the company's value increases, and so in turn, does the value attached to ownership of the company (its stock); when the company's value increases, your position as an investor can be very profitable.

But be cautious, many investment professionals maintain

Figure 2-1. *A Common Stock Certificate.*

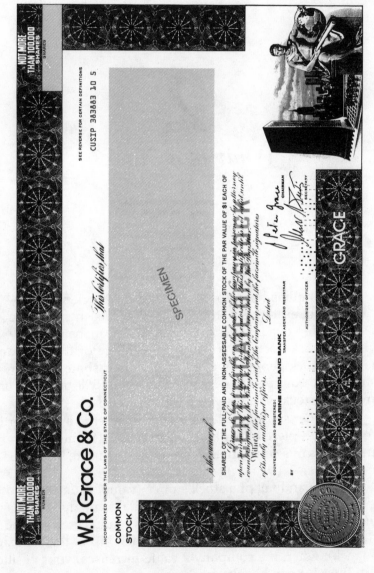

18

that to succeed in investing, you have to understand how business operates, that such knowledge is essential for success in selecting the investments most appropriate to your needs and goals. The following discussion gives some insight into the organization and capitalization of corporations—the businesses that issue stock.

Types of Business Organization

Three basic forms of business organization exist in the United States—the proprietorship, the partnership, and the corporation. Only the corporation can issue stocks to investors, but to better understand the distinctive features of the corporation, we also discuss the proprietorship (sole ownership) and partnership.

Sole Proprietorships and Partnerships

Did you ever wonder why you can't invest in your local restaurant, dry cleaner, or grocery store? The reason is that such enterprises are in most cases set up as sole proprietorships or partnerships and not as publicly traded corporations. As a matter of fact, the number of sole proprietorships and partnerships existing in the United States far exceeds the number of publicly traded corporations.

Your neighborhood dry cleaner provides a good example of a sole *proprietorship*. Whether such a venture succeeds or fails depends almost exclusively on the skill and efforts of its owner and/or family members. "Sweat equity" is a key ingredient here, as most such ventures entail long hours of work and a willingness on the part of all family members to sacrifice.

The owner of a dry cleaning shop is required to wear a number of hats. Dealing with the general public in a courteous and friendly manner is but one responsibility. The proprietor must also be familiar with all the technical aspects of the business and be able to direct the work of others in the actual cleaning process. The owner must deal with suppliers; maintain the financial, employee-benefit, and tax records on a day-to-day basis; and have a working knowledge of real estate and site location. In addition, the owner has unlimited liability; that is, liability extends to the owner's personal assets, not just to the assets committed to the business. In effect, the sole proprietor is like a one man band, marching to its own beat.

As time passes and business grows, many sole proprietorships evolve into partnerships. (Or a business may also start up in the partnership form). The *partnership* form of doing business has a number of advantages over the sole proprietorship, although it too entails unlimited liability. A partnership brings with it other sets of hands as well as a different perspective on the whole business. Hopefully, the personalities and skills of the partners complement each other. Also, the partner most likely brings additional capital. The typical sources of capital for sole proprietorships and partnerships are the owners, family and friends, and the local bank. Lack of capital is a prime reason why a number of sole proprietorships and partnerships fail, and it may be the reason for a change from sole ownership to partnership. Many owners look to partnership for the mechanical and financial resources needed for the business to grow and expand.

Corporations

Our neighborhood dry cleaner successfully conducted business as a sole proprietorship, perhaps later as a partnership. Business is good. Why, then, should incorporation be considered?

First, a *corporation* provides its owners with *limited liability*, that is, the owners' losses are limited to the assets that were committed to the venture. Creditors of the corporation cannot lay claim to any other assets of the owners. Limited liability also insulates owners of a corporation and their assets from suits brought against it. Even the owners of a small business such as a dry cleaning store might expect to be sued at some time. Operating as a corporation serves to protect the owners' personal assets from debts and legal battles. (Although limited liability is very important, in many cases, a bank requires the owners to personally guarantee the debts of the corporation before it will make a loan to a *small* corporation. However, by personally guaranteeing the corporation's debts, the owner forgoes the benefit of limited liability and allows the bank to attach all the owner's assets if necessary, to settle the corporation's debts.)

Another important feature of the corporate form of business is its *unlimited life*. If a sole proprietor dies or if partners die or separate, the business legally ceases to exist. A corporation, on the other hand, requires an act of law for its dissolution, so it can survive the death or disagreements of its owners. The unlimited life feature of a corporation makes it easier for the owners to formulate plans for the disposition of their estates and to pass control to their heirs.

Further, a corporation can raise capital much more easily than a sole proprietorship or partnership. Lenders are more familiar and comfortable with a corporate borrower. The corporate form of doing business is more acceptable to them because of its limited liability and unlimited life. Although a bank may ask for the personal guarantee of the owners of a small corporation, the decision to make the loan is based on the corporation's assets, sales, and earnings record.

Capitalization of Corporations

While sole proprietorships and partnerships typically have to look to internally generated funds and bank borrowings to finance business expansion, operating as a corporation offers a number of alternative sources of capital for growth and expansion. A corporation can "go public" and can raise capital in the stock and bond markets. Stocks are covered in this chapter; bonds in Chapter 4.

Perhaps 100,000 or more corporations conduct business in the United States today. They range in size from local businesses with sales of less than $1 million per year to giant corporations with sales of $1 billion or more; some of them have been in existence since Revolutionary War days.

Private Corporations

The vast majority of the nation's corporations are privately owned by a few large shareholders who in most instances are the founders of the corporation or their descendants. The manner in which they conduct their affairs closely parallels the approach used by sole proprietors and partners. Growth and expansion are financed primarily by internally generated funds or by bank borrowing. In the case of many of these *private corporations*, management does not wish to relinguish absolute control over the corporation's direction. Therefore, they do not offer their stock to the public. Instead, the company sells stock directly to the individual shareholder, who is generally expected to hold the stock as a long-term investment, rather than trade it in the secondary market. (Because this process involves no underwriter or investment banker as middleman, and therefore no commissions or other sales-related fees, the overall cost of this type of transaction is low.)

Publicly Traded Corporations

Some corporate managements—approximately 25,000 in the United States—have elected to *go public* by offering the investing public an opportunity to buy their shares. A decision to go public is made for one of several reasons. First and foremost, going public is an excellent way of raising large amounts of capital to finance expansion. The exclusive use of internally generated funds and bank borrowings limits the type of projects that can be undertaken. The demand for large amounts of capital may be particularly intense if the company is in an industry experiencing rapid growth, and such a company is likely to find an investing public eager to buy its shares.

Second, many corporate officers view going public as a way of "cashing in" on the value of their holdings—whether for personal use or for estate-planning purposes. Holdings in a private corporation are often difficult to convert to cold hard cash, and valuing a private corporation for estate-tax purposes is also difficult. Going public solves both of these problems.

Companies may also choose to go public to retain key employees and reward them for their contributions to the growth of the company. By granting stock options to such employees, the company links their personal wealth and fringe benefits to the performance of the company.

The Process of Going Public

As an investor, you should be aware that the agreement of the underwriting firm to take a company public can take one of two forms. In the case of a start-up company, the *underwriter* (the investment banking/brokerage firm that handles the public offering of the company's common stock from beginning to end) typically offers to distribute the company's stock on a *best-efforts/all-or-none* basis, meaning that the underwriting firm gives no guarantee that it will succeed in distributing the stock; if it is unable to distribute all of the shares, it will not distribute any. Further, none of the underwriter's own capital is committed to the offering. (This type of agreement is commonly offered by small *over-the-counter firms*—organizations that buy and sell stocks in the over-the-counter market, as discussed in Chapter 4.) If the company seeking to go public has substantial assets and/or is enjoying rapid growth, it might be able to obtain a firm commitment from an underwriter. With a *firm commitment*, the underwriting firm obligates itself and its own capital to take the company public. Obviously, this type of agreement offers the company a much better basis for going public.

Once the underwriting firm and the company agree on their respective responsibilities, the next step is *registration*. The *registration* process defines the legal requirements and standards a company must meet before it can offer its shares to the investing public. The registration process is administered by the Securities & Exchange Commission (SEC), the federal agency established by act of Congress to oversee the nation's financial markets. As a result of the abuses uncovered during investigations into the causes of the Market Crash of 1929, Congress mandated that "full disclosure" be a key element in all public stock transactions. *Full disclosure* means simply that all available pertinent data must be provided to investors so that they can base their decisions whether or not to make a particular investment on the most complete and accurate information. The laws of the state in which the company is incorporated also require certain information to be filed with the state authorities. These state laws afford additional protections to the companys' shareholders.

In a public offering, the *prospectus* or *offering circular* is the basic disclosure document. For a public offering of more than $5 million worth of stock, a prospectus is required. SEC regulations spell out the information required for inclusion in the prospectus—such as management aims and goals, the use to which the proceeds of the public offering will be put, financials, and management background. If a company wants to raise $5 million or less in its initial public offering, an offering circular (as opposed to a full prospectus) is prepared and submitted to the Securities & Exchange Commission. Referred to as a "Regulation A offering," such filings are designed so that small companies can easily gain access to the capital markets. The emphasis is to simplify the normal disclosure process. While a company must still describe the same type of information in its offering circular, a less sophisticated and detailed treatment of the information is required for a Regulation A filing.

During the registration process, the underwriter's employees organize the selling effort. In the case of a small offering, the underwriting firm may be the sole seller of the stock. If the offering is for a substantial number of shares, a *syndicate* may be organized that consists of a number of brokerage firms under the direction of the major underwriting firm Account executives involved in the selling effort (also referred to as registered representatives) are furnished with copies of a *preliminary prospectus*, but sales cannot be consummated until the buyers receive copies of the final prospectus. At this stage of the underwriting process, brokers and account executives solicit indications of interest in buying shares from prospective investors. From the response to this solicitation, conclusions are drawn as to whether the offering should proceed. In the case of a best-efforts offering, the underwriting firm may with-draw from the offering at this point, whereas with a firm com-mitment, withdrawal is generally not possible.

The last step in a public offering is essentially to bring together the registration and selling effort. With approval ob-tained from the SEC, the final prospectus is printed and ar-rangements are made for its distribution. Funds received from customers for the purchase of shares are held in an *escrow ac-count*, separated from the underwriting firm's other accounts. When the full number of shares offered is sold and the money received by the underwriting firm, the offering is closed. The proceeds, less fees and charges, are turned over to the com-pany issuing the stock, and at the same time, the company authorizes the *transfer agent*, who handles the physical distribu-tion and recording of ownership of the stock, to release the shares to the underwriter for distribution to the buyers. The SEC is advised that the offering is completed and the company moves from the status of a private company to a publicly traded corporation.

Once the public offering is completed, the underwriting firm does not disappear from the scene. The underwriting firm continues to "make a market" in the company's shares, and advises management regarding the responsibilities that come with public ownership, including periodically furnishing finan-cial information to the SEC and shareholders, and holding the annual meeting of shareholders.

How Do You Go About Investing?

Now that you know how a company becomes a publicly traded corporation, you're probably asking yourself, *"How can I invest in a publicly traded corporation?"* The question can be answered in two ways. One approach is through an *equity investment*: You could purchase common stock or preferred stock if it is avail-able. Alternatively, you could make a *debt investment* by invest-ing in the bonds of the public corporation. (Bonds are discussed in Chapter 3.)

Common Stock

When you hear people discussing stocks and the stock market, they are for the most part talking about *common stock*.

Earlier in this chapter, we explained what a corporation is and how it acquires public status. When a company goes public, it offers the investing public the opportunity to own a part of itself by purchasing shares of its *common stock*. The bulk of the trading on the various exchanges is in common stock.

When you, the investor, purchase the common stock of a public corporation you make an equity investment: You are buying a "piece of the action." If the company prospers, this should be reflected in the higher price its common stock commands in the marketplace. Alternatively, if the company's fortunes wane, the price of its common stock will most likely decline. In purchasing common stock you make a bet on the company's future growth and profitability.

The return on your investment comes principally in the from of price appreciation, referred to as *capital gains*. You also receive a return on your investment in the form of dividends paid by the company on its stock. Companies are not obliged to pay dividends to common stockholders and in the case of a company that is enjoying rapid growth in sales and earnings, investors probably prefer that the earnings be retained in the business to fuel further growth. Hence, rapid-growth companies typically pay few, small, or no dividends, or they may offer stock dividends. (When dividends are paid in the form of stock, the common shareholders receive additional stock but each shareholder's percentage of ownership in the company remains the same.) Only in the case of mature companies or companies in regulated industries such as utilities, do investors concentrate their attention on the value of cash dividends paid out by the company.

Certain rights and privileges come with ownership of common stock. The federal securities laws require a public company to supply its stockholders with timely reports (quarterly and annually) of the company's financial condition and progress. Shareholders must also be promptly informed of any significant event affecting the company, such as the destruction of a plant, the resignation of a senior officer, or an offer to buy the corporation.

In addition, a company's management must solicit the votes of its shareholders on a yearly basis. This solicitation is in the form of a *proxy* statement, which requests that stockholders vote to approve the continuation of existing management; provides information about the stockholdings of all company officers, directors, and 5% stockholders; and discloses the remuneration paid to management. Any change in the corporation's charter must be approved by the stockholders. A public corporation is required to have an annual meeting of shareholders, which provides an open forum for management and shareholders to meet and exchange views and opinions.

Common stocks have other characteristics important to you as an investor. For the most part, common stocks are *easily transferable*; that is, ownership can readily be passed from and between individual and corporate owners. Because ownership of common stocks is readily transferable, an active and dynamic market generally exists for them. Common stocks are one of the most *liquid* forms of investment an individual can make. Be aware, however, that in the case of a corporation's bankruptcy, the claims of common stockholders are subordinate to the claims of debt and preferred shareholders. This fact should rem,ind you that as a common stockholder you own a "piece of the action" and stand to gain or lose according to the company's good or bad fortune.

As an investor, you should be familiar with certain key terms and concepts relating to commons stocks.

In today's world, par value has little significance. Most corporations assign a nominal par value to their stock. Many years ago, it was customary for the initial public offering price of a corporation's common stock to be known as its *par value*. Nowadays, par value has no real significance, and it is utilized only for bookkeeping purposes. The par value of common stock is not related to its book value or market value. Most major corporations assign a par value to their common stock of one to ten cents. Some common stock has *no par*!

When a business is incorporated, management decides how any shares it will *authorize* the company to issue. Typically, management authorizes a greater number of shares than it plans to offer initially so that additional shares can be offered in the future. These shares are called *authorized-but-unissued* shares. With stockholder approval, management can increase the number of authorized shares at any time. *Issued-and-outstanding* shares represent the number of authorized shares distributed among investors.

To make a new stock more attractive, the corporation may attach a *warrant* to the authorized-but-unissued stock. This gives the shareholder a long-term privilege to *subscribe* to common stock (agree to buy a new issue), usually at a fixed price. Even though the subscription price of a warrant is higher at the time of the offering than the market price of the underlying stock, warrants are appealing to investors because of the possibility of a high-percentage gain.

At some point after a corporation has become publicly held, management may decide to buy back or repurchase some of its common stock. Shares that are reacquired, or in some instances acquired by donation, are called *treasury stock*. A company may buy back its own stock if the stock is selling at an extremely low price or if management is trying to prevent an unfriendly takeover, to provide stock for acquisition of other companies, or to fulfill stock option commitments. Reacquired stock is called treasury stock because it is thought of as held in the corporation's treasury, as part of its assets.

Treasury stock can be a two-edged sword in the hands of a corporation's management. On the one hand, an organized program by a company to repurchase its own shares provides a floor for the price of the stock because the company probably represents the most important and wealthy buyer obtainable. On the other hand, such a program makes the stock less liquid and inhibits a takeover, possibly perpetuating incompetent management.

The term "float" is frequently used in discussing common stock. The *float* equals the number of shares outstanding less the number of shares held by corporate insiders, institutions, or in the treasury. Thus, the float represents the number of shares available for trading in the public marketplace. You might be surprised at how few shares of a particular company's common stock are available for trading. The calculation of the float brings into focus the extent to which institutions and insiders dominate and control a company's fortunes. The float also tells you as an investor how difficult or easy it would be to "accumulate a position," that is, to purchase or sell a large amount of the company's common stock.

The reasons for investing in common stock are as diverse as the categories of common stock in which to invest. Those investors concerned with preservation of capital and a fixed dividend rate typically concentrate their attention in the area of utility stocks and blue chips (companies with a long record of steady growth and uninterrupted dividend payments). At the other extreme, investors willing to risk losing all the money they commit to the stock market in return for the possibility, however remote, of finding the next IBM or Xerox, concentrate their attention primarily in the area of *over-the-counter stocks* and *new issues.* Because of the diversity and liquidity common stocks offer, they are by by far the most popular investment vehicle.

Preferred Stock

Preferred stock is another type of equity investment, which first became popular during the 1920s and 1930s as a hybrid form of equity investment prossessing some characteristics of common stock and some of bonds.

As an investor, you should understand the important characteristics of preferred stocks. Preferred stock represents equity ownership in a corporation, but to a limited degree. Preferred stockholders have no voice in selecting a company's officers and directors, but owners of preferred stocks are guaranteed a fixed dividend payment that takes precedence over any dividend payment to common stockholders. Preferred stockholders also have a more senior claim on the company's assets in the event of liquidation or bankruptcy. Only bondholders (and other creditors) come before preferred stockholders in such cases.

In spite of the apparent advantages of senior claims to

dividends and company assets, preferred stocks also have some negative features that you should be aware of. While the common stockholder can look forward to dividend increases as the fortunes of the company improve and to possible stock dividends or stock splits, preferred stockholders generally do not enjoy any of the benefits of growth and expansion. Because investors typically look to preferred stock for current income rather than for growth (capital gains), they are particularly concerned about the dividends paid on such stocks. Hence, any increase in the prevailing interest rate has a greater impact on the price of preferred stocks than common stocks.

For the knowledgeable and astute investor, cumulative preferred stock and convertible preferred stock offer the possibility of significant capital gains. *Cumulative preferred* simply means that the dividend accumulates and becomes a debt of the company in those years in which the company is unable to pay the preferred dividend. Also, no dividend can be paid on the company's common stock while the preferred dividend is owed. For the shrewd investor who recognizes a turn-around in the company's business, the purchase of the cumulative preferred stock with a substantial dividend owed may represent a potential windfall profit when the company "cleans-up" all the outstanding preferred dividends before resuming payment of dividends on its common stock.

Convertible preferred stock (preferred stock that is convertible into common stock) can also offer special opportunities to the knowledgeable investor. An investor who feels that some time may pass before a company achieves recognition in the marketplace as a "growth" company may purchase convertible preferred stock if the company has such an issue outstanding. By purchasing convertible preferred, the investor is assured of a fixed dividend payment while providing the option of converting from preferred to common stock if and when the company is recognized in the marketplace and its common stock appreciates. Generally, convertible preferreds are more volatile than straight preferreds because their price is affected by the market performance of the common stock to which they can be converted.

What are the characteristics of the investor who purchases preferred stocks? Buyers of preferred stocks are characteristically cautious in their approach to investing and concerned for current income. Federal tax law allows many corporations and institutional investors to shelter a portion of the dividends they obtain from their stock holdings, and this provides an added incentive for these investors to purchase preferred stocks.

Reading Stock Tables in the Financial News

Newspapers such as the *Wall Street Journal* and the *New York Times* publish stock tables that appear daily in the financial pages. (Bond tables and mutual fund quotations also appear in the financial news. We discuss them in Chapter 3.) The ability to read, understand, and extract information from these tables is of vital importance for successful investing. Figure 2-2 is an example of such a stock table.

What information can you obtain from the stock tables and what significance should you attach to it? The first column on the far left in Figure 2-3 gives you the 52-week high and low for each alphabetically listed stock. From the 52-week high and low you can determine if the stock is selling close to its yearly high or yearly low. Many investors are hesitant to buy a stock selling close to its yearly high because they feel that it may be *fully priced*; that is, its price already reflects the positive factors of the company's future growth and prospects. Many investors also believe that when a company's stock is selling at its yearly high, any further price rise may encounter "resistance" as analysts and investors question whether the company's prospects warrant such a price for its stock. As an investor you should give special consideration to the present price of a stock compared with its yearly high and low.

The first column to the right of the company's name gives the annual dividend paid; next to this is the *percentage yield*. These two columns are of particular importance to the investor seeking current income as opposed to capital gains. Such an investor typically concentrates on utilities and blue chips. The

Figure 2-2. *NYSE Stock Quotations.*

New York Stock Exch

CONSOLIDATED TRADING

A B C D

52-Week High	52-Week Low	Stock	Div	Yld %	PE Ratio	Sales 100s	High	Low	Last	Chg.
26½	13½	AAR s	.44	2.0	17	130	22¼	21½	22	+ ½
30	21¾	ADT	.92	3.8	...	123	24⅝	24¼	24¼	...
33	11½	AFG s	.08i	.3	17	176	30¼	30⅛	30¼	− ⅛
25⅜	13¾	AGS		...	13	130	19⅜	19¼	19¼	+ ⅛
15	9⅞	AMCA		...	263	5	10½	10½	10½	...
60⅝	37½	AMR		...	14	1239	55¼	54½	55¼	+ ⅝
27½	23¼	ANR pf	2.67	10.5	...	29	25¾	25½	25½	...
24	19¼	ANR pf	2.12	9.0	...	6	23½	23½	23½	...
12½	8½	APL		...	6	165	11⅝	11½	11½	− ⅛
16¾	10	ARX	.71t	6.1	11	72	11⅞	11⅝	11⅝	− ⅛
44⅛	28¾	ASA	2.00a	6.2	...	566	33⅛	32⅛	32¼	− ⅜
18⅜	9¾	AVX		2.8	...	383	11⅜	11	11¼	+ ⅛
32	22⅝	AZP	2.72	8.7	9	2863	31⅝	31	31⅛	− ⅝
55	26⅜	AbtLb s	.84	1.7	23	3965	50⅜	49⅝	49¾	− ⅜
32	19⅝	AccoWd	.56	2.1	18	48	27¼	27	27¼	+ ⅛
14⅞	9	AcmeC	.40	3.9	...	111	10⅜	9⅞	10¼	+ ⅜
21¾	17	AdaEx	1.90e	8.7	...	92	21¾	21⅜	21¾	+ ⅜
33⅜	16	AdmMI	.40	1.3	13	6	30	29⅞	29⅞	...
20⅜	11⅝	AdvSys	.83t	5.4	14	77	15¾	15⅛	15½	+ ⅜
32⅞	14⅛	AMD		...	...	8097	18⅛	17⅛	18⅛	+1⅛
12⅝	5⅝	Adobe n		...	...	35	7	7	7	− ⅛
18⅜	13¾	Adob pf	1.84	12.3	...	43	15	14⅞	15	...
20¼	15¼	Adob pf	2.40	13.2	...	102	18¼	18	18⅛	...
18⅜	7⅜	Advest	.12a	.8	11	217	14½	14⅛	14⅜	− ⅛
66¼	42¼	AetnLf	2.64	4.2	10	4036	62⅜	62	62¼	− ¼
57½	51½	AetL pf	4.28e	8.1	...	165	53	53	53	+ ¼
28¾	9¾	Ahmns s	.46	1.8	8	2823	27¼	26	26¼	− ⅝
5¾	2½	Aileen		...	85	94	4¼	4⅛	4¼	+ ⅛
41⅝	25¾	AirPrd s	.80	2.4	60	1407	33⅞	33	33¼	− ¾
27¾	16	AirbFrt	.60	3.0	17	37	20⅛	20	20	− ⅛
2⅛	⅜	AlMoan	1.60c	...	...	86	7/16	7/16	7/16	...
29	25⅝	AlaP pf	2.12e	7.9	...	1050	26¾	26⅝	26¾	+ ⅛
10¾	7⅝	AlaP dpf	.87	8.5	...	112	10½	10¼	10¼	− ¼
103½	67½	AlaP pf	8.16	8.3	...	z70	98	98	98	−1
92	68¾	AlaP pf	8.28	9.0	...	z320u	92½	91	92½	+1
26⅛	14¼	AlskAir	.16	.9	19	322	18⅜	17½	17¾	− ⅝
25	9⅜	Albrto s	.21	1.1	19	25	18½	18½	18½	+ ⅛
23¼	15¾	AlbCulA	.21	1.2	18	156	17⅞	17½	17⅞	+ ⅛
49½	26⅞	Albtsns	.84	1.9	16	136	45¾	44¾	44¾	−1
34⅝	22¾	Alcan	.80	2.7	...	1503	29⅞	29½	29⅝	− ¼
46¾	32	AlcoStd	1.24	3.0	18	130	41⅞	41⅝	41¾	...
40⅞	26½	AlexAlx	1.00	2.6	...	2774	38⅜	37	37⅞	− ¾
47½	22⅞	Alexdr		...	26	18	37¾	37½	37⅝	+ ¼
02	75½	AllgCp	1.54t	1.5	15	140u	104	100⅜	103	+2⅞
29	25⅝	AlgCp pf	2.86	10.2	...	x16	28½	28	28	+ ¼
28¾	11⅜	AlgInt	.35i	1.9	...	442	18½	18⅛	18¼	+ ⅛
19¾	9½	AlgIn pf	2.19	16.1	...	11	13⅝	13⅜	13⅝	+ ¼
95½	39	AlgI pfC	11.25	18.9	...	19	59¾	59½	59½	...
53½	28⅛	AllgPw	2.80	5.3	13	860u	53⅞	52¼	52⅜	− ¾
27¼	16½	AllenG s	.56	2.9	18	176	19⅞	19½	19½	− ½
28⅞	23½	Allen pf	1.75	7.0	...	34	25	25	25	...
45½	16½	AlldPd		...	31	57	45	44⅞	45	− ⅜
49½	36¾	AldSgn n	1.80b	4.2	...	4309	42⅜	41¾	42⅜	+ ⅜
114⅜	101½	AldS pfD	12.00	11.7	...	29	102½	102	102½	...
53½	25⅛	AldStr s	1.16	2.3	15	1012	52⅝	51	51¼	− ⅝
10⅛	4⅞	AlldSup		...	...	231	7½	7⅛	7½	+ ¼
6¾	2⅞	AllisCh		...	...	240	3½	3¼	3¼	− ⅛
40¾	26[illegible]	AlisC pf		...	...	1	28¼	28¼	28¼	+ ½
40½	26½	ALLTL	1.96	4.9	12	109	40⅛	39¾	40⅛	+ ¼
46⅜	31½	Alcoa	1.20	3.3	...	1211	36½	36⅛	36⅜	+ ⅜
16⅜	10½	Amax		...	...	596	12¾	12½	12⅝	+ ⅛
36	27½	Amax pf	3.00	9.1	...	1	33	33	33	...
32¼	16½	AmHes	.27i	...	...	817	19⅞	19½	19¾	+ ⅛
1⅞	⅝	AmAgr		...	...	62	15/16	⅞	⅞	...
31¼	19½	ABakr		...	14	49	30½	30	30½	+ ⅜
105	53¼	ABrand	4.05	4.3	12	1366	95¼	94⅛	94¼	− ⅝
34⅜	28	ABrd pf	2.75	8.2	...	107	33⅝	33⅜	33⅜	...
29	20⅞	ABldM	.90	3.4	19	15	26½	26¼	26½	...
36⅞	25⅜	ABusPr	.76	2.6	15	23	28⅞	28⅝	28⅞	...
89¾	50¾	AmCan	2.90	3.2	14	932u	91⅞	89⅛	91	+1⅜
77	44⅞	ACan pf	3.00	3.8	...	3u	78¾	77	78¾	+1¾
25	19⅝	ACapBd	2.20	8.8	...	94	25	24⅞	25	...
32⅞	25¾	ACapCv	2.73e	8.6	...	33	32	31½	31¾	− ¼
24¼	18½	ACMR n	.15e	.7	15	122	21½	21¼	21⅜	+ ⅜
7⅞	3¾	ACentC		...	...	63	4	d 3⅝	4	+ ¼
87	48⅝	ACyan	1.90	2.2	27	2614u	87¾	86⅛	87⅛	+ ⅜
31½	19⅞	AEIPw	2.26	7.3	13	3705	31⅛	30¾	31	− ⅛
70⅛	40⅜	AmExp	1.36	2.1	12	3680	64⅛	63½	63⅞	− ¼
37⅜	16⅛	AFaml s	.40	1.1	21	780	36⅜	35⅞	36	...
44⅜	27¼	AGnCp	1.12	2.6	11	2974	42¾	42	42⅜	+ ½
23	10¼	AGnl wt		...	...	203	21½	21	21¼	...
56¾	51⅞	AGnl pfA	4.63e	8.7	...	2	53½	53½	53½	...
44⅛	32⅛	AHerit	1.32	3.2	14	9	41½	41½	41½	...
12⅞	6⅛	AHoist		...	...	51	6½	6⅜	6½	+ ¼
25¼	19¼	AHoist pf	1.95	9.8	...	41	20	19⅞	20	...
94⅞	54¾	AHome	3.10	3.4	19	1449	91⅞	91¼	91½	− ½
148⅞	86⅞	Amrtch	7.08	4.8	13	668u	149¾	148¼	148⅜	− ½
141	81¾	AInGrp	.44	.3	20	533	136½	135¾	135¾	−1¼
228	137½	AIGp pf	5.85	2.6	...	1	221¼	221¼	221¼	−1¾
24⅞	13⅜	AMI	.72	4.6	...	4166	15⅞	14¾	15¾	+ ¾
5	2¼	AmMot		...	...	2551	2¾	2⅝	2¾	...
25⅝	13⅞	APresd	.50	2.0	61	994	25	23⅞	25	+1
52¼	48½	APrsd pf	3.50	6.6	...	1057u	53¼	52	53¼	+1⅜
18⅝	6	ASLFla		...	...	825u	18⅞	17⅞	18½	+ ½
24¼	13¾	ASLFl pf	2.19	9.1	...	162	24⅛	23⅞	24	...
15⅝	8⅞	AShip	.80	8.0	10	229	10	9½	10	+ ½
46⅞	27	AmStd	1.60	4.3	15	284	37½	37⅛	37⅜	...
71¼	53⅛	AmStor	.84	1.4	14	911	61½	60	61⅜	− ⅜
81	66	AStr pfA	4.38	6.0	...	137	73	71½	73	+1½
61½	55½	AStr pfB	6.80	11.4	...	294	59½	58½	59½	+1¼

MARKET INDICATORS

N.Y.S.E. Issues

Consolidated Trading

Dow Jones Stock Averages

	Open	High	Low	Close	Chg.
30 Industrials	1879.78	1898.06	1868.11	1887.80	+ 6.61
20 Transports	757.38	765.50	754.25	761.75	+ 4.62
15 Utilities	217.89	219.15	215.96	217.39	− 0.82
65 Stocks	727.88	734.66	723.43	730.46	+ 2.14

S.&P. Index

	High	Low	Close	Chg.
400 Indust	275.63	274.22	275.24	+ 0.63
20 Transpt	191.09	189.05	191.06	+ 1.45
40 Utilities	123.24	122.69	122.79	− 0.34
40 Financl	29.86	29.49	29.78	+ 0.21
500 Stocks	250.61	249.27	250.19	+ 0.52

N.Y.S.E. Index

	High	Low	Last	Chg.
Composite	143.94	143.50	143.88	+0.27
Industrial	163.19	162.66	163.13	+0.42
Transport	113.83	112.98	113.83	+0.70
Utility	80.31	80.11	80.19	−0.27
Finance	156.03	155.13	156.01	+0.70

Most Active

	Vol.	Last	Chg.
Benefl Cp	2,872,800	73	+28½
USX Corp	2,509,000	19¼	− ½
DominResc	1,741,500	51⅜	− ¾
Safeway	1,621,300	66½	+ ⅝
ICN Pharm	1,492,000	28	−2¾
IrvngBk	1,406,200	52⅛	− ⅜
ContrData	1,351,200	25⅜	+1⅞
SearsRoeb	1,143,100	47¾	+ ⅞
HolidayCorp	1,133,700	61	....
NatSemi	1,053,100	10⅛	+ ¾
Phila Elec	1,000,000	23⅜	....
HouseIntl	942,900	46¼	+2¾
Amer T&T	912,900	23½	....
AndrsClay	834,100	57½	+1⅛
Consu Pow	819,700	12⅛	....

Changes—Up

	Last	Chg.	Pct.
Benefl Cp	73	+28½	64.0
Texfi Ind	4¼	+ ¾	21.4
viGlobMr pf	3¾	+ ½	15.4
NtMineSv	4¾	+ ⅝	15.2
viCLC Am	2	+ ¼	14.3
Benefl 5pf	32¼	+ 3¾	13.2
KDI Cp	16½	+ 1¾	11.9
Frigitronc	37¼	+ 3½	10.4
CtrlData pf	45	+ 4	9.8
Wean Unit	2⅞	+ ¼	9.5

Changes—Down

	Last	Chg.	Pct.
ICN Phrm pf	58	− 7½	11.5
ICN Pharm	28	− 2¾	8.9
Fieldcrd	75	− 6	7.4
GoldnNug wt	2	− ⅛	5.9
LVI Grp	4	− ¼	5.9
CBI Ind	28½	− 1¾	5.8
Gen Refrac	14⅛	− ⅞	5.8
Fedders	8¼	− ½	5.7
Savin 1.50pf	4⅛	− ¼	5.7
Sabine	13¼	− ¾	5.4

Volume by Exchanges

Markets	Shares
NYSE	118,130,000
Pacific	4,762,700
Midwest	9,283,700
NASD	4,104,830
Boston	2,293,700
Cinci	296,200
Phila	2,518,500
Instinet	15,000
Total	141,404,630

Volume Comparisons

Day's Sales	118,130,000
Thursday's Sales	135,180,000
Year Ago	75,270,000
1986 to Date	22,639,550,793
1985 to Date	17,451,442,471

Market Diary

	Today	Prev.
Advanced	846	922
Declined	738	701
Unchanged	439	416
Total issues	2023	2039
New highs	113	172
New lows	9	9

Up-Down Share Volume

	Advanced	Declined
N.Y.S.E.	55,244,600	45,033,100
Amex	3,291,440	3,790,810

Odd-Lot Trading

Previous Day's Trading

purchases of 298,339 shares; sales of 524,788 shares including 36,377 sales sold short.

MARKET INDEX (N.Y.S.E.)

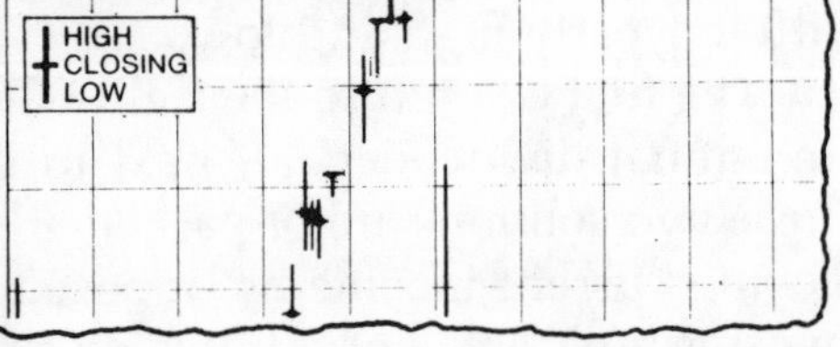
HIGH
CLOSING
LOW

Reprinted by permission of *Wall Street Journal.* © Dow Jones & Company, Inc., August 22, 1987. All rights reserved.

Figure 2-3. *Over-the-Counter Quotations.*

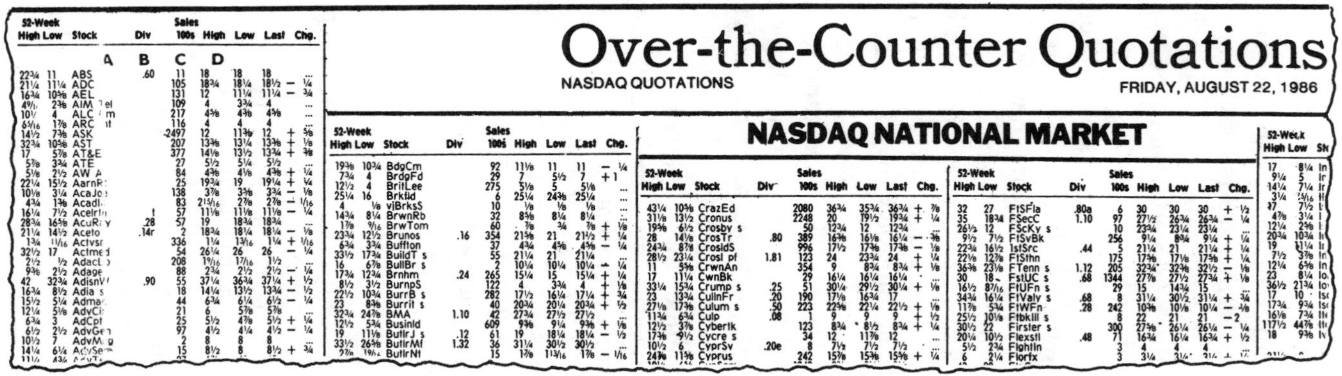

Over-the-Counter Quotations

NASDAQ QUOTATIONS

FRIDAY, AUGUST 22, 1986

NASDAQ NATIONAL MARKET

52-Week High	52-Week Low	Stock	Div	Sales 100s	High	Low	Last	Chg.
		A	B	C	D			

Reprinted by permission of Wall Street Journal. © Dow Jones & Company, Inc., August 22, 1987. All rights reserved.

percentage-yield column enables the investor to compare specific stocks in terms of the yields they offer.

The next column, price/earnings *(P/E) ratio*, is calculated by dividing the price of the company's stock by its current year's earnings per share. Price/earnings ratios vary, ranging from a low of 5 to 50 or more. Detailed studies have been conducted to determine whether investors should invest in low or high P/E stocks. Such studies seem to indicate that low-P/E stocks may ultimately become high-P/E stocks and are therefore a better investment. One reason given for this pattern is that low P/E stocks tend to be in industries followed by few, if any, analysts. When their growth is finally recognized, these stocks enjoy a rapid rise in price.

On the other hand, high P/E stocks tend to be the so-called institutional favorites. Stocks favored by a large number of institutional investors and followed by many analysts, are subject to wide price swings as their holders review their investments and react rapidly to changes in company prospects and/or earnings. Thus, in purchasing any stock, the current P/E ratio should be considered and compared to the P/E ratio of similar companies in the same or similar industries. If the P/E ratio deviates from the norm you should ask questions.

The remaining columns reflect the number of shares traded as well as stock price activity on the particular day. As an investor, you should focus your attention on the prevailing *trend* in volume and price rather than concern yourself with the details of what occurred on a particular day. Develop a feeling for what is the normal volume of trading in the particular stock and the normal price variation. If something occurs that does not seem quite right, think twice before you invest.

Over-the-counter stock information consists of two lists: the NASDAQ National Market Issues and the NASDAQ Bid and Asked Quotations. The NASDAQ National Market Issues listing is for the more actively traded stocks on the National Association of Securities Dealers Automated Quotation System (NASDAQ). Each trade must be reported to the National Association of Securities Dealers (NASD) within a minute and a half, so that up-to-date trading information about those securities is always available.

The second list for OTC stocks is the NASDAQ Bid and Asked Quotations, which describes less actively traded stocks. Because there is no central reporting of these trades, no up-to-date transaction prices are provided.

The stock pages also provide an analysis of the overall pattern of the market. Under the listing, Market Indicators, you can find a summary of the Dow Jones most active stocks and those stocks in the Dow Jones Average whose prices rose or fell the greatest percentage. This section highlights the overall direction of the market and what particular stocks and categories (NYSE, AMEX, OTC) of stocks are of greatest interest to investors at this time. This section is intended as a gauge for measuring market sentiment and you should use it for that purpose, rather than for choosing the most active stock or the industry currently in vogue.

In addition, the "Digest of Earnings Reports," published daily in the *Wall Street Journal*, reflects the value of securities. A typical earnings report gives the previous year's and the current year's net sales (revenues), net income (or loss), per-share earnings, and any extraordinary items taken into consideration during these fiscal periods. This report would certainly be worth a look if you have any doubts regarding the history of a particular stock.

3

There's More Than One Way to Invest

In Chapter 2, we discussed the world of stock investing. We explained the procedure a company must follow to change from a privately held corporation to a publicly traded company. We described common and preferred stock, and explained in some detail why individuals find stocks and the stock market attractive places to invest their savings. However, as an investor you should be aware of and familiar with another world—the world of debt and the bond market.

Corporate Bonds

What is the key difference between the stock and bond markets? The purchase of common or preferred *stock* represents an *equity* investment in the particular publicly traded company. As a stockholder, you are an *owner* of the company; how you fare as an investor depends on the company's success or failure. When you purchase a *bond* of the same publicly traded company you acquire a *debt instrument* and you become a creditor of that company. The only claim you have against the company is for the face amount of the bond itself plus the interest the company has promised to pay for the use of your money.

In general, if you buy a bond, a debt is owed you by the bond's issuer. As a bond owner, you are promised a fixed payment in the form of interest, usually paid on a semiannual basis over the life of the bond. The price of the bond varies, depending on whether interest rates rise or fall. For example, if interest rates rise after you purchase a particular bond, the price of the bond you bought must fall to bring the *yield* (the interest payment divided by the price) into line with the prevailing yield of similar bonds. The price of a bond maturing in thirty years reacts to changes in prevailing interest rates to a greater degree than the price of a bond coming due in a year or two. This disparity is due to the fact that the owner of a thirty-year bond is exposed to the impact of the higher interest rates for a much longer time.

For the most part, bonds are extremely liquid investment vehicles because an active marketplace exists for such investments.

Why would a publicly traded company issue bonds instead of stock? A company that goes public raises capital by offering its stock through an underwriter to the investing public. When additional capital is needed, management considers a number of factors in choosing a method for raising those funds. The condition of the company, the condition of the marketplace, the nature of the project for which the funds are needed, and the internal characteristics of the particular company are some of the factors that play a role in management's decision to offer stocks or bonds.

As a company grows in size and earning power, its bonds typically become more marketable, because the principal players in the bond market are large institutional investors or wealthy individuals whose major concern is to preserve their capital and to provide a predictable and adequate return for their assets. Such investors focus their attention on the company's assets and earning power rather than on future prospects. They rely on rating services such as Moody's Investor

Service Inc. and Standard & Poor's Corporation in deciding whether to purchase a particular bond or not. Thus, the majority of newer, smaller companies are excluded completely from the bond market.

Market conditions also play a major role in determining whether a company will raise capital through a bond or a stock offering. If the stock market is rising and the particular company's stock is performing well, the company's underwriter will most likely suggest a stock offering. Obviously, if the price of the company's stock is higher than normal, relatively few shares will have to be sold to raise the needed dollar amount, and the company's equity will be diluted to a lesser degree. Expressed another way, the assets behind each share of common stock will be reduced by a lesser amount. In a declining market, a stock offering may be extremely difficult, if not impossible, and a bond offering may be the only route available. Also, a stock offering in a declining stock market would result in a substantial dilution in the company's equity base. The current level of interest rates also plays a significant role in determining whether a stock offering or bond issue should be undertaken. If interest rates are rising or unusually high, the rate on a new bond issue (which represents interest expense to the issuing corporation) will be elevated. In such cases, a stock issue *might* be preferable.

The nature of the project also has a bearing on the way it will be financed. If the money to be raised is designated for a specific project, such as new plant construction or an existing plant's modernization, management and its investment banker will most likely select a bond issue because costs and returns can be specifically projected. However, if the funds are for general corporate purposes, rather than for a specific project, and if the stock market is particularly strong, an equity offering may be a more appropriate selection.

The peculiar characteristics of the company also influence the selection of financing alternatives. Management policy may dictate that the company carry very little debt and that the bulk of funds for financing growth and expansion come from internally generated funds and equity offerings. On the other hand, some corporate managements believe in the extensive use of debt and are willing to leverage (that is, borrow heavily against) corporate assets. The use of leverage has a dramatic effect because it magnifies corporate results, whether positive (increase in earnings) or negative (decline in earnings).

You as an investor should be familiar with some terms and concepts used by management and investors when describing debt and equity financing. The *debt-to-equity ratio* comes into play whenever a decision between debt and equity financing must be made. This ratio expresses in numerical terms what percentage of a company's capital structure is represented by debt, and what percentage is represented by equity. Managements seek to maintain a balance between the debt and equity components of their capital structure. For the investor, the debt-to-equity ratio gives a clue as to whether the company is excessively leveraged or is diluting its equity base by issuing too many shares. *Trading on the equity* (another term with which you should be familiar) means that a company is earning a higher rate of return in the business (equity side) than it is paying as the cost of the money it borrows (debt side). Expressed another way, trading on the equity means that the rate of return a company can earn in its business exceeds the rate of interest it has to pay to borrow the funds. In this case, it makes sense for a company to have a debt offering because it is able to earn a high rate of return on the borrowed funds.

Special Characteristics of Debt Offerings

The bond *indenture* contains a description of the key elements of any bond. For example, the indenture describes what items, if any, of the company's plant or equipment will secure the bond; which bank will act as trustee to represent the interests of the bondholders; what authority the trustee has to force the company into bankruptcy if it fails to comply with the terms contained in the indenture; what rate of interest will be paid to the bondholders; and how the payments will be made. Rather than examine the indenture itself, most investors rely on their financial advisers to inform them about the terms it contains. Only in the event of a *default* do bondholders focus their attention on the indenture (although many bonds sold and traded today are *debentures*, secured only by the "full faith and credit" of the borrower rather than by a particular asset of the company). (See Figure 3-1.)

Bonds used to be issued in two forms—bearer and registered. Bearer bonds are easily transferable from one individual or institution to any other individual or institution because the company assumes no responsibility for identifying or keeping track of the owners of its bonds. But in recent years only registered bonds have been issued due to governmental pressure to identify the holders of financial assets so that the income derived from these sources can be taxed. Registered bonds oblige the company to identify its bondholders, to pay to the registered owners all interest payments as they come due, and to advise the registered owners of any upcoming developments, such as redemption calls.

Par Value

Most bonds are issued in denominations of $1,000 and a bond selling at $1,000 is referred to as selling at *par*. The bond tables in the financial news would list a bond selling at par, or $1,000, as 100 (100% of its face value). A bond selling at $1,200 (at a *premium* above par) would be shown as 120. A bond selling at $780 (below par or at a *discount*) would be shown as 78. As with stock, corporate bonds trade at fractional prices in increments of eighths. Bonds issued by the federal government trade in a similar manner but the increments are expressed in thirty-seconds. For example, a government bond listed at 80.12 means 80 12/32 which translates into 80 3/8 or $803.75. (More information on how to read and understand bond tables in the financial pages can be found later in this chapter.)

Ratings

Bonds are given ratings by investors' services such as Moody's and Standard & Poor's. The rating assigned can play a crucial role in determining both the price at which the bond sells and its marketability. The rating of **Aaa** is the highest

Figure 3-1a. *A Bond Certificate (front).*

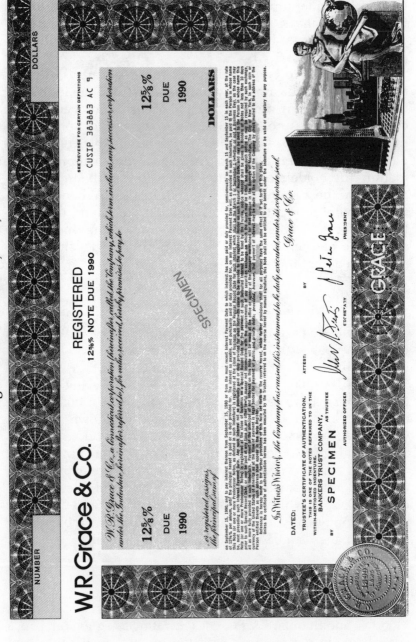

42

Figure 3-1b. *A Bond Certificate (back).*

12⅜% NOTE DUE 1990

This Note is one of a duly authorized issue of Notes of the Company designated as its 12⅜% Notes Due 1990 (herein called the "Notes"), limited (except as otherwise provided in the Indenture referred to below) in aggregate principal amount to $100,000,000, issued and to be issued under an indenture (herein called the "Indenture") dated as of September 15, 1980 between the Company and Bankers Trust Company, Trustee (herein called the "Trustee", which term includes any successor trustee under the Indenture), to which Indenture and all indentures supplemental thereto reference is hereby made for a statement of the respective rights thereunder of the Company, the Trustee and the Holders of the Notes, and the terms upon which the Notes are, and are to be, authenticated and delivered.

The Notes are subject to redemption, upon not less than 30 nor more than 60 days' notice by first-class mail, at any time on or after September 15, 1986, as a whole or from time to time in part, at the election of the Company, at a Redemption Price equal to 100% of their principal amount, together with accrued interest to the Redemption Date (but interest instalments whose Stated Maturity is on or prior to the Redemption Date will be payable to the Holders of such Notes, or one or more Predecessor Notes, of record at the close of business on the relevant Record Date referred to on the face hereof), all as provided in the Indenture.

In the event of redemption of this Note in part only, a new Note or Notes for the unredeemed portion hereof shall be issued in the name of the Holder hereof upon the cancellation hereof.

If an Event of Default, as defined in the Indenture, shall occur and be continuing, the principal of all the Notes may be declared due and payable in the manner and with the effect provided in the Indenture.

The Indenture permits, with certain exceptions as therein provided, the amendment thereof and the modification of the rights and obligations of the Company and the rights of the Holders of the Notes under the Indenture at any time by the Company and the Trustee with the consent of the Holders of 66⅔% in aggregate principal amount of the Notes at the time Outstanding, as defined in the Indenture. The Indenture also contains provisions permitting the Holders of specified percentages in aggregate principal amount of the Notes at the time Outstanding, as defined in the Indenture, on behalf of the Holders of all the Notes, to waive compliance by the Company with certain provisions of the Indenture and certain past defaults under the Indenture and their consequences. Any such consent or waiver by the Holder of this Note shall be conclusive and binding upon such Holder and upon all future Holders of this Note and of any Note issued upon the transfer hereof or in exchange herefor or in lieu hereof whether or not notation of such consent or waiver is made upon this Note.

No reference herein to the Indenture and no provision of this Note or of the Indenture shall alter or impair the obligation of the Company, which is absolute and unconditional, to pay the principal of and interest on this Note at the times, places, and rate, and in the coin or currency, herein prescribed.

As provided in the Indenture and subject to certain limitations therein set forth, this Note is transferable on the Note Register of the Company, upon surrender of this Note for registration of transfer at the office or agency of the Company in the Borough of Manhattan, The City of New York, duly endorsed by, or accompanied by a written instrument of transfer in form satisfactory to the Company and the Note Registrar duly executed by, the Holder hereof or his attorney duly authorized in writing, and thereupon one or more new Notes, of authorized denominations and for the same aggregate principal amount, will be issued to the designated transferee or transferees.

The Notes are issuable only in registered form without coupons in denominations of $1,000 and any integral multiple thereof. As provided in the Indenture and subject to certain limitations therein set forth, Notes are exchangeable for a like aggregate principal amount of Notes of a different authorized denomination, as requested by the Holder surrendering the same.

No service charge shall be made for any such transfer or exchange, but the Company may require payment of a sum sufficient to cover any tax or other governmental charge payable in connection therewith.

The Company, the Trustee and any agent of the Company or the Trustee may treat the Person in whose name this Note is registered as the owner hereof for all purposes, whether or not this Note be overdue, and neither the Company, the Trustee nor any such agent shall be affected by notice to the contrary.

The Notes are hereby designated as Superior Indebtedness for the purposes of (a) the Indenture covering the Company's 4¼% Convertible Subordinate Debentures Due March 1, 1990 issued pursuant to the Indenture dated as of March 1, 1965 between the Company and Chemical Bank New York Trust Company, Trustee, within the meaning of, and as defined in, Section 3.01 of such Indenture and (b) the Indenture covering the Company's 6½% Convertible Subordinate Debentures Due 1996 issued pursuant to the Indenture dated as of November 15, 1971 between the Company and The Chase Manhattan Bank (National Association), Trustee, within the meaning of, and as defined in, Section 3.01 of such Indenture.

Terms used herein which are defined in the Indenture shall have the respective meanings assigned thereto in the Indenture.

ABBREVIATIONS

The following abbreviations, when used in the inscription on the face of this Note, shall be construed as though they were written out in full according to applicable laws or regulations:

TEN COM —as tenants in common
TEN ENT —as tenants by the entireties
JT TEN —as joint tenants with right of survivorship and not as tenants in common

UNIF GIFT MIN ACT—........ Custodian........
(Cust)   (Minor)
under Uniform Gifts to Minors
Act........
(State)

Additional abbreviations may also be used though not in the above list.

FOR VALUE RECEIVED, the undersigned hereby sells, assigns and transfers unto

PLEASE INSERT SOCIAL SECURITY OR OTHER
IDENTIFYING NUMBER OF ASSIGNEE

PLEASE PRINT OR TYPEWRITE NAME AND ADDRESS OF ASSIGNEE

the within Note of W. R. GRACE & CO. and does hereby irrevocably constitute and appoint

_____Attorney

to transfer the said Note on the books of the within-named Corporation, with full power of substitution in the premises.

Dated_____

grade assigned by Moody's and indicates that the company selling the bond has an extremely strong capacity to pay principal and interest. At the other extreme, if a bond is rated by Moody's as **D**, the issuer is in default of the principal and/or interest payments. The rating scale utilized by Standard & Poor's is similar and both services generally track each other. Ratings are important because few investors have the time or the capability to arrive at their own conclusions about a company's ability to meet its financial commitments. Investors look to the rating services to perform this function. Further, many institutional investors, particularly pension funds and bank trust departments, are prevented by law or policy from investing in bonds rated below the **A** category. Thus, low-rated bonds are cut off from a major segment of the bond-investing community.

Convertible Bonds

The discussion thus far has focused in some detail on the characteristics and trading patterns of *straight* (nonconvertible) corporate bonds. *Convertible bonds* represent another area you should be familiar with—a special category of corporate debt. In essence, they combine some elements of both debt and equity offerings. The purchaser of a convertible bond is able to convert the bond from a debt of the issuing company into shares of the issuing company's common stock according to a formula provided in the terms of the convertible bond offering. In return for this privilege, the company is able to pay a lower rate of interest on the bond. The investor receives a "piece of the action" via the convertible feature, and at the same time enjoys the status of a debtor and the protection that status affords in the form of a fixed interest rate and protection in the event of default or bankruptcy.

To analyze a convertible bond issue, you must isolate the value of the bond as a straight debt offering and determine how much you are paying for the convertible feature. A number of financial advisory services, such as "Value Line" and "R.H.M.

Convertible Bond Survey" (to name just two), provide detailed information and advice on particular convertible bonds. While convertible bonds appear to provide the best of both worlds, individual investors should thoroughly examine them and seek competent advice and counsel before investing.

Call and Sinking Fund Features

As an investor, you should be aware of call and sinking fund features of bond offerings, because such features can have a significant impact on the total return (capital gains or losses plus interest).

A *call feature* requires a company seeking to refinance its debt, that is, "call" its bonds, to pay its bondholders not only principal and accrued interest, but also a premium. In the early years of a bond's existence, this sum can be fairly substantial. From the investor's point of view, a call on bonds means the forced reinvestment of money at a time when interest rates have declined from previous levels; for this reason the call feature provides for the payment of a premium over the face value of the bond.

Not all bond offerings have a call feature. To determine if a particular bond has such a feature, examine the bond's indenture or consult one of the standard reference sources such as Moody's or Standard & Poor's. Through their bond-buying patterns, investors have increasingly indicated that they prefer bonds without call features. This preference is principally a reaction to the volatile interest rates of recent years: Many investors saw high-yielding bonds "called away" from them as interest rates declined. In some instances they suffered a loss on their investments. If you own bonds in registered form, you will receive notice of any impending calls, but if the bonds are held in bearer form, you or your financial adviser must keep track of calls through the financial press and publications.

In the past, bond investors placed an emphasis on whether or not a particular bond had a *sinking fund* feature attached to it. A sinking fund provision means that the company is required to allocate a specific amount of its current earnings toward *retiring* the bond, that is, pay off a given amount of the bond each year. Investors like the sinking fund feature because it gives them some assurance that the company is working off its debt loan from current earnings rather than waiting until the bonds come due to meet its commitments. Such a provision also has an impact on the issue's market price. Because the company is under an obligation to retire a portion of its bonds on an annual basis, a floor is created for the price of the bond. Such demand by the company for its own bonds tends to smooth out adverse changes in interest rates and the bond market in general, and provides greater asset protection for the remaining bondholders.

In recent years, however, most investors have placed less emphasis on the sinking fund feature and more emphasis on the company's earnings and cash flow—the company's ability to service its debt. The rating services also have shifted their emphasis, focusing more on the ability of the company to service its debt and to show earnings and positive cash flow and less on the terms of the indenture itself.

Junk Bonds

In passing, you have probably seen or heard the term "junk bonds." This concept is new to the area of corporate bonds and debt financing and you should be familiar with it.

Drexel Burnham & Co., Inc., a major New York-based brokerage firm, pioneered the concept of junk bonds as a way to provide financing for merger and acquisition activity. Junk bonds get their name because of the low rating they carry (in most instances B or below). The assets securing the debt are highly leveraged and/or the proceeds are being raised for the specific purpose of financing a merger or acquisition.

The rating services view junk bonds as lacking a fundamental economic purpose. However, both individuals and institutions have made substantial profits from junk bonds. For example, at one point junk bonds offered a yield of 14% or better. As interest rates declined, the prices of the bonds appreciated to adjust to the new prevailing rates of 10% or below. Perhaps the best approach for an investor in junk bonds is to maintain a diversified portfolio of them.

Reading Corporate Bond Tables in the Financial News

The format for corporate bond tables in the financial news is shown in Figure 3-2. For purposes of this discussion, focus your attention on EasAir 17½ 99 in these tables. The first column to the right of the name gives the *current yield*, which is obtained by dividing the annual interest dollars by the current market price. Obviously, current yield varies as the price of the bond changes. A principal factor influencing bond prices (and, hence, current yields) is change in the prevailing level of interest rates—or even the perception in the marketplace that such changes are imminent.

In this particular case, EasAir offered to pay 17½% when it offered for sale bonds that will come due and be payable in 1997. Undoubtedly, 17½% was the prevailing rate on similar bonds when EasAir marketed these bonds, but changes in the pattern of interest rates now dictate a current yield of 15.9%. To understand the figures in the tables, you should be familiar with the following terms. *Nominal yield* is simply the rate of interest the bond carries on its face. *Yield-to-maturity* is an average rate of return that involves collective consideration of a bond's interest rate, current price, and number of years remaining to maturity. Yield-to-maturity comes into play when you are seeking to determine what the total yield of the bond would be if held to maturity. It is of greater significance to the professional investor than to the individual. For purposes of determining the yield-to-maturity, both bond tables and computer programs have been developed, eliminating the need for detailed manual calculations.

The next column to the right gives the number of bonds of the particular issue traded on this day. In this case, 6 bonds representing $6,000 were traded on the day in question. The

Figure 3-2. *New York Stock Exchange Bond Listings.*

Friday, Au

Total Volume $33,660,000

SALES SINCE JANUARY 1

1986	1985	1984
$6,779,092,000	$5,803,807,000	$4,322,698,000

Dow Jones B

	−1984−		−1985−		−1986−		
	High	Low	High	Low	High	Low	
72.92	64.81	83.73	72.27	91.84	83.73	20 Bon
70.31	59.43	82.88	68.62	92.57	81.85	10 Utili
76.22	69.61	84.58	75.61	90.86	84.82	10 Indu

Low	Close	Net Chg.	Bonds	Cur Yld	Vol	High	Low	Close	Net Chg.
102⅜	102⅜	+ ⅛	DiaSTel 7s08	8.5	5	82	82	82	− 1
99	99	...	Dow 8½s06	9.1	95	93½	93⅜	93½	+ 1¼
102	102	+ ½	duPnt 8.45s04	8.8	21	96½	95⅛	96½	...
103	103	...	duPnt 8½s06	8.7	56	97¼	96¼	97¼	+ 1
106	106	...	duPnt 14s91	12.3	2	114	114	114	+ ½
96	96	...	duPnt d6s01	7.6	120	78¾	78¾	78¾	− ⅛
109	110	+ 1¼	DukeP 7⅜s01	8.4	40	88¼	88¼	88¼	+ 1
102⅛	102⅛	+ ¾	DukeP 7¾s02	8.5	51	91½	89	91½	+ 2
110	110	+ 2	DukeP 7¾s03	8.6	10	89⅞	89⅞	89⅞	...
103½	103½	+ ½	DukeP 8½s03	8.8	16	92¼	92⅛	92⅛	+ ⅛
100¾	101	...	DukeP 9¾s04	9.4	7	104	104	104	+ 1¾
104⅞	105½	...	DukeP 9½s05	9.2	7	102⅞	102⅞	102⅞	− ⅜
106¼	106¼	+ ½	DukeP 9½s08	9.3	100	100½	100½	100½	− ¾
103½	105	...	DuqL 8¾s00	9.6	10	91	91	91	− ⅜
96⅜	96¾	+ ¾	ECL 9s89f	...	5	78	77	78	...
48¾	48¾	+ 2⅜	EasAir 5s92	cv	45	62	60⅛	60⅛	− 1⅝
18⅞	18⅞	− ⅛	EasAir 11½s99	cv	62	83	82	83	+ 1⅜
97½	98	+ 1	EasAir 11¾s05	cv	5	84	84	84	...
57	57	− 1	EasAir 17½s99	15.9	6	110	109	110	+ 1
94⅜	94⅝	...	EasAir 17½s98	15.9	14	110	110	110	+ 1
78	78	...	EasAir 16½s02	15.4	55	105	104½	105	+ 1¼
85⅛	85⅛	...	Eaton 8½s08	cv	110	118½	118	118¼	+ 1¼
96¼	96¼	+ 1¾	Ens 10⅜s00	10.3	10	103¾	103⅜	103⅜	+ 4⅛
101⅜	101⅜	+ 2½	Ens 10s01	cv	60	99⅛	97½	97½	− 3
95	95	− 3	Equitc 10s04	cv	5	96	96	96	+ 2½
89⅛	89⅛	− 1⅛	Exxon 6s97	7.0	41	85⅜	85⅜	85⅜	...
96⅜	96⅜	...	Exxon 6½s98	7.3	17	89	88½	89	+ ⅝
100	100⅛	+ ⅜	ExonFn 10½s89	10.0	45	104⅜	104⅜	104⅜	...
91¾	92	− ⅛	ExxP 9s04	8.9	21	101	100	101	− 1½
115⅝	115¾	+ 1¾	ExxP 8¼s01	8.4	5	98¾	98¾	98⅜	+ 1⅞
108¾	109½	+ ⅞	Feddr 5s96	cv	10	65¾	65¼	65¼	+ ¼
101	101⅞	+ ¼	FedN 4¾s96	cv	6	193	193	193	+ 2
109	109	+ ½	FedSt 7½s02	8.0	5	89	89	89	...
106½	106⅞	+ ⅛	FstChi 7¾s86	7.8	20	100	100	100	...
102	102	− ½	FtSec 8.45s99f	8.0	8	100¼	100	100¼	+ ¾
100	100	− ½	FUnRE 10¼s09	cv	11	122½	120	120	− 2
91½	91½	− 1½	FtWis 8½s96	8.7	10	97⅞	97⅝	97⅞	+ ⅜
90⅞	90⅞	+ 1⅛	FisbM 4¾s97	cv	1	69½	69½	69½	...
108¾	108¾	...	FleetFn 8½s10	cv	11	140½	139	139	− 1½
105½	105½	+ ½	FlowGn 14.30s04	14.0	1	102½	102½	102⅛	+ ⅜
101⅜	102	+ ⅝	Flwr 8¼s05	cv	71	124¾	123¼	124½	+ ½
100⅜	100⅜	− ½	Ford 9¼s94	9.1	103	101¾	101¾	101¾	+ ½
97¾	97¾	...	Ford 14⅛s90	13.4	26	106⅜	105⅜	106⅜	+ 1¼
90	90	...	FrdC 8½s91	8.4	35	101⅛	101	101	− 1
81⅜	81⅜	− ⅛	FrdC 4½s96	cv	10	217	217	217	− 1
74¼	74¼	− ½	FrdC 4⅞s98	cv	7	242½	242½	242½	− 1½
95	95	+ 2	FrdC 8.7s99	9.0	6	97½	97½	97⅛	− ¾
102	102½	+ ½	FrdC 7⅞s93	7.9	40	100	100	100	...
94⅞	95⅞	+ ⅛	FrdC 9½s01	9.1	5	100⅜	100¾	100⅜	...
93¼	93¼	− ¾	FrdC 8¾s02	9.0	25	93⅜	93⅜	93⅜	+ ⅜
99½	99½	+ 1	FreptM 10½s14	cv	98	100¾	99¾	100¾	+ ¾
85¾	85¾	+ 1½	Fruf 5½s94	cv	1	154	154	154	+ 2½
100⅜	101	− ½	Fuqua 9½s98	10.0	31	95¾	95	95¾	...
107½	107½	...	Fuqua 9⅞s97	10.1	12	98	98	98	+ 3
96	96	...	GATX 11½s96	11.6	221	99⅜	99⅛	99⅛	− ⅛
100	100	...	GTE 12¼s94	10.8	10	113½	111⅜	111⅜	− 2⅛
100¼	100¼	− ¾	Gelco 14⅜s99	13.9	4	105½	105½	105½	+ ½
95½	95½	− 1½	Gelco 14s01	cv	2	105	105	105	− ½
91½	91½	+ 1½	GnATr 5¾s99	cv	36	77	76½	77	+ ½
101½	101½	− ½	GnEl 7½s96	7.8	30	97½	96¾	96¾	...
106	106	+ 1⅛	GnEl 8½s04	8.7	75	98	97½	98	+ ¼
101	101	− ½	GEICr 7⅞s88	7.6	10	100⅞	100⅞	100⅞	+ ¼
99½	99⅞	...	GEICr 11½s90	11.2	76	102½	102⅜	102⅜	...
87	88⅜	+ 1⅜	GEICr 14s90	13.2	1	106	106	106	+ 1⅛
97¾	98⅜	− ⅛	GEICr 13⅜s91	12.5	20	109¼	109¼	109¼	− ½
96	96	+ ⅝	GnInst 5s92	cv	3	108	108	108	...
104¼s22	− ⁷⁄₃₂		GMills zr88s	...	7	90	89⅜	89⅜	+ ⅛
107	107⅜	− ⅛	GMA 4⅞s87	5.0	5	98	98	98	...
118	118	− 2½	GMA 6¼s88	6.3	10	98¾	98¾	98¾	− ⅛
114	114	− 1⅜	GMA 7½s90	7.2	71	99½	98⅞	98⅞	− ¾
109⅜	109⅜	− ⅛	GMA 8s93	7.9	120	100¾	100⅜	100¾	+ ½
114	114	− 1¾	GMA 7¾s94	7.8	147	99¾	99	99½	...
135	135	− 1			39	100		99½	− 1½

Bonds	Cur Yld	Vol	High	Low	Close	Net Chg.
Hawn 9s2000	9.0	6	100	100	100	+ 2
HlIUSA 8¼s03	cv	50	70¾	70¾	70¾	+ ¾
Heilm zr03	...	155	32¾	32½	32½	− ½
Hellr 8.1s87	8.1	5	99⅞	99⅞	99⅞	...
Hercul 6½s99	cv	10	156	156	156	+ 2
Hercul 8s10	cv	30	136½	135½	135½	+ ½
HerCm 7s11	cv	2	113	113	113	...
Holdy 9½s95	9.4	2	101	101	101	+ 1
HmeDp 8½s09	cv	78	101½	101	101½	+ ½
HomFSD 6¾s11	cv	6	107¾	107¾	107¾	+ 1⅛
HoCp 8½s08	cv	55	106	106	106	+ ¼
HoCp 9s98	cv	18	103½	103	103	− 1
HousF 7½s95	7.8	10	96	96	96	+ 4
HNG 8.7s01	9.7	10	91	90	90	− ⅛
HugheT 9s00	11.5	20	78	77¾	78	− 2½
HugheT 14¼s88	14.0	5	101½	101½	101½	+ ½
HugheT 9½s06	cv	38	82	81¾	82	+ ½
Humn d13½s02	13.1	32	103½	103	103	− 3
Humn 8½s09	cv	32	104½	104	104	− ¾
Hutton 12s05	11.4	30	105½	105	105½	+ ¾
Hum 8⅞s96	8.9	10	100	100	100	...
IBM Cr 9½s90	9.1	15	105½	105½	105½	+ 1
ITTF 8½s02	9.1	25	93¾	93¾	93¾	+ ¾
ITTF 14¾s91	13.0	1	113½	113½	113½	...
IdelB 9¼s00f	...	50	66¾	66	66	+ ¾
IIIBel 7⅞s06	8.5	12	89⅞	89½	89½	+ ⅞
IIIBel 8s04	8.6	6	93¾	93¾	93⅜	+ ⅝
IIIPw 8⅜s06	9.3	10	94	92½	92½	− ¾
Inco 6.85s93	8.0	10	85½	85½	85½	...
IndBel 8½s11	8.8	30	92¾	92¾	92¾	+ 1¾
IndBel 10s14	9.6	10	104¼	104	104	− ¼
Inexc 8½s00	cv	15	79¾	78¾	79¾	+ 1¼
IngR 8.05s04	9.2	21	87⅛	87½	87½	+ ¼
InldStl 4½s89	5.2	5	86⅞	86⅞	86⅞	...
InldStl 9½s00	12.2	23	81	78	78	− 3
InldStl 7.9s07	11.6	37	68¼	68¼	68¼	− 1¾
InldStl 11⅛s90	11.4	90	98½	98½	98½	+ ½
Intlgc 14½s95	...	10	100	100	100	+ ½
Intrfst 7¾s05	cv	132	68½	68	68½	+ ¼
IBM 9¾s04	9.1	125	102¼	102½	102½	− ¼
IBM 7⅞s04	cv	286	118½	117½	117½	− 1
IBM 10½s15	9.5	20	110½	110½	110½	...
IPap d5⅛s12	...	17	58⅜	58⅜	58⅜	− ⅛
IntRec 9s10	cv	10	81	81	81	− 2

Reprinted by permission of *Wall Street Journal.* © Dow Jones & Company, Inc., August 15, 1986. All rights reserved.

number of bonds traded gives you an idea of how liquid the market for this bond is (how easy or difficult it would be to buy or sell this bond). Certain bonds can be very illiquid and the small investor may pay a heavy penalty if an attempt is made to sell them before maturity date. Small orders (5 bonds or less) can also present a problem at the time of sale. For this reason many small investors are best served by investing in bonds via a bond fund.

The next four columns to the right describe the events that occurred during the trading day. In this particular case, the high, low, and close for the day were 110, 109, and 110. One investor, either an individual or an institution, probably purchased all 6 bonds that traded on this particular day. The last column indicates that the price of the bond rose 1 point for the day.

From this same trading table, you can see that EasAir has a number of bonds outstanding with different maturity dates and different nominal yields. In addition to the influence of interest rates, the time remaining until the bond matures and becomes payable affects the current yield. The holder, who must wait until 1997 to receive the face amount of the bond, will demand a higher current yield than if the bond bears the same nominal yield but comes due in 1990. Likewise, the price of a longer-term bond is more volatile than that of shorter-term bonds.

U.S. Government-Issued Securities

The Treasury Department issues U.S. government securities to pay for running the government. Interest payments are partially tax-free: free from state but *not* from federal income taxes.

As an investor, you are probably familiar with one form of treasury offering—the *savings bond*—which is sold directly to the public. Patriotism and safety of principal were the reasons most people purchased savings bonds, however, and few financial advisers recommended savings bonds as a means of investment. But in recent years, declining interest rates and tax law changes have made savings bonds more desirable. For one thing, the interest rate paid on savings bonds is no longer fixed for extended periods of time, but is adjusted to prevailing market rates on a periodic basis. Also, the tax laws allow the owners of savings bonds to decide whether to pay tax on the interest earned as it is accrued, or to postpone all tax on interest earned until the bonds are cashed in. For these reasons, savings bonds offer an attractive investment vehicle for the portion of assets the investor wants to set aside as a security umbrella.

In recent years, many investors have become familiar with another important category of government debt: *Treasury bills, notes,* and *bonds*.

Treasury bills, or *T bills* as they are called, are sold in multiples of $5,000 with a minimum face value of $10,000, and in maturities of 91 days, 182 days, and 52 weeks. All purchases of T bills are recorded in *book entry form*—the receipt given at the time of purchase is the only evidence of the purchase. For all practical purposes, T bills are the equivalent of cash. While institutions dominate the market, many small investors purchase T bills because they are available in relatively small dollar amounts. T bills do not pay interest on a semi-annual basis as do Treasury notes and bonds. Instead, they are sold to investors at a discount from par value—in effect, at a dollar price that is less than the redemption value at maturity.

All categories of treasury offerings have certain common characteristics: ready marketability, excellent liquidity, the safety of the full faith and credit of the United States government. In most instances, the spread between the bid and asked prices of Treasury notes and bonds shows that an active *secondary market* exists for these securities. Transactions costs, and thus brokerage fees, are fairly low. Probably the most important characteristic of treasury offerings is their exemption from state and city income tax, which makes them more attractive than most conventional bank CDs (certificates of deposit) subject as they are to such taxes.

A significant difference between T bills and Treasury notes and bonds is in the length of time to *maturity*. Treasury notes mature in one to ten years, while Treasury bonds are issued in maturities ranging from ten to thirty years. Because they have a longer life span, treasury notes, and treasury bonds in particular, are more likely than T bills to fluctuate violently at the mere indication of a change in interest rates.

Treasury notes and bonds typically require a minimum investment of $10,000. Only with the development of zero-coupon bonds has the small investor been able to readily invest in these instruments. *Zero-coupon bonds, or stripped securities,* are simply Treasury notes or bonds which are sold to investors with their coupons "stripped" or detached. Such notes and bonds are especially suitable for long-range goals such as providing for retirement or a child's education, because you can determine ahead of time the actual dollars you will receive when the security matures. As an investor you must report annually the interest you earn on a zero-coupon bond, even though you do not receive it until the bond matures. For this reason, zero-coupon bonds are considered most appropriate for *Keogh* and *IRA* accounts.

While the wealthy can't escape taxes even at death, Uncle Sam provided some help in the form of so-called flower bonds. Flower bonds are outstanding Treasury bonds which, if held at the time of death, can be redeemed at face value to pay estate taxes—even if they were purchased at a deep discount from face value. Flower bonds are no longer issued, although some that were previously issued are still outstanding and will survive until 1998.

Municipal Bonds

State, county, and local governments, like corporations, may issue bonds. Funds from municipal bond issues may be spent on the government's general financing or on special projects. The key characteristic of muncipal bonds, or "muni's," is that the interest on certain types of them is exempt from federal taxation. Whether the bond is tax-exempt depends on how the funds are spent by the issuing government. Be *certain*, if you

Figure 3-3a. *A Municipal Bond Certificate (front).*

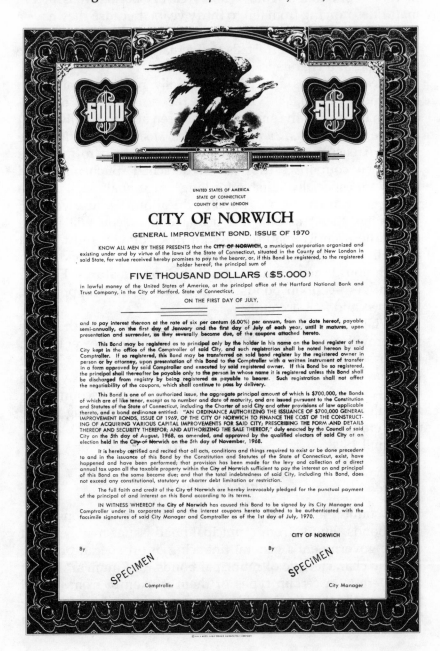

Figure 3-3b. *A Municipal Bond Certificate (back).*

No.

UNITED STATES OF AMERICA
STATE OF CONNECTICUT
COUNTY OF NEW LONDON

CITY OF NORWICH

6.00%
GENERAL IMPROVEMENT BOND,
ISSUE OF 1970

DATED JULY 1, 1970

PRINCIPAL DUE JULY 1,

INTEREST PAYABLE
JULY 1 and JANUARY 1

PRINCIPAL AND INTEREST PAYABLE
AT THE PRINCIPAL OFFICE OF THE
**HARTFORD NATIONAL BANK AND
TRUST COMPANY**
IN THE CITY OF HARTFORD
STATE OF CONNECTICUT

SECURITY-COLUMBIAN BANKNOTE COMPANY

CERTIFICATE OF HARTFORD NATIONAL BANK AND TRUST COMPANY

The Hartford National Bank and Trust Company hereby certifies that this Bond is one of the issue of Bonds described in said Bond; that the signatures of the City officials and seal thereto affixed are genuine and that Messrs. Mudge Rose Guthrie & Alexander, attorneys at law, New York City, and Sabino P. Tamborra, Corporation Counsel of the City of Norwich, Connecticut, have rendered opinions approving the legality of such issue of Bonds, and that such opinions may be inspected at our principal office at any time.

_____
Authorized Officer

Figure 3-3c. *Coupons on a Municipal Bond Certificate (front).*

$150.00	COUPON No. 19	$150.00
ust Company, in the 00 Dollars ($150.00), ue that NUMBER	ON THE FIRST DAY OF JANUARY, 1980, the CITY OF NORWICH, Connecticut, will pay to bearer, at the principal office of the Hartford National Bank and Trust Company, in the City of Hartford and State of Connecticut, the sum of One Hundred Fifty and No/100 Dollars ($150.00), in lawful money of the United States of America being the semi-annual interest due that day on its General Improvement Bond, Issue of 1970, dated July 1, 1970, NUMBER	COMPTROLLER CITY MANAGER

$150.00	COUPON No. 17	$150.00
ust Company, in the 00 Dollars ($150.00), ue that NUMBER	ON THE FIRST DAY OF JANUARY, 1979, the CITY OF NORWICH, Connecticut, will pay to bearer, at the principal office of the Hartford National Bank and Trust Company, in the City of Hartford and State of Connecticut, the sum of One Hundred Fifty and No/100 Dollars ($150.00), in lawful money of the United States of America being the semi-annual interest due that day on its General Improvement Bond, Issue of 1970, dated July 1, 1970, NUMBER	COMPTROLLER CITY MANAGER

$150.00	COUPON No. 15	$150.00
ust Company, in the 00 Dollars ($150.00), ue that NUMBER	ON THE FIRST DAY OF JANUARY, 1978, the CITY OF NORWICH, Connecticut, will pay to bearer, at the principal office of the Hartford National Bank and Trust Company, in the City of Hartford and State of Connecticut, the sum of One Hundred Fifty and No/100 Dollars ($150.00), in lawful money of the United States of America being the semi-annual interest due that day on its General Improvement Bond, Issue of 1970, dated July 1, 1970, NUMBER	COMPTROLLER CITY MANAGER

$150.00	COUPON No. 13	$150.00
ust Company, in the 00 Dollars ($150.00), ue that NUMBER	ON THE FIRST DAY OF JANUARY, 1977, the CITY OF NORWICH, Connecticut, will pay to bearer, at the principal office of the Hartford National Bank and Trust Company, in the City of Hartford and State of Connecticut, the sum of One Hundred Fifty and No/100 Dollars ($150.00), in lawful money of the United States of America being the semi-annual interest due that day on its General Improvement Bond, Issue of 1970, dated July 1, 1970, NUMBER	COMPTROLLER CITY MANAGER

$150.00	COUPON No. 11	$150.00
ust Company, in the 00 Dollars ($150.00), ue that NUMBER	ON THE FIRST DAY OF JANUARY, 1976, the CITY OF NORWICH, Connecticut, will pay to bearer, at the principal office of the Hartford National Bank and Trust Company, in the City of Hartford and State of Connecticut, the sum of One Hundred Fifty and No/100 Dollars ($150.00), in lawful money of the United States of America being the semi-annual interest due that day on its General Improvement Bond, Issue of 1970, dated July 1, 1970, NUMBER	COMPTROLLER CITY MANAGER

$150.00	COUPON No. 9	$150.00
ust Company, in the 00 Dollars ($150.00), ue that NUMBER	ON THE FIRST DAY OF JANUARY, 1975, the CITY OF NORWICH, Connecticut, will pay to bearer, at the principal office of the Hartford National Bank and Trust Company, in the City of Hartford and State of Connecticut, the sum of One Hundred Fifty and No/100 Dollars ($150.00), in lawful money of the United States of America being the semi-annual interest due that day on its General Improvement Bond, Issue of 1970, dated July 1, 1970, NUMBER	COMPTROLLER CITY MANAGER

$150.00	COUPON No. 7	$150.00
ust Company, in the 00 Dollars ($150.00), ue that NUMBER	ON THE FIRST DAY OF JANUARY, 1974, the CITY OF NORWICH, Connecticut, will pay to bearer, at the principal office of the Hartford National Bank and Trust Company, in the City of Hartford and State of Connecticut, the sum of One Hundred Fifty and No/100 Dollars ($150.00), in lawful money of the United States of America being the semi-annual interest due that day on its General Improvement Bond, Issue of 1970, dated July 1, 1970, NUMBER	COMPTROLLER CITY MANAGER

$150.00	COUPON No. 5	$150.00
ust Company, in the 00 Dollars ($150.00), ue that NUMBER	ON THE FIRST DAY OF JANUARY, 1973, the CITY OF NORWICH, Connecticut, will pay to bearer, at the principal office of the Hartford National Bank and Trust Company, in the City of Hartford and State of Connecticut, the sum of One Hundred Fifty and No/100 Dollars ($150.00), in lawful money of the United States of America being the semi-annual interest due that day on its General Improvement Bond, Issue of 1970, dated July 1, 1970, NUMBER	COMPTROLLER CITY MANAGER

SPECIMEN

Figure 3-3d. *Coupons on a Municipal Bond Certificate (back).*

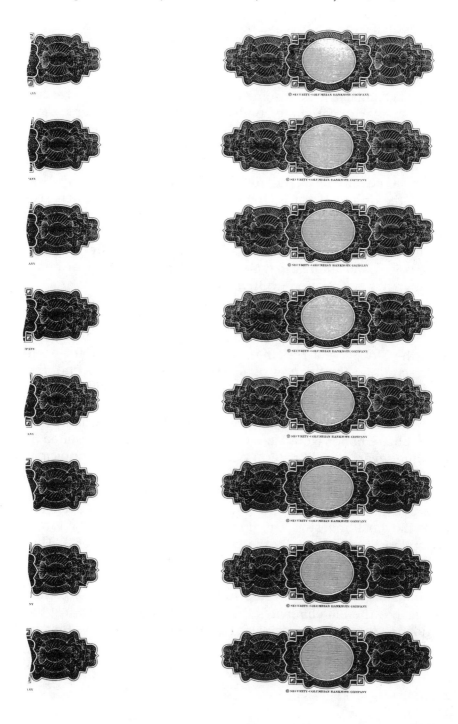

are purchasing a municipal bond because you wish tax-exempt income, that the bond you buy is indeed tax-exempt. In some cases, interest on a muni can also be exempt from state and city taxation.

Let's take a look at some characteristics of municipal securities. As with corporate bonds, municipal bonds cover a wide range of safety and liquidity. The bonds of large, well-known, state and local authorities are fairly safe investments. Likewise, if the initial offering is of a decent size, it should be relatively easy to acquire or dispose of a particular municipal bond. Unless the "piece" (that is, the dollar amount) of the purchased bond is small or the offering is that of a little-known municipality, it should not be difficult to dispose of. Further, many municipal offerings achieve added creditability by insuring principal and interest payments through the Municipal Bond Insurance Association (MBIA).

At one time, municipal bonds did not fluctuate much in price and few questions were raised about their creditworthiness, but several factors led to a change. The near bankruptcy of the City of New York in the early 1970s highlighted the need to scrutinize the finances of all issuing authorities. Second, the volatile pattern of interest-rate changes caused major upward and downward movements in the prices of municipal bonds as they tried to adjust to the prevailing rates. A prevailing fear that these bonds would lose their tax-exempt status, resulted in some severe but short-term declines in the prices of municipal securities.

The Tax Reform Act of 1986 made changes that render municipal bonds one of the last remaining tax shelters available to the small investor. The first significant change is the lower top bracket called for by the tax overhaul (28% vs. 50%). This lower top bracket makes the tax-exempt feature worth less to the individual investor. But the prices of many municipal bonds have already adjusted to take this change into account. Second, the bill eliminates the incentives for financial institutions to invest in municipals. Historically, banks and other financial institutions dominated the market for intermediate-term—7 to 20 years—tax-exempt issues. With the principal players "out of the ball park," the individual investor may perhaps find some real buys in this category of tax-exempt issue. The impact of these factors is already reflected in the marketplace.

But the marketplace has not come to grips with the impact of the third area of change. The tax-overhaul bill calls for the creation of four categories of municipal bonds in order to grant tax-exempt status based on the "social usefulness" of the project the bond is designed to finance. The first category includes securities issued directly by state and local governments to provide essential services. The second category includes bonds issued for so-called "non-governmental purposes." Housing and student loans fall into this category and have a cap on the dollar amount of bonds that can be issued for such purposes. The third category consists of taxable municipals. Bonds issued by a municipality to finance such things as a sports facility would fall into this third category. The fourth category consists of those tax-exempt bonds issued prior to August 7, 1986, which for the most part will not be taxed.

As you can see from the preceding discussion, the area of tax-exempt securities is fairly complex and for many individual investors the best route to investments in municipal bonds may be through the selection of a well-managed mutual fund specializing in these securities.

U.S. Government-Sponsored Securities

Price information for most U.S. government, government-agency, and quasi-governmental debt securities can be found in the daily newspaper. (See Figure 3-4.) Some papers, however, publish this information only weekly. The listings are categorized by issue: U.S. government bills, notes, and bonds comprise one list and government-agency, and miscellaneous securities comprise another. Each list is arranged in order of maturity; the earliest maturation dates are first. Bid and asked prices are shown in increments as small as 1/32% of the issue's par value. Bid changes (*Bid Chg.*) are given for Treasury issues.

Figure 3-4. *U.S. Treasury Listings.*

TREASURY BONDS, NOTES & BILLS

Tuesday, January 20, 1987
Representative mid-afternoon Over-the-Counter quotations supplied by the Federal Reserve Bank of New York City, based on transactions of $1 million or more.
Decimals in bid-and-asked and bid changes represent 32nds; 101.1 means 101 1/32. a-Plus 1/64. b-Yield to call date. d-Minus 1/64. k-Nonresident aliens exempt from withholding taxes. n-Treasury notes. p-Treasury note; nonresident aliens exempt from withholding taxes.

Treasury Bonds and Notes

Rate	Mat.	Date	Bid	Asked	Bid Chg.	Yld.
9¾s,	1987	Jan p	100.2	100.6	− .1	1.99
9s,	1987	Feb n	100.5	100.9	− .1	4.50
10s,	1987	Feb n	100.12	100.16	− .1	4.89
10⅞s,	1987	Feb n	100.9	100.13	− .2	4.42
12¾s,	1987	Feb n	100.13	100.17	− .2	4.34
10¼s,	1987	Mar n	100.26	100.30	− .1	5.02
10¾s,	1987	Mar p	100.29	101.1	− .1	5.01
9¾s,	1987	Apr p	101.2	101.6	− .1	5.19
9⅛s,	1987	May p	101.5	101.9	.....	5.37
12s,	1987	May n	101.31	102.3	− .1	5.07
12½s,	1987	May n	102.2	102.6	− .2	5.25
14s,	1987	May n	102.20	102.24	− .1	4.93
8½s,	1987	Jun p	101.7	101.11	.....	5.34
10½s,	1987	Jun n	102.3	102.7	.....	5.30
8⅞s,	1987	Jul p	101.20	101.24	+ .1	5.45
8⅞s,	1987	Aug p	101.26	101.30	.....	5.56
12⅜s,	1987	Aug p	103.20	103.24	− .1	5.55
13¾s,	1987	Aug n	104.14	104.18	.....	5.45
9s,	1987	Sep p	102.4	102.8	.....	5.62
11⅛s,	1987	Sep n	103.17	103.21	.....	5.64
8⅞s,	1987	Oct p	102.7	102.11	.....	5.64
7⅝s,	1987	Nov n	101.12	101.20	.....	5.56
8½s,	1987	Nov p	102.5	102.9	.....	5.73
11s,	1987	Nov p	104	104.4	.....	5.74
12⅝s,	1987	Nov n	105.10	105.14	.....	5.69
11¼s,	1987	Dec n	104.29	105.1	+ .1	5.68
7⅞s,	1987	Dec p	101.26	101.30	+ .1	5.73
8⅛s,	1988	Jan p	102.6	102.10	+ .2	5.77

Reprinted by permission of *Wall Street Journal.* © Dow Jones & Company, Inc., January 20, 1987. All rights reserved.

These figures are also expressed in thirty-seconds. The figure in the *Yield* column is a yield-to-maturity, not a current yield. Yield-to-maturity gives a more relevant number for institutional investors—for whom these securities have greatest appeal.

Government-sponsored securities and agency obligations usually offer a slightly higher rate of return than the previously described *direct* obligations of the Treasury. In spite of this fact, they are usually viewed as a step down from Treasury offerings because they are neither as safe nor as liquid as Treasury offerings.

Just what are federal agency securities?

They are usually not *direct* obligations of the U.S. government but are considered moral obligations and carry an implied guarantee. Approved amounts of these securities are issued and payable through the Federal Reserve Bank, thereby enjoying federal sponsorship, but not necessarily strong guarantees of safety.

Some agency securities include:

1. Government National Mortgage Association (GNMA, or "Ginnie Mae"),
2. Federal National Mortgage Association (FNMA, or "Fannie Mae"),
3. Federal Home Loan Banks (FHLB, or "Freddie Mac"),
4. U.S. Postal Service (USPS),
5. Tennessee Valley Authority (TVA).

Is there a place for agency securities in the portfolio of an individual investor? The answer to this question is yes, because, like Treasury offerings, agency securities provide a safe haven for the portion of an individual's portfolio designated to provide a security umbrella. While agency securities are not directly guaranteed by the federal government, none have ever been allowed to fail.

Mortgage-Backed Securities

One of the most popular forms of agency securities is *mortgage-backed securities*. In recent years, you have probably heard and read about Ginnie Mae, Freddie Mac, and their various step-children such as Sallie Mae (Student Loan Mortgage Corp.). In this section, we explain what these securities offer the individual investor and why they have become increasingly popular in recent years.

Ginnie Mae, Freddie Mac, and their step-children are referred to as *pass-through securities*. When you purchase a Freddie Mac or a Ginnie Mae bond or invest in a mutual fund consisting of such securities, you are purchasing an undivided interest in a pool of mortgages. As an owner of such an interest, you are entitled to receive on a monthly basis a pro rata share of the interest and principal payments collected on the particular pool of mortgages.

The creation of pass-through securities such as Freddie Macs and Ginnie Maes has helped the federal government and the nation's citizens by providing a medium through which the federal government can market the mortgages it guarantees. Hence, the government can expand its efforts to provide all its citizens with decent housing at a reasonable price.

You as an individual investor might find pass-through securities an attractive investment vehicle for a number of reasons. The first reason stems from the role of the federal government in the issuance of such securities. Second, an attractive feature for many people is that payments from such investments are received on a monthly basis, making it easier to balance income and expenses. Such securities also provide a high degree of liquidity, as well as a slightly higher yield than other Treasury offerings.

But as an investor you should be more than a little cautious when you see newspaper ads and other advertisements offering you what appear to be exceptional yields on Ginnie Maes. Such high yields may be the result of a fluke in the system. Because a Ginnie Mae represents a participation in a pool of mortgages, a particular pool might have a very high speed. *Speed* is professional jargon for the rate at which the pool of mortgages is liquidated. A pool has a high speed if by chance a number of mortgagees die or decide to liquidate their mortgages for various other resons. This high speed is temporary, and eventually the speed of liquidation reverts to normal. So yields that are advertised as substantially above the prevailing rate will hold only for a short time. Such advertisers usually note somewhere that the rate shown in the ad is good only as of the date of the ad's placement.

Although we are attempting to alert you to some of the pitfalls of mortgage-backed securities, you should realize that such securities can be a valuable part of an individual investor's portfolio.

Mutual Funds

Mutual funds should be considered as part of an overall investment program. They offer diversification and the expertise of an investment company.

Diversification is a key concept behind mutual funds. By investing in a variety of bonds, stocks, or a mixture of both, you reduce your overall level of risk and smooth out the radical downward and upward movements of stocks and bonds. The return on mutual fund shares is generally lower than on the stocks and bonds themselves, but the risk of capital loss is also less.

Expertise is a second factor behind the growth in mutual funds. An individual investor with limited assets may not have access to highly skilled investment analysts and managers but by combining assets with those of other small investors in a mutual fund, access to skilled professional management becomes available.

Mutual funds are a highly liquid investment vehicle because a central marketplace exists for them. Many different types of mutual funds are available; the trick is to find one that's right for you and your investment goals. (A widow with limited assets should probably not purchase an aggressive-growth mutual fund. Likewise, for a businessperson whose objective is long-term growth of capital, an income or blue-chip fund would not be suitable.) First determine what you want your money to do for you, and how much risk you are willing to take. Then discuss your personal objectives, needs, and means with a broker or account executive who is familiar with the various types of funds.

Market statistics for the most popular mutual funds are published daily in the financial pages. Figures for small funds, and other investment companies such as publicly traded funds (closed-end companies), specialty funds, and dual-purpose funds, usually appear once a week. The funds are arranged alphabetically and by management group (see Figure 3-5).

The bid price in the quotation of a mutual fund is identified as its net asset value (NAV). As is the case with any OTC stock, holders of these shares can usually dispose of them at the bid

Figure 3-5. *Mutual Fund Quotations.*

MUTUAL FUND QUOTATIONS

Tuesday, January 20, 1987

Price ranges for investment companies, as quoted by the National Association of Securities Dealers. NAV stands for net asset value per share; the offering includes net asset value plus maximum sales charge, if any.

Name	NAV	Offer Price	Chg.
DTR Inv	9.98	N.L.+	.01
GNMA	9.26	9.72-	.01
US Govt	9.25	9.71+	.01
TxFr Pa	8.13	8.54+	.02
TFr USA	11.89	12.48+	.02
TF USAl	11.05	11.60+	.04
Delw Fd	20.28	22.16+	.01
Delta Td	8.22	8.98	...
Destiny I	13.81	(z) -	.03
Destiny II	17.64	(z) -	.02
D.I.T.			
Cap Gr	14.52	N.L.-	.03
Cur In	10.34	N.L.+	.02
Gov Sec	10.26	N.L.	...
OTC Gr	27.05	N.L.+	.08
DFA FxIn	101.86	N.L.+	.06
DFA Small	9.58	N.L.	...
D G DvSrs	27.27	N.L.-	.03
DodgC Bal	35.27	N.L.-	.01
DodgC Stk	35.54	N.L.-	.01
Double Ex	11.93	12.43+	.02
Drexel Burnham:			
DB Fund	22.67	23.49+	.01
DSTGv r	10.71	N.L.+	.03
DSTOp r	10.44	N.L.-	.01
DST Cv r	10.09	N.L.+	.03
DSTBd r	11.86	N.L.+	.05
DST Gr r	12.75	N.L.-	.05
DST E r	14.50	N.L.-	.01
FenInt r	12.57	N.L.-	.12
TxFr Ltd	10.90	11.07	...
Dreyfus Group:			
A Bonds	15.23	N.L.+	.08
CalT Ex	15.71	N.L.+	.05
Cap Val	20.31	N.L.-	.04
Cnv Sec	9.16	N.L.-	.02
Dreyf Fd	13.49	14.74-	.02
Dreyf Lv	17.27	18.87-	.04
GNMA	15.78	N.L.+	.01
Growth	11.30	N.L.-	.04
Insr TE	18.77	N.L.+	.13
Intrmd	14.25	N.L.+	.08
Mass Tx	16.99	N.L.+	.08
New Ldr	22.38	N.L.+	.07
NYT Ex	16.14	N.L.+	.07
Str Inc	13.83	14.26+	.07
Str Inv	14.05	14.48	...
Tax ExB	13.18	N.L.+	.04
Third Cn	7.05	N.L.-	.01
Eagle Gth	7.73	8.45-	.01
Eaton Vance Funds:			
Cal Mn r	10.78	N.L.+	.01
EH Stk	14.27	15.39+	.03
Gov Obli	12.32	12.93+	.01
Growth	7.67	8.05-	.02
Hi Inc r	10.18	N.L.	...
Hi Mun r	10.56	N.L.+	.02
High Yld	5.27	5.53	...
Inc Bost	10.59	11.12	...
Invests	8.16	8.57+	.01
Muni Bd	9.36	9.83+	.03
Naut Fd	13.68	14.36-	.06
Spc Eqty	18.14	19.56+	.01
Tot Ret	11.03	11.58+	.02
VS Specl	11.97	12.57+	.01
Empir Bld	17.91	18.80+	.04
Equitec Siebel:			
AgarGr r	12.74		

Name	NAV	Offer Price	Chg.
GenAgg G	21.28	N.L.+	.03
Genl Elec Invest:			
Elf TxE	11.48	N.L.+	.01
Elfn Inc	11.64	N.L.+	.04
Elfn Tr	28.95	N.L.-	.05
S&S LT	12.09	N.L.+	.03
S&S Pro	37.05	N.L.-	.03
GenlSec r	11.88	N.L.-	.08
Genl TxEx	15.10	N.L.+	.05
Gintel Group:			
Cap App	11.60	N.L.-	.07
Erisa	47.45	N.L.-	.37
Gintl Fd	69.03	N.L.-	.45
Grad EstG	16.48	N.L.+	.03
Grad Opp	12.63	N.L.+	.02
GIT Investment:			
Eq Spec	17.62	N.L.+	.03
Income	9.61	N.L.+	.01
TxFr HY	11.59	N.L.+	.04
Grth IndSh	9.97	N.L.-	.02
GrF Wash	12.07	12.71+	.03
GT Global:			
Europe	20.21	N.L.+	.06
Intl	18.85	N.L.+	.06
Japan	20.23	N.L.	...
Pacific	30.05	N.L.-	.09
Guardian Funds:			
Bond	(z)	(z)	...
Park Av	(z)	(z)	...
Stock	(z)	(z)	...
Hamilton Group: Hamilton Group:			
Hamltn Fd	7.36	8.04-	.02
Harbor G	11.53	N.L.-	.03
Hartwll Gt	13.92	N.L.+	.11
Hartwll Lv	19.49	N.L.-	.01
Heartlnd	15.43	16.16+	.07
Hrtg Cap	11.69	12.05+	.08
HorcM Gr	23.82	N.L.+	.24
Hutton EF Group:			
Bond r	12.39	N.L.+	.05
Growth r	14.40	N.L.-	.02
Optnln r	9.04	N.L.-	.02
GovSec r	10.53	N.L.+	.02
BasVal r	12.84	N.L.-	.08
Cal Muni	11.25	11.72+	.02
Nat Mun	12.21	12.72+	.04
NY Muni	11.44	11.92+	.02
PrecMt r	13.93	N.L.-	.27
SplEq r	14.18	N.L.	...
IDEX	13.44	14.69+	.04
IDEX II	11.16	12.20+	.04
IndsFd Am	3.32	N.L.	...
Industrial Group:			
Ind Am	9.92	10.84-	.07
Ind Govt	9.40	10.08+	.01
Ind Opt	9.22	10.08+	.01
Integrated Resources:			
CapAp r	14.17	N.L.-	.05

Name	NAV	Offer Price	Chg.
Ltd Mat	9.92	10.02	...
Munil r	10.10	N.L.+	.01
NatRes r	14.28	N.L.-	.06
Pacific	37.66	40.28-	.20
Phoenx	13.12	14.03+	.03
Retire r	11.59	N.L.	...
RetInc r	10.09	N.L.+	.01
RetGIB r	10.54	N.L.-	.09
Sci Tech	12.77	13.96-	.05
Sp'l Valu	15.36	16.43-	.01
MetL Eqlc	9.92	10.39	...
MetL HI	7.57	7.93+	.01
Mid Amer	6.59	7.20+	.06
MidA HGr	4.83	5.28	...
Midas Gld	8.88	9.45-	.25
Monitrd	19.83	20.55+	.10
MSB Fund	(z)	(z)	...
Mutl Beac	19.88	N.L.	...
Mutl BnFd	14.76	16.13-	.03
Mutual of Omaha Funds:			
Amer	10.79	N.L.+	.01
Growth	7.81	8.49	...
Incom	9.31	10.12-	.01
Tax Free	11.96	13.00+	.06
MutlQl Fd	21.24	N.L.	...
Mutl Shars	63.95	N.L.+	.03
NtlAvia Tc	12.13	13.26+	.06
Natl Ind	12.59	N.L.-	.13
National Securities Funds:			
Balanc	14.66	15.81-	.01
Bond	3.27	3.53+	.01
Cal TEx	13.43	14.17+	.06
Fed Sec	11.41	12.24+	.04
Preferd	8.84	9.53-	.01
Income	8.22	8.86+	.01
Real Est	10.39	11.26-	.01
Stock	9.72	10.48+	.02
Tax ExB	10.47	11.05+	.04
Totl Ret	7.85	8.46+	.01
Grwth	12.23	13.19-	.03
Fairfld	9.71	10.61+	.02
Natl Telcm	15.45	16.89+	.07
Nationwide Funds:			
Fund	14.61	15.79-	.01
Growth	9.17	9.91-	.05
Bond	10.41	11.25+	.03
Tax Free	10.09	N.L.+	.01
New England Funds:			
Equity	(z)	(z)	...
Grwth	(z)	(z)	...
Income	(z)	(z)	...
Gvt Sec	(z)	(z)	...
Ret Eqtv	(z)	(z)	...
Tax Ex	(z)	(z)	...
Neuberger Berman Mngt:			
Energy	20.11	N.L.-	.03
Guardn	41.76	N.L.-	.07
Liberty	4.78	N.L.	...
Ltd Mat	10.20	N.L.	...

Reprinted by permission of *Wall Street Journal.* © Dow Jones & Company, Inc., January 20, 1987. All rights reserved.

Figure 3-6. *Front Page of a Mutual Fund Prospectus.*

PROSPECTUS

GLOBAL YIELD FUND

57,000,000 Shares
The Global Yield Fund, Inc.
Common Stock

The Global Yield Fund, Inc. (the "Fund") is a newly incorporated, non-diversified, closed-end management investment company. The Fund's objective is to achieve high current yield relative to current yields available from U.S. dollar debt securities by investment in debt securities denominated in other specified currencies expected by the Investment Manager to be stable or to appreciate versus the U.S. dollar. The Fund may also achieve incidental capital appreciation in periods when interest rates decline. The Investment Manager intends that the Fund will normally have at least 65% of the Fund's total assets invested in governmental, semi-governmental or government agency securities, or in short-term bank securities or deposits. The remainder will be invested in corporate securities or longer term bank securities. The Fund will not normally invest in debt securities denominated in a particular currency, if immediately thereafter debt securities denominated in such currency would exceed 40% of total asset value. All of the Fund's investments will be rated A or better by Moody's or Standard & Poor's or will, in the Investment Manager's judgment, be of equivalent quality. No assurance can be given that the Fund's investment objective will be realized.

Investment in the Fund's shares requires consideration of certain factors that are not normally involved in investments denominated in U.S. dollars, such as the effect of changes in currency exchange rates on the U.S. dollar value of the Fund's assets and yield. See "Investment Objective and Policies" and "Special Considerations".

The Fund's Investment Manager is The Prudential Insurance Company of America ("Prudential"). Prudential is one of the largest investment management firms in the United States, with portfolios under management, including its general account assets, totalling approximately $50.6 billion as of December 31, 1985. Prudential-Bache Securities Inc. will act as the Fund's Administrator. The address of the Fund is One Seaport Plaza, New York, New York 10292, and its telephone number is (212)-214-1215.

Prior to this offering, there has been no public market for the Common Stock of the Fund. Investors are advised to read this Prospectus and to retain it for future reference.

Application has been made to list the Common Stock on the New York Stock Exchange.

THESE SECURITIES HAVE NOT BEEN APPROVED OR DISAPPROVED BY THE SECURITIES AND EXCHANGE COMMISSION NOR HAS THE COMMISSION PASSED UPON THE ACCURACY OR ADEQUACY OF THIS PROSPECTUS. ANY REPRESENTATION TO THE CONTRARY IS A CRIMINAL OFFENSE.

	Price to Public	Underwriting Discount	Proceeds to the Fund(1)
Per Share........................	$10.00	$.70	$9.30
Total(2)	$570,000,000	$39,900,000	$530,100,000

(1) Before deduction of expenses payable by the Fund estimated at $1,420,000.

(2) The Fund has granted the several Underwriters an over-allotment option to purchase up to 8,550,000 additional shares on the same terms and conditions as set forth above. If all 65,550,000 shares are purchased by the Underwriters, the total Price to Public, Underwriting Discount and Proceeds to the Fund will be $655,500,000, $45,885,000, and $609,615,000 respectively. See "Underwriting".

The Shares are offered by the several Underwriters when, as and if issued by the Fund and delivered to and accepted by the Underwriters, subject to prior sale or withdrawal, cancellation or modification of the offer without notice. Delivery of the shares to the Underwriters is expected to be made at the office of Prudential-Bache Securities Inc., 100 Gold Street, New York, New York 10292, on or about July 8, 1986.

Prudential-Bache
Securities

June 30, 1986

SMThe mark is a service mark of The Prudential Insurance Company of America.

---

price, by redeeming them rather than selling them to another investor. The *offering price* is a fixed price dependent on the bid and includes the maximum sales charge used when selling those shares to the investing public. (This sales charge may be subject to discounts for quantity purchasers.) Some offering prices do not have a dollar figure, just the letters *N.L.* (no load), indicating that there is no sales charge for the fund, and the offering price is the same as the bid price.

Commodities/Futures

Up to this point, we have discussed investment vehicles with which you probably feel some degree of familiarity and comfort. Commodities may present a totally different picture.

Just what are commodities? How and under what circumstances do commodities fit into an individuals' financial planning?

When someone speaks of commodities, you may think of wheat, corn, soybeans, and other farm products. Commodities also include such things as gold, silver, platinum, and even lumber and heating oil, to name just a few.

Originally, farmers simply sold their crops as they were harvested and had to be content with whatever they earned from their labors. Some of the nation's produce is still sold on this basis in the cash (actual) market.

However, when people speak of commodities as investment vehicles, they are referring to *commodity future contracts*. Large grain dealers and end-users of grain products (for example, food processors and manufacturers) use future contracts to assure themselves of a given supply of a particular commodity on a specified future date at a fixed price. Many of the nation's farmers liked the idea of selling their crops ahead of harvest time at a given price. Commodity future contracts came into being as a third participant—investors and speculators— entered the marketplace created by farmers and grain dealers and provided liquidity.

To understand what commodity future contracts represent you must understand that a contract gives the holder the right to buy or sell a given amount of a specific commodity at a set price on a fixed date. A contract represents only the right to buy or sell—it does not represent ownership. For example, if you as an investor feel that a certain commodity will rise in price in the future, you would "go long" a future contract, that is, purchase a future contract that entitles you to buy the commodity in question at a set price on a fixed day. If you feel that a certain commodity will decline in price in the future, you would "go short" a future contract, that is purchase a future contract that entitles you to sell the commodity in question at a set price on a fixed day.

Because an active market exists for them, commodity future contracts are a liquid form of investment. Beginning with the formation of the Chicago Board of Trade (CBT), the marketplace for future contracts has continued to expand and now includes more than eleven exchanges around the country as well as trading locations in the major financial centers of the world. Likewise, future contracts have developed far beyond the original commodity categories and include such things as financial futures, that is, Treasury bills, bonds, currencies, and Ginnie Maes.

Although future contracts get a plus for their liquidity, you should be aware that they carry a high degree of risk. The risk exists because weather and world conditions are unpredictable and can lead to either an excess of a commodity or a shortage of it. Radical price movements in future contracts is the norm rather than the exception.

Options

Options are another of the newer and more interesting investment vehicles. The buyer of an option obtains, for a limited period of time, the right to either buy or sell 100 shares of a company's common stock at a fixed price. However, an option does not confer ownership, merely the ability to control a specified number of shares for a designated period of time.

Option contracts are of two basic types. The buyer of a *call* option has the right to call (acquire) 100 shares of a company's common stock at a specified price for a limited period of time. The buyer of a *put* option has the right to put (sell) 100 shares of a company's common stock at a specified price for a limited time. If you believe that the price of a company's common stock will rise in the future, you would want to buy call options because calls give you the right to purchase the stock in the future (when you expect it to be selling at a higher price) at today's lower price. Conversely, if you believe that the price of a company's common stock will decline in the future, you would want to buy put options because puts give you the right to sell the stock in the future (when you expect it to be selling at a lower price) at today's higher price.

The concept of *leverage* (which is discussed in more detail in Chapter 5) is at the cornerstone of the development of options as an investment vehicle. It would cost you $3,000 to acquire 100 shares of a stock selling at $30 per share ($30 per share times 100 shares), but for that same $3,000 you might be able to purchase 10 call options that are selling for $300 each. This purchase would allow you to purchase 1,000 shares for a specified time (typically 3 to 9 months) at a specified price per share (typically the price of the stock at the time you buy the option). Before you run out and buy options though, be aware that if you have not exercised your option by the date specified in the contract (referred to as the *expiration date*), the contract loses all its value and any money you committed to the investment is lost. When you purchase an option you are gambling that your prediction—whether for a rise or a decline in the stock's price—will occur within the time specified in the option contract.

Options are traded on the Chicago Board of Options Exchange (CBOE) as well as on most of the leading stock exchanges; thus options are among the most liquid investment vehicles. But as we indicated in the preceding paragraph, investments in options carry a high degree of risk and should be approached with caution.

Savings Accounts

Have you ever considered that a market exists for your savings? Probably not. But commercial banks, savings and loan associations, and money market funds all compete for your savings. This market does not exist at any specifically designated location, such as a Wall Street; the marketplace is national in scope.

A market for your savings exists because financial institutions actively compete for your deposits and stand ready to pay them out on demand. Thus your savings deposits have *liquidity*—a *key characteristic* of any *marketplace*.

Liquidity is an important concept for first-time investors to grasp because the presence or absence of liquidity in a particular investment vehicle in most instances determines what if any money should be committed there. By definition, liquidity is simply the ease or difficulty one experiences in purchasing or selling a particular investment. Because an active and highly competitive marketplace exists for savings accounts, they are considered the most liquid form of investment.

At the outset of *any* investment program, you should set aside a given amount of money in a savings or money market account to provide for unexpected emergencies. Likewise, you should actively shop around for the bank offering the best rate of interest for a specified period of time. Many investors seek to have their CD/savings accounts come due between March 1 and April 15 because banks seeking to obtain IRA deposits often engage in rate wars during this time.

Insurance

Once you have set up a savings account to meet unexpected emergencies, you are ready to consider another investment vehicle: insurance.

Insurance should be at the core of any financial planning program. The purpose of insurance is to provide *protection* for an individual or, in the case of death, a financial safety net for survivors. You should purchase insurance policies for the protection they offer not, as most insurance agents recommend, as a tool for savings. For most individuals, term insurance is the best choice because it provides maximum coverage at the lowest cost.

Remember that insurance is a relatively illiquid investment vehicle because no central marketplace exists and because it is difficult to compare the policies issued by one insurance company with those issued by other companies.

Real Estate

The most significant investment you make in your lifetime may be the purchase of the home you live in. After savings and insurance, most people look to the purchase of their own home as a core element of long-range financial planning. Besides providing shelter and a pleasant living environment, in recent years the family home has been a significant contributing factor to growth in personal net worth. In certain sections of the country, particularly in the Northeast Corridor during 1985, single-family homes appreciated at an annualized rate of more than 50%. No one can be certain that the prices of single family homes will continue to rise or at what rate they will appreciate, but the purchase of a home has proved for many individuals to be the best investment of a lifetime.

The purchase of rental property, whether a single condo unit or a multi-unit dwelling, may also be a suitable investment vehicle. Such properties generate returns that are largely dependent on the price buyers pay as well as on the amount of time and "sweat equity" they are willing to invest in management and upkeep of the properties. The nature, interests, and characteristics of the potential investor—not simply an analysis of earnings and appreciation potential—determine whether rental property is a suitable investment vehicle for a particular individual.

Real estate is basically an illiquid investment vehicle because each property is unique. You cannot determine how much time it will take to sell a property or at what price it can be sold. Further, no central marketplace exists where buyer and seller can easily and quickly be brought together.

Collectibles

Collectibles consist of any tangible asset, whether jewelry, paintings, stamps, coins, furniture, and so forth—that a person acquires with an expectation of appreciation in its value. The best investments in collectibles are usually made by individuals who purchase a particular article because they like it and enjoy it. Individuals with an expert knowledge of and familiarity with a particular category of collectible have a substantial advantage over the investor who lacks such knowledge.

Appreciation of collectibles is closely linked to the rate of inflation. The extremely high rate of inflation that characterized the mid-1970s encouraged many individuals for the first time to look at collectibles as possible investment vehicles. During this period financial publications developed various indexes and averages—much like the stock tables—to record the rise or fall in the price of collectibles. A number of investment managers formed partnerships to invest in various categories of collectibles. Within a few years collectibles gained a reputation as legitimate investment vehicles and, for some investors, replaced stocks and bonds as core elements of their overall financial plans.

In their enthusiasm for collectibles, however, investors lost sight of the fact that the marketplace for collectibles is extremely illiquid. Because each work of art or piece of jewelry is one of a kind and must be bought and sold as such, no one can predict how easy or difficult the disposition of a particular item will be. Also, because each collectible is one of a kind, a central marketplace has been impossible to develop despite the efforts of auction houses and dealers to achieve one. Further, collectibles, as opposed to stocks and bonds, are creatures of fashion and can thus experience radical changes in value and price.

When the Reagan administration succeeded in controlling

the rate of inflation, the prices of a number of collectible items, as well as investor interest in collectibles in general, declined sharply. This fact should remind you that investments in collectibles, like investments in commodities and options, require a high degree of knowledge and expertise and should perhaps be left to the professional dealer and expert.

4

There's More Than One Market

Barter, the earliest form of commerce, is defined as the exchange of commodities or services for other commodities or services, rather than for money. The earliest societies relied on barter for the exchange of the goods and services necessary for human existence. As trade expanded, the use of money became the norm, and later the concept of the corporation developed. The corporation was an improvement over other forms of business organization because it enjoys unlimited life. (It can only be detroyed by act of law.) Furthermore, corporations provide their owners (shareholders) with limited liability. (The shareholders, stand to lose only those assets committed to the corporation.)

Wall Street—Where It All Began

Securities are traded in a variety of forms and in diverse trading places. Wall Street is where it all began, but you will see that the nation's financial marketplace today bears little resemblance to its origins there.

According to historians, prior to the Revolution, New York City's leading merchants met daily under a buttonwood tree located at what is today the corner of Wall and Broad Streets. These early merchants traded in commodities such as furs, tobacco, and currencies and provided services, such as insuring ships' cargoes.

As companies were organized to conduct different types of commercial activities such as banking, retail trade, or shipping, an informal market in shares of these companies developed among the merchants who controlled them. Twenty-four of these early merchants, or stockbrokers as they came to be called, entered into a formal agreement on May 17, 1792 to trade only among themselves and to maintain agreed-on commission rates. This marked the founding of what is today the New York Stock Exchange.

The development of the New York Stock Exchange as the nation's major financial marketplace parallels the economic development of the United States. Growth and development of the railroads resulted in the predominance of railroad stock trading during much of the 1800s. Names such as Harriman,

Figure 4-1. *Wall Street in the Early 1800s.*

Fiske, and Gould dominated the financial news and these people became the heroes or scoundrels of their day. Many of these railroad tycoons were called "robber barons" because of their aggressiveness in establishing their empires, and their blatant disregard for rules of fair play.

The 1900s were characterized by a pattern of merger and consolidation, during which a majority of the nation's key industries came under the domination of a few powerful individuals. Names such as Carnegie, Rockefeller, and Swift replaced the railroad tycoons as the foci of public interest.

Until 1929, much of the trading on the New York Stock Exchange was controlled and dominated by pools. These *pools* were informal associations of wealthy and influential businessmen and stockbrokers who banded together to influence prices of particular stocks. (Joseph Kennedy, the father of President John F. Kennedy, was the first Chairman of the Securities & Exchange Commission and one of the most effective pool operators.) A pool sought to control a block of the target company's stock by striking a deal with the company's controlling stockholders. Once control of a block was established, favorable press releases were to be issued and a conscious effort was made to solicit the interest of small investors. When small investors bought shares of the company's stock (causing its price to rise) the pool members would sell out their positions and reap their profits, leaving the small investor to wonder why the stock's price suddenly collapsed.

Pools also conducted *bear raids*—efforts to undermine the price of a company's stock that allowed pool members either to buy the whole company at an artificially depressed price or to profit by buying stock cheaply to cover *short positions* (positions established by the sale of stock that was not actually owned; short positions are covered in Chapter 8.)

The Crash of 1929 and the reaction of Congress and the nation to the financial abuses uncovered in its wake led to federal regulation of the financial marketplace. This marked the end of the pools and in many ways prompted the development of the New York Stock Exchange as we know it today.

Figure 4-2a. *Order Clerks at Work on the Floor of the NYSE.*

Photo courtesy of Edward C. Topple, NYSE photographer.

The New York Stock Exchange (NYSE)

One of the ways to acquire an understanding of finance, the stock market, and the stock exchange is to visit one of the exchanges. Often guided tours are provided by the staff, who answer your questions clearly and succinctly.

From such a tour you would learn about the standards a company must meet to have its shares *listed*, and about trading

Figure 4-2b. *A Post.*

volume and the individuals and institutions that play a major role in the operations of the Exchange.

To be *listed* on the NYSE, a company must have substantial assets, an excellent earnings history, and a significant number of common shares outstanding and eligible for trading. Figure 4-3 is a compilation of the current listing standards.

Because of these stringent listing requirements, most companies whose shares are traded on the NYSE are household names. People refer to many of these NYSE-listed companies as *blue chips*, referring to the highest quality company you can invest in. Expressed another way, widows and orphans, persons the least able to sustian a loss of assets, should invest in the kind of company. This assertion does not imply that the prices of NYSE-listed stocks do not fluctuate or that some of these companies have not over the years gone bankrupt. In-

Figure 4-2c. *NYSE Specialists at Work.*

Photo courtesy of Edward C. Topple, NYSE photographer.

Figure 4-3 *Minimum Qualifications for Stock Listing.*

Criterion	Initial Listing	Continued Listing
1. Earning power	$2.5 million pretax and $2 million for the preceding 2 years	$600,000 after-tax for the preceding 3 years
2. Net tangible assets	$16 million	$8 million
3. Aggregate market value of common stock publicly held	$8-$16 million	$2.5-$5 million
4. Publicly held shares	1 million	600,000
5. Number of shareholders	2,000 round-lot holders	1,200 round-lot holders

Over the past ten years the volume of trading on the NYSE has risen dramatically. Ten years ago the average daily volume was between 20 and 30 million shares. One hundred million shares or more are now traded on a normal business day.

A change in the ownership of common stock accounts for this marked jump in volume. Until recent years, small investors were the dominant players in the market. Brokerage firms survived and prospered by catering to them. Today, however, 70% of all transactions are done on behalf of institutions. (When we speak of *institutions* we refer to mutual funds, pension plans, and insurance companies—to name just a few.)

Institutions not only dominate trading today but they own the majority of shares of common stock. As small investors liquidated their stock holdings, institutions took their place.

How does the stock market's domination by institutions affect you as an investor? For one thing, the NYSE current daily trading volume of over 100 million shares reflects the market's dominance by institutions. Unlike the typical individual investor, institutions are active in the stock market on a day-to-day basis, buying and selling large blocks of stock (10,000 shares or more)

Institutional investors tend to follow the herd instinct, concentrating their investments in stocks that are presently in vogue. Institutions find it easier to defend their investment decisions to their own clients if other institutional investors have holdings in the same industry or the same stock. Also, institutions typically concentrate their activities in companies that have a large number of shares outstanding and whose shares are actively traded. Such investments provide the liquidity and flexibility these institutions need to be able to acquire and dispose of large blocks of stock without disturbing the market price, and hence to place the ever-increasing sums turned over to professional management.

Listed stocks—blue chips in particular—have been the market leaders in recent years primarily because institutional investors dominate the stock market. Blue chips typically have large numbers of shares outstanding and are actively traded and widely held—characteristics important to an institutional investor. The name recognition of blue chip companies, the abundance of information they provide to securities analysts, and the fact that they are closely followed by such analysts have also led to their choice as institutional favorites.

Institutional dominance of the stock market leaves the individual investor with two alternatives. One possibility is to seek the professional management provided by a mutual fund. Many individual investors have selected this alternative as shown by the dramatic increase in fund sales over the past few years.

Alternatively—if you have the necessary interest, time, knowledge and personal characteristics—you can make your own investment decisions. In that case, you should be aware of the impact and influence that institutions have on the stock market and select your investments accordingly. Individual investors must determine how institutions operate and adjust their investment practices to deal with the dominant role the institutions play in today's stock market. By all means, read up on the subject.

As a prospective investor in or observer of the stock market, you must understand the persons and processes involved in the trading of stock. The trading process consists of many "players." You must learn to identify them and understand how they fit into the overall trading process.

The specialist is the key player on the floor of the Stock Exchange. Each stock traded on the Exchange is assigned to a specialist who operates from the center of the many trading posts located on the trading floor. Specialists provide an orderly and liquid market for the stocks they specialize in, buying when the price is falling and selling when the price is rising. Specialists are like auctioneers who buy and sell from inventory; they act as buffers against market excesses.

Further, the specialist is placed in a unique position by virtue of "running the book" in the stocks assigned by the Exchange. *Running the book* refers to the specialist entering on a computer terminal those orders that require special handling, typically orders to buy or sell stock at a price different from the prevailing market price. When and if that price is reached, the order is executed. Because of their positions, specialists have access to highly significant information: the numbers of shares and prices at which orders are awaiting execution. In other words, they know the supply and demand for a particular company's stock and to some degree can predict the direction the stock's price is headed.

Historically the specialist's role has proven very profitable but it requires substantial capital, particularly because such large blocks of stock are traded today. The specialist is required to act without emotion and contrary to irrational market sentiment or the public's overreaction to internal corporate developments.

The Exchange uses various statistical techniques to gauge how effectively specialists are performing their duties. If the results show that a particular market is not being stabilized, the Exchange may remove the specialist. The close monitoring of the specialist's activity shows how important to the trading process the Exchange considers this role.

The *floor broker* is another significant player in the trading process. To understand the role played by the floor broker, you must realize that the Exchange functions as an auction market with its sole function being to bring together buyer and seller. The *floor brokers* act as agents of and on behalf of buyers and sellers of stock. Each floor broker or firm represented by a floor broker owns a "seat" or membership on the Exchange, which entitles that firm or broker to transact business on the trading floor.

For example, if you place an order for 100 shares (referred to as a *round lot*) of General Motors common stock, the order is transmitted from the registered representative or account executive (the person you, as a customer of the brokerage firm, deal with) to the brokerage firm's floor broker. The floor broker who receives the order takes it toward what is called the *crowd* (the other floor brokers) surrounding the specialist handling General Motors stock. The buy order for 100 shares of General Motors common stock is shouted out, specifying price and number of shares. Hopefully, a floor broker is in the crowd who has an order from a customer seeking to sell 100 shares of General Motors on similar terms. If a trade is made, identification numbers, price, and number of shares are exchanged between the floor brokers representing buyer and seller. Within minutes of the transaction's occurrence, the trade is reported on the stock ticker or tape. The *tape* records on a minute-by-minute basis all transactions occurring on the Exchange.

The floor broker turns to the specialist if a selling floor broker cannot be found in the crowd. As market stabilizer, the specialist must sell the 100 shares of General Motors common stock from his or her own account. The specialist also executes all *odd-lot* transactions (trades of 99 shares or less) at the price of the next round-lot transaction, charging a nominal fee for the execution of the trade.

Registered traders and operational staff are the two remaining categories of players on the exchange floor. *Registered traders* are a dying breed whose original purpose was to provide depth and liquidity to the marketplace. They own seats on the Exchange and trade solely for their own personal accounts. The argument has been made that registered traders serve no useful purpose, and that their position on the floor of the Exchange, by placing them so close to the "action," gives them an unfair advantage over other investors and traders.

Operational staff account for most of the other people on the floor of the Exchange. These range in function from floor clerks and specialists' assistants to floor governors who represent the administration of the Exchange. The floor governors make day-to-day decisions about operational practices and procedures and enforce the rules and regulations of the Exchange.

Once you understand the players and their roles, you can more easily understand the stock market and investing in general.

The American Stock Exchange (AMEX)

Many investors refer to the American Stock Exchange as the
"Curb Exchange," because it began as an informal group of
stockbrokers and dealers who conducted their business on the
curb in front of the New York Stock Exchange and from the
windows and doorways of the surrounding buldings. By the
late 1890s, the American Stock Exchange had been organized
and moved indoors to its own building. In the late 1950s, the
AMEX moved to its present location behind Trinity Church just
blocks away from the NYSE.

The requirements for listing a corporation on the AMEX

Figure 4-4. *The Floor of the American Stock Exchange.*

Photo courtesy of AMEX.

are substantially less stringent regarding assets, earnings, and number of stockholders. The AMEX has traditionally been the trading place for shares of the smaller and newer of the nation's public companies. A pattern has been that as a company grew in assets, showed a proven record of sales and earnings, and gained greater public recognition, it met the standards for listing on the NYSE and moved over to that exchange.

The reasons for switching to the NYSE have much to do with the added recognition and liquidity that many investors and corporate managers feel a NYSE listing gives a company. However, if you run down the names of the AMEX-listed companies, you will find a number of familiar names and companies of substantial size. For that matter, many companies have been listed on the AMEX for thirty or forty years; the idea of switching exchanges does not appeal to all company managements.

The mechanical process of executing orders on the AMEX is effectively the same as on the NYSE. The specialist, floor broker, registered trader, and operational staff play the same roles and have similiar importance as on the AMEX.

However, some important differences exist between the two exchanges. For one thing, the volume of trading on the AMEX is much less than that on the NYSE, because institutions find that many of the stocks listed on the AMEX do not meet their investment criteria. The AMEX has historically been, and continues to be, the investment domain of the small investor.

Second, the prices of stocks listed on the AMEX tend to be lower and the price action more volatile than those of NYSE-listed stocks. Many companies listed on the AMEX are smaller and more subject to economic downturns and competition. The AMEX has proven to be aggressive in developing and marketing new investment products such as options. It was the AMEX that first developed an option trading program in New York.

If you are a risk-oriented investor, one who is willing to live with the possibility of substantial loss of assets in the hope of substantial gains (see Chapter 5), the AMEX may be the place to look when investing in stocks.

Regional Stock Exchanges

Regional stock exchanges were developed to meet the need for trading places for the stocks of local companies. Companies can be listed on more than one exchange as long as they meet the respective market's listing requirements. Dual listings are common on the regional exchanges where transactions are usually based on current NYSE or AMEX prices. While the Boston, Philadelphia, Midwest, Cincinnati, and Pacific Stock Exchanges still exist, as time passed the New York Stock Exchange, American Stock Exchange, and the Over-The-Counter market (described later) came to account for approximately 90% of all trading activity. This pattern appears likely to continue in the future. Regional exchanges, however, help to increase the overall liquidity of the marketplace. Some of the larger regional exchanges have been linked by computer to the NYSE and AMEX, providing a truly national listing for many stocks.

The Chicago Board Options Exchange (CBOE)

The exchanges discussed thus far provide marketplaces for trading stocks and bonds. The Chicago Board Options Exchange, commonly referred to as the CBOE, provides a marketplace for trading stock *options*. Prior to the establishment of the CBOE in the mid 1970s, brokerage firms referred all their stock-option business to the Put and Call Dealers Association. All option dealers were members of the dealers association and all options—whether *calls* (rights to buy) or *puts* (rights to sell)—were created (written) to fit the needs of the particular customer. The sole function of the member firm was to guarantee that the dealer writing the option was financially capable of fulfilling the option's terms.

This system changed when the CBOE came into existence. For the first time, an active marketplace was available for trading put and call options on the majority of listed stocks. Option trading was no longer relegated to an obscure corner of the investment picture; rather, the volume of option trading on the CBOE has grown so much in recent years that the NYSE, AMEX, and certain of the regional exchanges voted to permit option trading on their respective trading floors.

Institutional investors have also become a major force in option trading and a number of brokerage firms and investment advisers have developed sophisticated computer-based trading strategies for options. Orders are processed on the CBOE in much the same fashion as stock orders are processed on the exchanges (as described earlier), and the specialist, floor broker, registered trader, and operational personnel play much the same roles.

Futures Exchanges

Commodity trading is one of the most volatile areas of the financial marketplace. In today's world, the commodities market is not limited to traditional commodities such as precious metals and crops, but includes lumber, fuel oil, and even financial products such as Treasury bills and GNMAs. Dealers in commodities buy and sell *futures* contracts—agreements to make or take delivery of a commodity at a specified future time and price. The terms *commodities* and *futures* can be used interchangeably.

You can trade commodities with a small amount of money down (usually a 5% *margin* deposit); this leverage attracts many people to commodity trading. But leverage (discussed in Chapter 5) is a two-edged sword that can magnify losses as well as gains. In commodity trading, like options trading, fortunes can be made or lost in a matter of minutes.

The method of order execution and the players on the futures exchanges are much the same as on the other exchanges, except that futures exchanges do not have specialists. Also, commodities exchanges place an artificial cap called a *limit*, that sets a maximum day-to-day variation in price. The limit is simply the greatest price change permitted by the Exchange for any particular commodity during the trading day.

The different futures exchanges and their various product concentrations are shown in Figure 4-5.

The Over-The-Counter Market

The Over-The-Counter (OTC) market got its name from the manner in which securities were bought and sold: Buyer and seller passed securities over the counter in a brokerage house, rather than trading them on the floor of an exchange.

As an investor, you *must* be aware of the difference between an exchange market and the OTC market. The exchange is an *auction* market, in which a stock, bond, or other type of security is traded in a bidding process, by open outcry on the

Figure 4-5. *Futures Exchanges.*

Exchange	Principal Contract
Chicago Board of Trade	grains
	financial futures
Chicago Mercantile Exchange	livestock
	financial futures
Commodity Exchange, Inc. (NYC)	metals
New York Mercantile Exchange	petroleum
	potatoes
	metals
New York Cotton Exchange	cotton
	orange juice
New York Coffee, Sugar, and Cocoa Exchange	coffee
	sugar
	cocoa
Kansas City Board of Trades	grains
	stock indexes
Mid America Commodity Exchange	("mini" contracts in:)
	grains
	gold
	financial futures
Minneapolis Grain Exchange	grains
New York Futures Exchange	financial futures

Source: *Handbook of Investment Products and Services*, 2nd ed., by Victor L. Harper (New York: New York Institute of Finance, 1986).

exchange floor. In the over-the-counter market, two broker/ dealers arrive at a transaction price one-on-one, usually over the phone. Hence this market is regarded as *negotiated*.

What kinds of companies are traded in the Over-The-Counter-Market? Traditionally, companies lacking the necessary assets, earnings, or number of shareholders to meet an exchange's listing requirements are traded over the counter. Start-up companies, penny stocks, and companies on the verge of bankruptcy can be found trading over the counter. But some of the nation's largest and most prestigious banks, insurance companies, and industrial companies can also be found there. Companies such as American Express Co. and Anheuser-Busch Co., Inc. traded over the counter for many years. The managements of these companies did not view exchange listing as a plus and preferred the less restrictive environment of the OTC.

How are buyers and sellers brought together on the OTC? For many years, the National Quotation Bureau, Inc. (NQB) published a daily listing by name of all OTC stocks on which a quote was offered. The quote could take the form of simply a "name only" (NO) listing, meaning that the brokerage firm listed was interested in any offer (buy or sell) in the particular stock. Alternatively, a brokerage firm interested in trading in the particular stock (referred to as a *market maker*) might list a *bid* (a price at which it would buy) or an *offer* (a price at which it would sell) for a minimum of 100 shares. In the brokerage community, the NQB sheets are referred to as the "pink sheets" because of the pink paper on which they are printed.

Typically, when a customer gives a stockbroker or registered representative an order to purchase or sell a stock traded over-the-counter, three market makers (listed in the pink sheets as trading or "making a market" in that particular stock) are telephoned. Operating on the customer's instructions, the broker *negotiates* the best price.

Because these transactions are executed over the telephone rather than in the open forum of a trading floor, many investors have been hesitant to trade in OTC stocks.

The introduction of a computerized central trading system provided customers with an alternative to the NQB for over-the-counter transactions and eliminated much of this reluctance. In recent years, much of the trading in the OTC market has been executed through the National Association of Securities Dealers Automated Quotations System (NASDAQ). NASDAQ is an electronic data terminal that provides instant identification of market makers and their current *quotations* for many stocks. Companies that meet the requirement regarding assets, earnings, and number of shareholders are eligible for inclusion in the NASDAQ system. An ever-increasing number of OTC stocks have applied for listing on the NASDAQ system and have met the system's standards and requirements.

Market makers in NASDAQ-listed stocks are required to report all transactions to NASDAQ. Because of this reporting feature, adjustments can be made instantaneously as bid and asked prices change. Thus, the market for NASDAQ-listed stocks is much more liquid than that for stocks listed only in the pink sheets. Very often the spread between the bid and asked prices of NASDAQ-listed stocks is fairly narrow. The NASDAQ system provides information about volume, up-to-the-minute bid and asked prices, and access to a greater number of market makers than those listed in the pink sheets. As a result, ownership of OTC stocks by individuals and institutions has increased dramatically.

5

General Investment Goals And Guidelines

For many people, an investment program begins and ends with a stock tip. The tip may come from a friend who works for a company that developed a new product, obtained a government contract, or is experiencing rapid growth. Or it may come from a conversation overheard in a barber shop, restaurant, or on the subway. The first purchase of common stock is often the result of just such a tip. Tips do not usually pan out, but instead, result in the loss of a substantial portion if not all of the money invested.

Why is investing on the basis of a tip usually destined to fail? This approach to investing puts the cart before the horse. Before purchasing stocks, bonds, real estate, or any of the investment products now available, investors should decide what their long-range goals are. Once long-range goals have been determined, it is easy to decide whether the purchase of a particular stock fits into the overall plan. Long-range plans also force investors to come to grips with how much risk they are willing to live with to obtain specific rewards (risk/reward ratio) and to decide whether they want to make their own investment decisions or prefer that professional management handle their investments.

In this section, we define and explore some of the long-range goals and objectives of typical investors. We point out some of the alternative ways to reach these long-range goals and the trade-offs necessary along the way.

Investment Objectives

Starting with an objective (a goal) makes it easier to formulate a long-range plan for achieving that objective.

Two basic investment goals are, first, the *accumulation of assets* and, second, the *derivation of income from accumulated assets*.

Most people occupy themselves throughout their working lives with the accumulation of assets and never really recognize it as an investment goal. Typically, the first asset a person accumulates is a savings account and for some people this continues to be their core asset throughout their working lives. Many people never progress to the second stage in the accumulation of assets, which is typically the purchase of a home. Along the way, the majority of people acquire some luxuries, such as an expensive car, a VCR, jewelry, and so on. Most people reading this book are concerned with the third stage in accumulating assets; the accumulation of *financial* assets. The starting point for the accumulation of financial assets is a systematic program for setting aside a portion of an invididual's after-tax income in order to build up the capital that is the core of any investment program. Most people falter at this stage, either because of life's many pressures or because there are many attractive alternatives to the dull chore of saving and accumulating capital.

How can you accumulate the necessary capital to begin an investment program? The easiest way is to have a portion of your salary directly deposited with a savings institution so that you never actually see the money. Also, money that comes to you as a surprise in the form of a tax refund, or an inheritance, could provide the core capital you need to begin an investment program.

Once you have accumulated this basic core capital, you are ready to initiate a program to *accumulate financial assets*. Most of this book is concerned with describing and explaining the nature of the financial investments available today. However, before you can select from the alternatives available to you, you must answer a number of questions about yourself.

Some of these questions relate to your own personality and how much uncertainty and risk you can live with. A later section of this chapter helps you answer this question, to find what professional investors refer to as your *risk/reward ratio*. Another question you have to answer for yourself is, "Why are you seeking to accumulate financial assets?" Do you want to provide for your retirement or for a college education for you children, or simply to accumulate the money for its own sake and for the luxury and power that might come with it? You must answer this question so that you have a time frame in which to operate—that is, you need to know how much time you have to accumulate the specific dollar amount you need to fulfill the designated goal. Knowing the dollar figure and the time frame makes it easier to select particular financial products (stocks, bonds, real estate, and so on).

Once individuals have accumulated the needed financial assets and have used them to meet their aims or goals, they typically turn to a second investment objective—deriving income from accumulated assets. We do not mean that people never seek income from their financial assets during their working lives, but most people can meet their goals only through substantial capital appreciation—not simply from investment income. (Leverage—increasing return without increasing investment—is the key here and is discussed in greater detail later in this chapter.) As an investor gets older, emphasis typically shifts from seeking capital gains and growth in financial assets to preserving capital and maximizing the return from the assets accumulated over a working lifetime. To meet the needs of an aging population, investment professionals have developed a number of products that meet this need for a stable and predictable income stream. Portions of this book identify and explain the nature and character of these income-producing products, particularly the nature of bonds. Older investors should be cautious: They may tend to be more vulnerable if they are trusting and they do not have a lifetime to replace assets lost through bad or fraudulent investments.

Risk/Reward Ratio

The risk/reward ratio is a new term applied to an old concept. Without consciously thinking about it, most people realize that to achieve a given return on an investment they have to be willing and able to assume some degree of risk. The risk/reward ratio focuses attention on the process of evaluating risk.

The risk/reward ratio relates the level of risk a particular investor is willing and/or able to accept, to the reward achievable from such an investment. For example, let's assume that an investor Mary Richards is seeking to obtain a 200% return on her money in one year. Mary might best be described as a high level *risk-taker*. Investments that could yield such a high return over a one-year period would be highly speculative, including perhaps low-priced "penny stocks," new issues, and issues of companies on the verge of bankruptcy or just coming out of bankruptcy. To achieve such a high return, an investor must be willing to live with the possibility that all the money placed into such investments could be lost. Investors who will not take more than minimal risks confine their investing to savings accounts, T bills, and similar financial products and are described as *risk-avoiders*. Most people fit somewhere between these two extremes, and will accept a moderate degree of risk for a moderate return on their investment.

What makes a particular individual a risk-taker or a risk-avoider? To answer this question, a number of academic studies on individuals' risk tolerance have been conducted that lead to the following conclusions. First, the level of risk an individual is willing to assume is directly related to personality traits and age. Some individuals are uncomfortable with any risk in their investment life. Persons who lie awake at night worrying about their investments, have obviously chosen ones that are inappropriate for them. On the other hand, some people thrive on the excitement and challenge of the marketplace.

The same studies found that most older investors tended to be risk-avoiders because they believe that they could not recover from investment losses and are concerned about not having an adequate retirement fund. Further, these studies found that *net worth* (assets minus liabilities) has a bearing on the level of risk a person is comfortable with. Typically, a wealthy individual will accept a greater degree of risk than will an investor with moderate income and net worth. This fact is attributed to the wealthy individual's concern for the tax consequences of investment strategies. Many individuals acquired wealth because they were willing to take chances and accept risks.

How can you as an investor make use of the risk/reward ratio in making investment decisions? Rather than make an investment and then try to determine its anticipated return, you should calculate the risk/reward ratio before you make any investment. As an investor, you must be satisfied that the return you may derive from a particular investment is in line with the attendant risk and fits your investor profile as a risk-taker or risk-avoider.

Leverage

Leverage is another name for borrowing; in today's world of investing, leverage has been elevated to a high art form. Every year *Forbes* magazine publishes a list of the nation's wealthiest individuals. If you examine the business history of most of these individuals, you will find that they accumulated their wealth by using other peoples' money, that is, by knowing when and under what circumstances to use leverage.

To understand how leverage, the use of borrowed funds, works for such individuals and can work for you, you should understand the concepts of concentration and diversification. If you seek to reduce your risk of loss (thereby also reducing your possibility for gain as well), you must *diversify* your portfolio, in effect, spread your risk around. The concept of diversification is the cornerstone of the mutual fund industry. Diversification has merit for the individual who seeks an average return from an investment portfolio and is willing or unable to assume a high degree of risk. Chapter 3 discusses mutual funds and explains how they fit into an investment program.

Concentration is the flip side of the coin. Concentration is a term that describes an investment pattern in which substantial assets are committed to one or a small number of investments. Professional investors call this type of investment "betting the ranch." Many people who made the "Forbes list" bet the ranch on a single idea, concept, or industry. First-time investors usually overdiversify—by buying a few shares of a number of companies, often based on the "stock tip of the day." As an individual investor, you should avoid this approach to investing; if you err, err on the side of concentrating your investments.

How does leverage fit into a program of concentrating your investments? Identifying a particular investment as clearly undervalued (when the value of its underlying assets is compared with market price) is the most difficult part of concentrating your investments. Chapter 9 describes some of the techniques securities analysts use to identify such undervalued investments. When you have read it, you should be familiar with the methods used to uncover such situations. In recent years, however, the marketplace has become more and more efficient and the duration of inequities between value and price has become shorter and shorter. Therefore, you must act promptly when you uncover such a situation.

Once you identify an undervalued situation, concentrate your investment dollars on that particular investment. But realize that leverage is a two-edged sword; it can magnify losses as well as gains. For this reason, you must investigate a situation thoroughly before you invest. The next sections explain some of the leverage techniques and devices available to individual investors.

Margin Account Techniques

When investing, the first leverage technique you will probably encounter is the *margin* account. Utilizing a margin account enables you to make your dollars work harder for you by financing your securities transactions. For example, a 50% margin requirement is currently in effect for the initial purchase of all stocks listed on the New York Stock Exchange, American Stock Exchange, and for certain qualifying over-the-counter securities. To purchase $10,000 of such securities, in a margin account, you need only $5,000; the remaining $5,000 is financed by the brokerage firm that maintains the customer's account. Interest is charged on the outstanding balance at a rate slightly above the prevailing prime rate. (Margin accounts are explained more fully in Chapter 7.)

However, you should be familiar with some other aspects of the margin account. A customer will receive a maintenance call if the stock purchased in the account drops substantially in price. A maintenance call requires the customer to put up additional cash or securities to bring the account into balance, that is, at least to the 25% equity position. In the case of corporate or government bonds, less money is required "up front" because the brokerage firm is allowed to finance more of the transaction.

The majority of small investors are not aware of another aspect of stock-secured or collateralized borrowing. This is the nonpurpose loan. A *nonpurpose loan* allows you to borrow against your fully paid-for securities to finance a venture, such as a real estate transaction, a new business, an educational expense. Commercial banks make such nonpurpose loans at rates substantially below the rates charged on conventional consumer loans and generally lend between 70% and 90% of the market value of all fully paid-for securities. However, many commercial banks place restrictions as to the size of such a loan (usually a minimum of $25,000) and the type of securities required as collateral (e.g., government or corporate bonds or listed stocks selling above a certain price). Obviously, the nonpurpose loan is a useful tool for getting more mileage from your assets.

From the foregoing discussion, you can see how margin works to magnify losses as well as gains. Margin allows you to purchase a greater number of shares because you are able to finance a portion of the transaction. If the stock you purchased on margin increases in value you will be building *buying power* in your account. This allows you to buy additional shares of the same security or any other security as the equity in your account increases. But margin is something you should handle with the respect due any form of borrowing—use it but don't abuse it.

Warrant Technique

The purchase of a *warrant* represents another way that you can make your investment dollars work hard for you.

A warrant does not represent an actual ownership position in a company as does a share of common stock. Rather, a warrant represents the right to purchase a specified number of shares of a company's common stock at a certain price for a designated period of time. As a nonowner, the holder of a warrant has no say in the company's management and is not entitled to any dividends. Typically, warrants have a life span of at least two years, although they can be extended, and some perpetual warrants do exist. Warrants are a source of potential capital to the issuing company. When an investor exercises a warrant, the stock is issued by the company and the proceeds go to the company itself.

For what reasons do companies issue warrants? Besides providing a source for potential new capital for the company, warrants are frequently used as "sweeteners" of stock and bond offerings. By attaching a warrant to its debt or preferred stock offering, a company may stimulate the market for it and reduce the rate it must pay to borrow the funds. Many small start-up companies find that the only way they can go public is through the offering of units consisting of common stock and warrants. Many of the warrants in existence today were "spun off" from comanies coming out of bankruptcy as managements sought to compensate their creditors and stimulate interest in the reorganized company.

How do warrants fit in as a leverage device? When you find a company you want to invest in, you should consult one of the standard financial reference sources (Standard & Poor's or Moody's) to determine if the company has any warrants outstanding and what their terms are. The purchase of a company's warrants enables you to control a greater number of shares for the same number of dollars. Warrants provide a way to leverage your capital and make it work harder.

For example, at the time of this writing, the common stock of Eli Lilly & Co. Inc, a major pharmaceutical company listed on the New York Stock Exchange, is selling at $66 3/8 per share. The purchase of 100 shares of Eli Lilly's common stock would cost $6,637 plus brokerage commissions. Eli Lilly also has a warrant outstanding which entitles the holder to purchase one share of Eli Lilly common stock at $75.98 per share. At the time of this writing, the warrant is selling at $19 1/4. Thus, for the same dollars it costs to purchase 100 shares of Eli Lilly's common stock, you can purchase 345 warrants, each representing the right to purchase a share of Eli Lilly's common stock at the aforementioned price of $75.98 per share.

From this example, you can see how the warrant, for the same dollar amount, lets you control a greater number of shares. By purchasing a warrant as opposed to the underlying common stock, you can magnify your gain if the stock appreciates in price or your loss if it declines.

Before you rush out and invest in every available warrant, be aware of some of their negative aspects. First, warrants tend to be more volatile than the underlying stock they represent because the typical purchaser of a warrant is a short-term trader who reacts quickly to any change in the company's stock price or earnings picture. Second, because warrantholders are not owners of the company, they have no standing in the event of the company's bankruptcy or liquidation.

A number of financial services and publications monitor warrants. Two of the more popular are "Value Line" and "The R.H.M. Survey of Warrants, Options, & Low Price Stocks."

Options Technique

The packaging and marketing of options as respectable investment products has probably been the most significant development on the investment scene in the last fifteen years

Years ago, options were traded exclusively through the Put and Call Dealers Association. If you wanted to purchase a call option on IBM common stock, (the right to purchase 100 shares of IBM common stock at a specified price for a designated period of time usually ranging up to one year), you would have to arrange through the brokerage firm that the particular call be written by the Put and Call Dealers Association. Likewise, an investor who wished to purchase a put on IBM, (the right to sell 100 shares of IBM stock at a specified price for a designated period of time), would have to follow the same procedure.

Such a system presented a number of problems. Because each trade was "custom made," there was little liquidity in the marketplace for put and call options. Each transaction was handled on a negotiated basis, with no set fees. For these reasons, options were viewed by most professional investors as a somewhat shady part of the investment business best left to the small-time speculator and trader. It was unheard of for institutions to trade in options.

All of this changed about fifteen years ago with the founding of the Chicago Board Options Exchange (CBOE). The founding of the CBOE marked the development of a centralized marketplace for option trading. Each option was no longer a separate item; but a uniform set of fees, expiration dates, and stocks on which options were written. Clearing procedures were established and implemented.

Options are now actively traded on all the principal exchanges and the number of stocks on which options are written grows day by day. Institutions are active in the option market and sophisticated computer programs have been developed to analyze and devise option-trading strategies.

How can options be used as a leverage tool by the small investor? As with warrants, options enable you to leverage your limited capital by enabling you to control (for a limited time) a larger amount of a company's common stock than if you purchased the underlying stock. Essentially, options are "time instruments": They give you rights that are short in duration. Warrants, on the other hand, are issued with a minimum of two years life and can be extended at the discretion of the company. For this reason, the option buyer must guess the direction of the overall market, as well as forecast a stock's price appreciation. If the timing is off, the investor may lose whatever money was invested in the option.

The foregoing explains why options are perhaps the most *sophisticated* and *dangerous* investments. Although more and more small investors trade in options, much of this activity is unsatisfactory. Before you invest in options, become familiar with the overall operations of the securities marketplace and find an investment adviser in whom you have confidence. Options are not for the unsophisticated and unknowledgeable investor.

Market Averages

The stock market and its performance ranks high as a popular topic of conversation these days. In newspapers and on television you hear frequent references to the dramatic·swings in the market averages (Dow Jones and Standard & Poor's 500) that have occurred with increased frequency over the past few years. *Just what are these averages and how much weight should you give them in making your investment decisions?*

The market averages we hear of today trace their existence to the late 1800s and to the work of Charles H. Dow, one of the founders of Dow Jones Company and the first editor of the *Wall Street Journal*. Dow thought that a market "average" of a group of selected stocks could be used to gauge the level and trend of stock prices. Initially, he included only industrial stocks in his average, but later, performance measurements included transportation and utility stocks. These averages, particularly, the Dow Jones Industrial Average, are the most widely followed stock market averages in the world.

The Dow Jones Average is simply an average of the market prices of a selected group of thirty industrial, twenty transportation, and fifteen public utility common stocks. The prices of the stocks included are adjusted in cases of stock splits or stock dividends.

Some criticism of the Dow Jones Industrial Average (DJIA), relates to its being a price-weighted average: Movements in the average are influenced by different prices. The argument has been made that the DJIA is heavily weighted towards the higher-priced well-capitalized companies, that is, blue chips, as opposed to the lower-priced stocks of smaller companies. Another criticism is that, while attempts have been made to adjust for stock splits and stock dividends, those companies that have not split their stock continue to have greater influence in the overall average.

In response to these criticisms, new indexes have been developed. The Standard & Poor's 500 Index is value-weighted. This type of index derives the value of all the stocks used in the series; this figure is then used as a "base" and assigned a value of 100. A new market value is calculated daily and compared to the base to determine the percentage change in the value of the index. The S&P 500 Index includes stocks traded on the American Stock Exchange, as well as OTC stocks, and uses this weighting concept to eliminate the dominance of the blue chips and to obtain a better gauge of the price trend of the overall market.

Severe market swings have increased in recent years due to the growing institutionalization of the marketplace. This process has left the investment decision-making process in the hands of fewer and fewer individuals. Institutional investors tend to overreact to corporate and economic developments and in many instances have a short-term viewpoint regarding investments. Because of the large sums controlled by institutional investors, a change in institutional sentiment about market direction can drive the DJIA up or down fifty or more points at a single session.

Another reason for the recent pattern of violent swings in the DJIA relates to the development of index options and programmed trading. Index options are simply that—options based on the performance of an overall stock market index, for example, the S&P 500. The purchaser of such an option is forecasting where the overall market will be in three to nine months. Programmed trading refers to the utilization of computers to analyze trading situations for the purpose of uncovering inefficiencies in the marketplace. For example, if the price of an index option is out of line with the prices of the stocks comprising the Dow Jones Average or S&P 500 Index, such a situation would trigger massive sales of the stocks comprising the index and purchases of the option. A substantial number of institutions would act at the same time on the same computer-generated advice, magnifying the decline in the averages with no consideration for the value or investment worth of the stocks themselves.

Averages and indexes may give you a feel for the general condition of the marketplace, but do not depend too heavily on their data for plotting your investment goals.

What is Behind Market Performance?

The typical first-time investor makes a purchase of a particular common stock based on a feeling about the company's management, its products, or the stock's performance. The professional investor takes the opposite approach, focusing first on the overall economy, then on the particular industry, and finally, selecting a company to invest in.

How do you as an investor keep yourself informed about economic indicators? The financial pages of most daily newspapers feature changes in economic indicators and devote substantial space to analyzing the indicators and their implications for the overall economy. The Federal Reserve Bank, as well as many of the major money-center banks, publish monthly newsletters analyzing economic indicators.

Professional investors utilize economic indicators to signal changes in the direction of the economy. For this reason, indicators have been divided into three categories: leading, lag-

ging, and coincidental. *Leading indicators* usually reach peaks or
bottoms before the rest of the economy. Analysts and professional investors place the greatest emphasis on leading indicators and find them the most useful. Common stock prices
and the money supply in constant dollars are examples of two
leading indicators. *Lagging indicators* have their peaks and
troughs after the peaks and troughs actually occur in the overall
economy. *Coincidental indicators* have their peaks and troughs at
the same time or coincidentally with the economy.

*How accurate are economic indicators in predicting turns in the
overall economy?* These indicators, no matter how refined and
mathematically sophisticated, cannot predict turns in the overall economy in all instances. One reason lies with the *variability*
of the leads and lags. On the average, a particular economic
indicator may lead or lag the economy by five or six months,
but the range may vary over the years from two to ten months.
Another limitation on the accuracy of such indicators is related
to the difficulty of gathering the data and revising it. The reason indicators are so widely relied on despite their inaccuracies
is that they are the only game in town and, in a general sense at
least, point in the direction the economy is headed.

The first step in any investment plan is to determine the
direction of the economy. From this decision about whether the
economy will improve or decline, flow a number of other decisions, including the decision whether to invest any money at all
in the equity or bond markets at this time. If you do decide to
invest, the economic outlook you foresee will influence the size
and timing of your investments. Rational investing requires
economic projections.

Industries

If you have decided that the time is suitable for you to
invest in common stocks, the next question that confronts you
concerns the choice of industries to invest in.

Like people, industries pass through stages. The first stage
of the industrial life cycle is referred to as the pioneering stage.

This stage is characterized by rapid growth in sales and earnings, followed by increased competition as more and more companies recognize the possibilities of the industry and enter it. Networking, the linking together of computers at diverse work locations, is an example of an industry in its pioneering stage.

The investment maturity stage, which follows the pioneering stage, is characterized by the domination of the industry by a relatively few companies. The investment maturity stage can be relatively long in duration (running into the decades), and characterized by mergers and consolidation. Cable television would be an example of an industry in the maturity stage. While the rewards of investing in industries in the investment maturity stage are less than the rewards of investing in industries in the pioneering stage, so are the risks.

The final stage in the industrial life cycle is the stabilization stage, which can last for many decades. Most of the nation's companies are in this stage of industrial development. It is characterized by a slowdown in the rate of growth of sales and earnings and by the actual bankruptcy of some of the weaker companies.

Now that you are familiar with the industrial life cycle you probably wonder how to identify industries in their pioneer and investment maturity stages so that you can choose investments in industries that will grow and expand. Identifying industries in these stages of growth is time-consuming for professional investors and security analysts. There are some basic guidelines to identify such industries, but no method is foolproof.

One technique for identifying such industries requires you to follow scientific breakthroughs closely, looking for the industries that emerge from such developments. Other individual investors as well as professional investors are constantly on the lookout for such developments; therefore such developing industries rarely stay undiscovered for long. Professional investors also rely on computer techniques to survey industries, looking for industries whose sales and earnings are growing at an above-average rate. Further, financial institutions employ technologists on an ongoing basis to visit and examine numerous industries and companies, looking for what may be the next IBM or Xerox.

Where does this leave the individual investor? For the most part, unless you have some insight into a particular industry, you are probably better off having your investment adviser formulate ideas and suggestions about pioneering or growth industries. But you should keep informed so that you can properly evaluate and act on the information supplied by your adviser.

Companies

Once you have selected an industry to invest in, the next question you face is which *company* in that industry is suitable for your investment.

Chapter 9 of this book is devoted to the analytical tools security analysts utilize to select the "right" company. As a matter of fact, the analyst usually selects a specific company first, then uses these analytical tools to determine its investment merits. Therefore, in this chapter we describe the different categories most companies fit into, rather than discuss specific techniques.

Most investors, both individual and professional, spend their time trying to discover growth companies and the stocks they represent. A *growth stock* is simply one in which the growth rate of sales and earnings is well above the norm. Note that emphasis is placed on both sales *and* earnings, because a major increase in sales is significant only if the results are brought down to the bottom line—earnings. Likewise, for a stock to qualify as a growth stock, the pattern must continue for a period of time rather than appear as the result of a one-time event or accounting "adjustments."

Why is it so difficult to identify growth stocks? Growth stocks are difficult to identify because you are competing with the whole world. Many of these other investors have capabilities and contacts that are not available to you.

What are the dangers in investing in growth stocks? When you invest in growth situations, you must realize that frequently such stocks sell at a high *price-to-earnings ratio*. Such a high ratio may already include a substantial portion of future growth. Also, many growth stocks are heavily owned by institutional investors who plan to liquidate their positions if growth in earnings and sales is less than outstanding. Thus, the price movements of growth stocks can be particularly volatile. This is not to say that growth stocks are not suitable for the individual investor, but you must be sure that you are buying into a growth situation "early on."

Cyclical stocks and the companies they represent are another important category. The term *cyclical stocks* refers to companies in such industries as auto and steel. Investing in companies in these industries is a matter of timing. To be successful in this area, you need a knowledge of or a feeling for industry and economic cycles and a willingness to be a *contrarian*, that is to invest in what no one else wants at this particular time and wait until business and market climates change. In effect, investing in cyclical stocks means buying them at the bottom of the business cycle and selling them at the top. Many individual investors have done well in this area of investing because they have more staying power than institutional investors.

Defensive stocks and the companies they represent are another important category. Defensive stocks are stocks of companies such as tobacco, liquor, and food, which perform well in an economic downturn. (Such companies are thought of as supplying the necessities of life and continue to perform well in terms of sales and earnings during economic downturns because people cannot live without their products.) Again, these investments are a matter of timing. Individual investors tend to dominate this area both in terms of interest and ownership.

A final area where you might concentrate your research effort is in the area of *low price-to-earnings (P/E) stocks*. Low P/E stocks represent the orphans of the marketplace. Stocks selling at P/Es of ten or below fall into this category and represent stocks and companies in which few individual investors and institutions have an interest. Typically, such companies are not followed by security analysts and for the most part are not heavily owned by institutional investors. Many of these companies are "thinly traded," meaning that few shares are held in public hands and financial information is not readily available. But a number of studies have shown that low P/E stocks have outperformed many of the so-called growth (high P/E) stocks. Some analysts have turned their attention to what is called "bottom fishing," that is, to looking for such marketplace orphans. But the small investor can still prosper in this area by devoting the time and effort necessary to research such companies and by holding such stocks until developments, either internal or external, change the market's perception of their real worth.

Certain general observations can be made about approaches to deciding which companies and industries you should invest in. First, it is generally held that the worst company in an industry that is performing well, will perform better in the marketplace than the best company in the worst industry. However, if you decide to invest in an industry performing poorly, have patience and select a company with the financial capability to survive the downturn. Second, after you have analyzed the numbers, but before you invest in a company, read and learn as much as you can about the management. Management plays a key role in the success or failure of any company. Third, see if the company and the stock have "sponsorship," that is, the interest of nonretail investors. Many companies remain undiscovered because they have no institution or analyst sponsorship. Although buying stocks that have no following may prove profitable, it is always worthwhile to figure out who might buy the stock from you and why it is undiscovered.

6

Determining Your Investment Goals

Investment Preparation

In the first five chapters, we discussed investing in general—the different types of investments, the types of advisors, and the reasons for investing, including the goals and risks involved. The next step is to coordinate your *assets* and *liabilities*.

To develop your own road map for financial success, you must know what your assets and liabilities are: *How much money do you have available to work with? How much risk can you take with how much of this money? What debts or moral obligations do you have?* For example, you may have no legal obligation to take care of your mother-in-law or to educate your cousin, but if you want to do these things, then they become goals of yours as well as moral obligations.

Your assets and liabilities are invariably interrelated and eventually they affect each other. The illustration in Figure 6-1 shows this interrelationship. As you coordinate your assets and liabilities, with the help of suitable advisors, you must understand how your assets and liabilities are related in order to

Figure 6-1. *Investing Is Only One Aspect of Your Overall Financial Situation.*

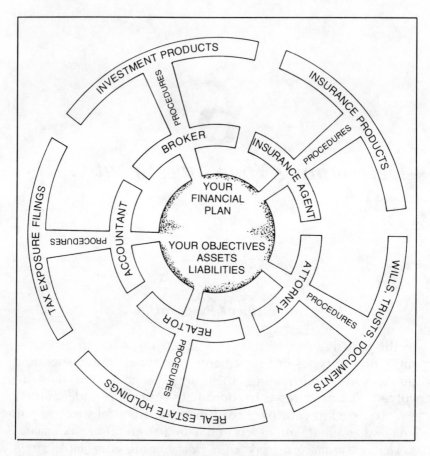

Reprinted from Victor L. Harper, *Handbook of Investment Products and Services,* 2nd ed. (New York: New York Institute of Finance, 1986), p. 13.

match your assets and investments to your resources and liabilities and to accomplish your financial goals.

Develop Your Net Worth Statement

To develop a suitable investment program, you must complete a net worth statement. This process enables you and your financial advisor(s) to fully understand your present financial circumstances and to design an appropriate map to your financial success.

Figure 6-2 shows an example of a simplified net worth statement. It lists assets and liabilities in a way similar to that required for a financial statement you submit to a bank when applying for a loan. However, your net worth statement should be more detailed than a financial statement to a banker.

Figure 6-2. *Simplified Net Worth Statement.*

Total Assets

Current Assets

Cash
   On hand and in checking account
   Savings accounts
      Regular
      Certificates of deposit
   Savings bonds
   Treasury bills, notes, and bonds
Marketable securities including stocks, corporate bonds, municipal bonds, mutual funds, etc.

Noncurrent Assets

Real estate (residence)
Real estate (investment property)
Pension plans—vested
IRS/Keogh plan contributions
Life insurance
Tax shelters-liquidation value
Annuities & inheritances
Personal effects
Miscellaneous

Total Liabilities

Current Liabilities

Credit cards
Bank lines
Auto loans
Home improvement loans
Miscellaneous loans

Noncurrent Liabilities

Mortgage

Recapitulation

Total Assets
Total Liabilities
Net Worth

Develop Your Cash Flow Statement

Your cash flow statement should list all your income and expenses. Depending on your profession and the number of people in your family who work, you may find it difficult to project all income and expenses. However, if you can make a reasonable estimate, you should have a fairly good idea of where you stand.

If you are like most people, you had no idea of your *real* worth until you calculated it: You probably had no idea how your assets are distributed or what your liabilities are. For this reason you *must* calculate your net worth *before* you invest in financial vehicles such as stocks, bonds, mutual funds, and so on; or before you add to such investments you have already made.

Draw Up a Will

One thing that should not be overlooked in any financial planning program is *drawing up a will*. Many people, even today, are hesitant to draw up a will because doing so arouses fears that they are growing old or that death is imminent. But a will is a "living document"—a way of planning and managing your assets to protect your loved ones and reduce tax liability. For these reasons, consider having an attorney draft a will for you at the time you are calculating your net worth, when you are thinking in terms of acquiring financial assets. You should also review your will periodically to decide what, if any, changes should be made. A note of caution: Using the services of an attorney to draft a will is preferable to purchasing one of the "will drafting kits" that are extensively advertised, because an attorney is able to advise you about your personal situation.

Evaluate Your Life and Disability Insurance Needs

In connection with any financial planning program you should examine *the adequacy of your life insurance and disability coverage*. (Chapter 3 discusses some aspects of life insurance.)

In today's world it is not out of line for the head of a family to carry $250,000 or more in life insurance; in a two-income family this figure may approach $500,000. For the person starting out, *term life insurance,* a "pure" form of insurance that does not accumulate any cash value in the policy, offers the best buy. As you grow older, the cost of term insurance grows and for this reason most term policies offer the option of converting to whole life or some other form of insurance. The universal life or variable life policy is a new product that is being offered by more and more insurance companies. This policy offers the insured a combination of life insurance and participation in the debt and equity markets. Certain tax rules allow the owner of such a policy to borrow against the equity built up in the policy without incurring any capital gains liability. Before you purchase any life insurance policy, you should compare the costs and benefits of different policies offered by a number of insurance companies.

Disability coverage is another area you should review before implementing any financial plan. Most employers provide some form of disability insurance for their employees, either as a fringe benefit or under the terms of a union contract. However, the coverage provided under such plans should be reviewed before the need for it arises. If the coverage seems inadequate for your circumstances, individual disability insurance is available. Because the commissions paid on such policies are relatively low, many insurance agents do not actively sell them; however, they are available. If purchased, an individual disability policy should include a clause that makes it noncancellable and renewable. Take time to compare the cost and coverage of different policies offered by various insurance companies. Be sure you understand the coverage provided by the policy you purchase.

Establish an Emergency Fund

One last step before you put any financial plan into effect is to *set up an emergency fund.* An emergency fund consists of savings bonds or money set aside in a savings account or money market fund that is available to you to meet emergencies such as the loss of your job, a sudden illness, or any unplanned expense. For most people, such an emergency fund should contain $2,500 to $5,000, although wealthier individuals may require the equivalent of six months to a year of net earnings.

Even if your net worth statement shows an accumulation of financial assets, do not neglect these steps when embarking on any financial plan. Only after you have adequately provided for your economic health by drafting a will, obtaining adequate life and disability insurance coverage, and setting up an emergency fund, are you ready to take the first step in forming a financial plan or program.

Your Financial Profile

The first step in any financial plan or program is the selection of a goal—a reason for accumulating financial assets. Examples of such goals range from the accumulation of financial assets for their own sake, to the accumulation of assets in order to make a down payment on a house, start a business, or prepare for retirement. Once you come to grips with your reason or purpose for accumulating financial assets, you can use your net worth statement to help you reach your goal(s).

When you work up your net worth statement, you create a snapshot of your financial profile. Your financial profile will change over time just as the subject of any snapshot. A young person's assets are usually concentrated in the category of current assets; that is, cash, savings accounts, and certificates of deposit (CD). As people grow older and marry and raise their families, the concentration of assets may shift from current assets to noncurrent assets—principally homes or condominiums. The inflation of the past few years, together with a demand for housing as the "baby boomers" came of age, resulted in substantial appreciation of the value of most residential property. For most individuals in their 30s and 40s, home ownership has contributed the largest increase in net worth.

For middle-aged and older persons, with most home-buying and child-rearing expenses behind them, the placement of financial assets generally shifts from the noncurrent to the current category, as these individuals become able to accumulate capital for investment and prepare for retirement. While every reader does not fit this pattern, it can serve as a guideline or benchmark in discussing how particular financial assets fit into your lifestyle and stage of life.

The net worth statement tells you a number of things about your financial profile. In particular, the net worth statement tells you how much capital you have to work with. If you know how much capital you have and if you have an approximate time frame for reaching your dollar goal, you can determine what rate of return you must obtain from the capital you invest. The rate of return you need largely dictates the types of investment (for example, blue chips vs. new issues) you should make, and highlights the amount of risk you must be willing to accept in order to reach your goal. By calculating your net worth on an annual basis, you can judge your progress toward your goal. Finally, your age and personality (your psychological profile) should be considered with your net worth statement and investment goals to determine whether the investment program you have selected is appropriate for your needs and resources.

Your Psychological Profile

An interesting and informative book discussing the psychological profiles of a sample of investors is entitled *Winning*. The author of the book is Dr. Srully Blotnick, a research psychologist, author of a number of business-related books, and a frequent contributor to *Forbes* magazine.

In writing his book, Dr. Blotnick seeks to develop a profile of the "successful investor." He studied the activities of a number of individual investors, ranging in age from young to old and in wealth from those of modest means to the very wealthy. Likewise, the investors ranged in education and employment. Dr. Blotnick reached some interesting conclusions from his study of successful and not-so-successful investors.

The first conclusion he reached that has a bearing on *your* investor profile, is that the most successful investors tend to concentrate their investments in a few areas or stocks. One stock that performed remarkably well typically made the investor a large amount of money. According to this study, concentration , not diversification, was the route to wealth and success in the stock market. Concentration brings with it a greater degree of risk than is acceptable to many investors. As an investor, you must be confortable with your investments; such a high degree of risk does not fit every investor's psychological profile.

A number of other conclusions were drawn from Dr. Blotnick's study of "successful" investors. Many of these investors did not review and change their stock holdings frequently. Some of the most successful investors averaged four or five trades a year and rarely followed the financial pages. This brings home another point about the psychological profiles of individual investors. Many small investors are guilty of excessive trading, chasing one investment fad after another. Because many of the most successful investors did not follow the market closely, they "let their profits run" rather than sell out too soon. What this means for you as an individual investor is that once you have made a decision to invest in a particular company's common stock you should not be influenced by short-term market swings. To be a successful investor you must be willing and able, psychologically, to make a long-term commitment to whatever investment you select.

The final common thread Dr. Blotnick found that links successful investors is a tendency to invest in industries they were employed in or had some direct familiarity with. The classic case was the computer analyst who invested in a small start-up computer operation, basing the choice on a knowledge of the industry and the company's management and technology. An investment of $20,000 turned into $1,000,000 in a few years. While this example is extreme, it brings home the point that as an individual investor you should become psychologically tuned in to developments in the industry you work in. This source may well provide the best investment ideas available to the individual investor, but to capitalize on it you need the psychological profile that will lead you to seek out such investment opportunities.

A final conclusion Dr. Blotnick drew from his study of investors is that there is no proven road to success. While concentrating holdings, investing in industries you are personally familiar with, and avoiding excessive trading make you more likely to succeed in the market, following these rules does not give an absolute guarantee of success. What the study *does* bring out is that you need to be comfortable with long-range planning and willing to invest time and effort to analyze a particular investment, rather than simply act on the advice of others.

Budgeting

In any book that deals with investing, some space should be devoted to the budgeting process, as it is the cornerstone of any investing or financial-planning program.

Budgeting is simply analyzing what your living expenses are at the present time and deciding what, if any, changes should be made in your spending pattern. If you feel that you are not allocating your total income in the proper fashion, then you must consider changing your spending pattern accordingly. For most people, developing a workable budget is the first step toward accumulating capital and investing in financial assets.

The budgeting process begins with determining your gross family income from all sources. Next, you must calculate the federal, state, and local taxes paid on the gross family income. This process emphasizes the need to take steps to reduce the family tax burden through better tax planning or the purchase of tax-sheltered investments.

Net income is what is left after you deduct taxes from your gross earnings. From your net earnings, you must pay both the fixed and variable expenses associated with day-to-day living. Utilities, transportation, and housing are examples of fixed expenses. The nature of some of these expenses doesn't allow you to shop around for a better deal or a cheaper cost. However, for items such as appliances, insurance, food, and clothing, you can find a variation in cost and can improve your situation by becoming a more astute shopper and consumer. The budgeting process helps you to focus on your expenses vis-à-vis your net income and on the costs attached to individual areas and items. While most people are fairly good at controlling and budgeting fixed expenses, they fall down when it comes to disposable income.

Disposable income is what you have left to spend or to save after all the family's fixed costs are covered. The easiest way to see how the family handles the disposable income it has available is through a daily diary that lists all expenditures no matter how small. You need maintain such a diary for only a short time to determine if a substantial amount is spent on what professional consumer counselors refer to as "miscellaneous expenses." Entertainment, business lunches, and "walking around money" fall into this category and by simply tightening up in this area, most people can save a substantial amount of money that can be put to better use elsewhere in the family budget.

Many strategies and services are available to help in budgeting. A number of free consumer counseling services are available that can assist you in formulating a budget. These services will contact your creditors if necessary, to work out revised payment plans. Also, a number of computer software packages are available that deal with the budget process and make it more workable. Many professional consumer counselors advise their clients to place excess funds in savings accounts from which it is inconvenient or difficult to make withdrawals, such as accounts in out-of-town banks.

As an individual investor and consumer, you should know that the tax law changes have a real impact on consumer spending. The new tax law eliminates the blanket deduction for all interest expense. On a gradual basis, the deduction of interest expense associated with credit card purchases is being phased out; all such deductions will have been completely eliminated in a few years. Certain limits are placed on the deduction of interest expenses associated with "equity" financing. Deductible interest is directly related to the purposes for which the financing is used as well as the total dollar amount of financing which the consumer can utilize. This amount is based on the original cost of the house plus any improvements.

Tax Planning

In today's complex world, tax planning must be an integral part of any financial-planning effort. In this section, we discuss some ways an individual investor can save taxes as well as the impact of the law changes on these tax shelters.

IRA

Perhaps the greatest tax shelter available to the small investor is the IRA. Originally, an IRA could be set up by any gainfully employed individual, even if the individual was covered by an existing pension plan. A single individual could contribute $2,000 per year to an IRA; a married couple with only one party working, $2,250 per year; and a married couple with both parties working, up to $4,000 per year. All contributions to an IRA were deductible from the gross income of the individual or the couple making the contribution. Further, all income earned on an IRA, whether from capital gains or interest, was sheltered from taxes until the money was drawn from the IRA. You could begin drawing from your IRA account at age 59 1/2 but you had the option of waiting until age 70 1/2, when you were required to begin withdrawing from the account.

However, the new tax law changes most of the ground rules covering IRA accounts. First, working individuals and couples who are not active participants in a pension plan continue to be able to make the maximum contributions to their

IRA accounts and deduct those amounts from their income. Second, and probably most significant for small investors, working individuals with adjusted gross incomes over $35,000 and working couples with adjusted gross incomes over $50,000 are no longer allowed any IRA deductions if they actively participate in an employer-sponsored pension or profit-sharing plan. Adjusted gross income is determined before any deduction is made for IRA contributions.

What does this change in the rules governing IRA contributions mean for the average investor? How will this change be implemented? The change effectively means that the average investor loses the benefit of one of the best tax shelters available. The changes will be implemented as follows: For every $1,000 of income over $25,000 (or $40,000 for couples) the $2,000 deduction is reduced by $200. For example, a single filer with an adjusted gross income of $30,000 who makes the full contribution of $2,000 to an IRA, is able to deduct only $1,000 when filing taxes.

Not only do these changes eliminate the IRA as an effective tax-sheltering device, but they also influence the types of investment most appropriate for existing IRAs. In the past, IRA investments had been concentrated in the areas of certificates of deposit and savings accounts. But the changes will cause the emphasis to shift toward stocks and bonds; in other words, to those areas capable of producing capital. Because under the new tax changes, all capital gains are taxed at the same level as ordinary income, the only way to shelter capital gains is through the IRA. So in the future IRA accounts may become the home for speculative investments, thus subverting the whole concept of an IRA.

401(K) Plans

For many individual investors the 401(K) plans remain the only avenue for sheltering income. Many employers established such plans to encourage their employees to save and to provide an added tax-sheltered fringe benefit. In the typical plan, an employee would authorize a given amount of money to be deducted from salary, the employer would match or contribute on a sliding scale, and the employee would be able to reduce adjusted gross income by the amount of the contribution to the 401(K) plan. The employee was also allowed to borrow against the contributions to a 401(K) plan.

The new tax law allows the 401(K) to continue as a tax-sheltering device. For this reason, many more such plans will probably come into existence, as employees press for something to replace the IRA. However, the new tax law shrinks the maximum amount an individual can contribute to such a plan each year from $30,000 to $7,000. Borrowing from such plans is no longer easy as a penalty is attached to any future withdrawals.

Before you make any decisions about IRA and 401(K) plans, consult with your tax adviser. Each situation is different and the laws are always subject to change.

Capital Gains

One of the most significant changes in the tax laws that has a bearing on the individual investor is in the treatment of capital gains. The new tax law effectively eliminates the preferential treatment given capital gains in the past and also eliminates the distinction between long- and short-term capital gains. Under the new law, capital gains are treated as ordinary income, although because the overall tax rates have been lowered, the impact is not as severe as it would seem at first glance.

What does this change mean to the average investor? It means that the average investor is no longer bound by the six-months rule to establish long-term capital gains or losses. It means that there will probably be a more rapid turnover by individual investors of the stocks and bonds they hold. Overall, an acceleration in the volume and activity on both the listed and over-the-counter markets is likely. For the individual investor there is less reason to "be married" to stock or bond investments.

Uniform Gift to Minors Act

The new tax law radically changes the rules governing the gift of financial assets to minor children. The changes were directed at eliminating "generation-skipping" loopholes in the tax laws that allowed wealthy individuals to pass on their accumulated or inherited wealth with little or no tax liability.

How does the Uniform Gift to Minors Act (UGMA) help the small investor? The act allows an investor to shift assets, whether long-term growth investments or interest-generating assets such as savings accounts or certificates of deposit, to minor children. While the new tax law places limits on the amount of assets that can be transferred to a minor child, such limits will not have much impact on the average investor. Such interest income and capital gains must be reported on a tax return filed for the minor child, and net unearned income is taxed at the parent's rate if the child is under age fourteen.

What are the negative aspects of the UGMA? Once such a gift to a minor child is given, the transaction cannot be reversed. In effect, ownership passes from the adult to the minor. For this reason, before any such transfer is made, the parent should consider carefully whether the assets will be needed in the future.

Parent and Student Savings Accounts (PASS Accts)

For a resident of New York State, the Parent and Student Savings Account (PASS) represents a way of creating a monetary fund to finance a child's higher education. Enacted under the laws of the State of New York, the PASS provides that up to $750 per year per minor child can be deposited in such an account. The amount deposited can be deducted from the adjusted gross income reported to the State of New York. The PASS account in effect provides a way to reduce the income you report to the state. Further, any interest earned on such an account is free from state tax. Thus, the PASS account is a useful way of building a fund to pay for higher education.

From the point of view of the small investor, the negative aspects of the PASS account is the fact that the money is effectively locked up and cannot be easily withdrawn if an emergency arises. Also, such an account is not deductible from the adjusted gross income reported on your federal income tax—any interest earned on a PASS account is subject to federal tax.

Self-Employment

One last area that many small investors overlook when considering ways of sheltering income is to start their own business.

While starting your own business on a full-time basis may be difficult if not impossible, for many small investors the possibility of turning a hobby into a part-time business is a worthwhile idea. Even under the new tax law, a number of advantages exist in being self-employed even on a part-time basis. Certain retirement plans can be set up and business-related expenses can be deducted. Talk to your tax adviser about the benefits and possible drawbacks to becoming self-employed.

7

Opening An Account

After you have reviewed your personal financial situation, determined your financial goals, and decided that securities investment may be right for you, you are ready to select a brokerage firm and open an account.

Choosing A Brokerage Firm

The purposes and types of brokerage firms were discussed in Chapter 1. You must decide what services you need to achieve your goals and then choose a firm that meets your needs.

Finding the appropriate brokerage firm requires a little research on your part. The first step is to ask a friend, business associate, your lawyer, or tax adviser if they know a reputable firm and/or broker. Such recommendations may be worth following up.

Once you have a name or names to work with, you must do a little reading on your own. Read professional opinions of these firms or brokers. Go to the library and research back issues of magazines like *Financial World, Forbes, Money, Money Maker,* and *Barron's.* Articles on top-ranking brokers may give you additional insight into performance records, success routes, and success rates of firms you may want to do business with. Other sources of information include the *Wall Street Journal's* weekly column "Heard on The Street" which heavily quotes brokers and fund managers, and the December issue of *Financial World,* which usually lists the year's top ten brokers.

The third step involves reading advertisements for brokerage firms in the financial pages of newspapers. Pay close attention to members of the New York Stock Exchange, as they are subject to strict regulation and surveillance.

The fourth and final step in choosing a brokerage firm is to telephone the most likely candidates from your list. Tell them your name, who recommended you to them and the amount of money you have available to invest at this time. Find the one who is most interested in helping clients within your income and net worth group.

Also consider the following questions:

- What is the range of their services?
- Will you be matched to a broker specializing in your needs? (If not, or if you feel you are being "turned off," pursue another firm.)
- How long has the firm been in business?
- Is research available to you?
- What products (stocks, bonds, options) do they deal with?
- What is their margin rate?
- Does the firm underwrite new issues of stocks or bonds and make them available to their customers?
- Has anyone in the firm ever been censured by an official regulatory agency?
- Do you feel pressured? (Never allow yourself to be pressured into acting immediately with this first call.)

Based on the feedback you receive from these calls, choose a firm you feel comfortable doing business with.

Choosing an Account Executive

How NOT to Find An Account Executive

One way *never* to select an account executive is to respond to a cold call and buy an investment product in a single phone conversation. Any legitimate sales representative who calls should be *glad* to answer your questions because they signal that you are interested enough to want to know more. Be very suspicious of any cold-calling salesperson who:

- asks leading questions, such as "As the provider for your family, you want to do the very best you can for them—don't you?"
- promises you quick, large profits (*No one* can make that guarantee.);
- hurries you to make a decision before you "miss out on this great opportunity;"
- will not agree to talk with your accountant and/or lawyer;
- does not seem interested in knowing about you and your finances before opening an account or accepting an order for you (The AE is bound *by law* to make sure your investments suit your financial capabilities and investment goals.); or
- gives you cagey answers.

Ask these questions of any salesperson who calls:

- Where did you get my name?
- Will you send me a prospectus, an investment proposal and/or risk disclosure statements?
- If I am interested in the investment, are you willing to speak with my lawyer/accountant?
- What risks are involved?
- Which regulatory agency governs your firm?
- Is the investment traded on a regulated exchange?
- When can I meet with you?

- May I get references from your firm's bank or attorneys?
- What happens if I want to get out of the investment?

If the caller answers your questions forthrightly, agrees to be checked out, and arranges to meet with you, you're probably dealing with a legitimate firm and representative. The next question is whether the investment is the right one for you, and an honest account executive will help you with that decision too.

One last note about being cold-called: The likelihood is all but nil that a perfectly suitable account executive is going to call you. More likely, you will have to actively search for the AE who will meet your personal and financial needs.

Prospecting

One way to start the search for an account executive is to ask your friends about their AEs. Don't be content with a blanket recommendation like, "My account executive is John Smith. He's great. You ought to try him." John Smith might be the perfect advisor for your friend, but totally unsuitable for you, because your investment goals may differ from your friend's. For example, in the next ten years you may need cash for your children's education, while a childless couple about to retire would be looking ahead to monthly income payments from their investments. These differing investment goals entail different investment products and perhaps varying levels of risk. The same account executive might be able to handle both objectives, and, therefore, your account as well as your friend's. Such is not always the case, however, and you may have to look further for an AE.

Here are some questions to ask about a friend's AE:

- What are your investment goals?
- How have your advisor's recommendations helped you to achieve your goals?
- Is the AE responsive? Are your calls returned? Do you receive information you requested?

- Have you changed advisors many times?
- Is the firm prompt and accurate in executing orders?
- Do you get a confirmation by phone from the AE? Is the confirmation by mail prompt and accurate?
- Is your monthly statement on time and accurate?
- Does the firm correct its mistakes without your having to constantly follow up?
- Do you think your AE would be able to handle my investment goals?

If you cannot get a recommendation from a friend, then you have to do some prospecting, that is, you must call and screen a number of brokerage firms. (Before making any calls, however, be sure that you are aware of the wide selection of investments, the types of accounts available to you, and, most importantly, your own investment goals.) Each call should enable you to determine whether a face-to-face interview with the AE is worthwhile for both of you.

Interviewing Your Account Executive

Whenever the phone conversation leads you to believe that a meeting with the AE might be beneficial, set up an appointment.

Once you have chosen a firm, it is a good idea to meet with the account executive (AE), broker, or registered representative who will be handling your account.

A face-to-face meeting between yourself and your prospective broker or AE helps to ensure that the two of you get along and understand each other. *You* must understand how the AE will handle your account, what will be done with your money, and whether you will be notified in the event of a mistake or if a quick decision must be made. The *broker* must be clear about your overall financial picture—not just the amount you are investing, your risk tolerance, and your understanding of the industry and how it works. Avoid an AE who is patronizing or condescending, promises to make you rich, claims to be an expert in *all* areas of finance, or doesn't take time to discuss your financial goals or the amount of risk you are willing to take.

Suppose It Doesn't Work Out?

Despite everyone's best efforts, sometimes the relationship between broker and customer simply does not succeed. Perhaps the AE is not helping you achieve your goals. Perhaps your goals or financial status have changed and require the services of an AE with different qualifications. Perhaps your AE has moved to another firm, and you don't want to change accounts. Or perhaps the two of you just don't see eye to eye.

Whatever the reason, the decision to change AEs is yours to make whenever you feel it's necessary. However, first ask yourself whether the AE or the firm is at fault. Assuming that the firm's other services—execution, clearing, and so on—are satisfactory, consider changing to another AE within the firm.

You can make this change simply by finding a new account executive and authorizing the release of assets and information from your current AE. Your new AE does everything else. This procedure is the same whether you change AEs within a firm, or change from one firm to another.

Types of Accounts

The process of opening a brokerage account is similar to that of opening a bank account or a charge account. However, the two basic types of accounts—cash accounts and margin accounts have different requirements.

Cash Account

A *cash account*, in which all transactions are settled on a cash basis, is the most popular type of account opened by a new investor. Several forms must be filled out, but these may differ among brokerage firms. The new account application (see Figure 7-1) asks for your name, address, social security

Figure 7-1. *A Typical New Account Information Form.*

● ● ● ● ● ● ● ● ● ● ● ● ● ● ● ● ● ● ●

Snowden Winter
Incorporated

New Account Information (Confidential)

ACCOUNT NUMBER

Branch	Account	Type	Ck.	RR

RR REGISTERED IN STATE OF CUSTOMERS RESIDENCE ☐ YES ☐ NO

ACCOUNT TITLE (in full as it should appear on billings; if JT Acct. specify JT/WROS or Ten. in common)

NAME _____

ADDRESS _____
CITY _____ STATE _____ ZIP _____

SOCIAL SECURITY OR TAX IDENTIFICATION # ⌐ ⌐ ⌐ ⌐ ⌐ ⌐ ⌐ ⌐ ⌐

RESIDENT OF N.Y. STATE ☐ YES ☐ NO

CITIZENSHIP (Country) _____ AGE _____

INSTRUCTIONS (SEE EXPLANATION ON BACK) CHECK ONE

☐ HOLD SECURITIES IN FIRM NAME AND HOLD FUNDS (3/7)

☐ TRANSFER AND MAIL SECURITIES AS BILLED REMIT FUNDS (1/8)

☐ SETTLE TRADES C.O.D. THROUGH CLIENT'S AGENT (5/6) ☐ SAME AS ABOVE
AGENTS NAME, ADDRESS, DEPARTMENT, CLIENT'S IDENTIFICATION NUMBER

_____

☐ FOLLOW SPECIAL INSTRUCTIONS ON BACK (Check appropriate instructions)

☐ ALTERNATE NAME - DUPLICATE STATEMENTS, CONFIRMATION, ALTERNATE TRANSFER NAME,
ALTERNATE DIVIDEND PAYEE (SEE BACK)

*INSTITUTIONAL A/C FILL IN SHADED AREAS ONLY

INITIAL TRANSACTION	AMOUNT OF DEPOSIT $	TRF or A/C ☐	FORMER BROKER

DIVIDENDS
☐ PAY MONTHLY
☐ HOLD

TYPE OF ACCOUNT
☐ CASH
☐ MARGIN
☐ EMPLOYEE RELATED
☐ DISCRETIONARY
☐ OPTION (PROSPECTUS FURNISHED
_____ DATE

PAPERS NEEDED
☐ JOINT ACCT. AGREEMENT
☐ MARGIN AGREEMENT
☐ TRUST AGREEMENT
☐ ESTATE PAPERS
☐ CORPORATE RESOLUTION
☐ PARTNERSHIP AGREEMENT
☐ N.Y. NON RESIDENT WAIVER
☐ FIRST PARTY TRADING AUTHORITY
☐ THIRD PARTY TRADING AUTHORITY
☐ OPTION AGREEMENT
☐ INVESTMENT CLUB AGREEMENT
☐ INVESTMENT ADVISOR
☐ OTHER

EMPLOYER NAME and ADDRESS (IF UNEMPLOYED, SOURCE OF INCOME)	OCCUPATION/POSITION OR TYPE OF BUSINESS
	BUSINESS PHONE
HOME ADDRESS (IF NOT ALREADY GIVEN)	HOME PHONE
NAME OF BANK REFERENCE (IF BRANCH BANK INCLUDE LOCATION)	TYPE OF BANK ACCOUNT ☐ CHECKING ☐ SAVINGS ☐ COMMERCIAL ☐ OTHER

IS THIS ACCOUNT TO BE OPERATED BY ANY OTHER PERSON THAN THE OWNER? ☐ NO ☐ YES, NAME _____ A/C # _____

RELATION TO CUSTOMER _____ OCCUPATION _____

ADDRESS _____ EMPLOYER _____

EXPERIENCE OF PERSON HOLDING THIRD PARTY TRADING AUTHORITY if APPLICABLE

DOES CLIENT OWN ANY UNREGISTERED STOCK? ☐ NO ☐ YES, COMPANY

DOES CLIENT OR MEMBER OF IMMEDIATE FAMILY HAVE ANY DIRECT OR INDIRECT
CONTROL RELATIONSHIP WITH A PUBLICLY OWNED COMPANY? ☐ NO ☐ YES, COMPANY

HOW WAS ACCOUNT ACQUIRED? ☐ SOLICITED ☐ CALL IN ☐ AD LEAD ☐ RE-OPENED ☐ PERSONALLY KNOWN TO RR _____ YEARS

REFERRED BY

MARITAL STATUS ☐ M ☐ S SPOUSE'S NAME _____ AGE OF DEPENDENTS _____

SPOUSE'S EMPLOYER _____

APPROXIMATE NET WORTH $	ANNUAL INCOME $	APPROX. TAX BRACKET %	AMOUNT LIFE INSURANCE $
CUSTOMER'S MAIN INVESTMENT OBJECTIVES ☐ SAFETY OF PRINCIPAL	☐ INCOME	☐ LONG TERM GROWTH	☐ TRADING PROFITS

ADDITIONAL INFORMATION FOR CLIENTS INTENDING TO WRITE UNCOVERED OPTIONS

DOES CLIENT HAVE ANY PREVIOUS EXPERIENCE IN OPTION/COMMODITY TRADING? ☐ NO ☐ YES HOW LONG? ☐ CALLS ☐ PUTS ☐ SPREADS ☐ COMMODITY

HAVE YOU DISCUSSED TO CLIENT'S UNDERSTANDING THE RISK OF WRITING UNCOVERED OPTIONS? ☐ NO ☐ YES

ESTIMATED LIQUID NET WORTH	CASH $	SECURITIES $	OTHER $

OTHER RELEVANT FINANCIAL INFORMATION,

DOES CLIENT MAKE HIS OWN INVESTMENT DECISIONS? ☐ NO ☐ YES ☐ OCCASIONALLY

THE ABOVE IS CORRECT TO THE BEST OF MY KNOWLEDGE AND BELIEF (SIGN FULL NAME)

DATE _____ SIGNED _____ DATE _____ SIGNED _____
REGISTERED REPRESENTATIVE OFFICER/ROP

ORIGINAL

number, occupation, citizenship, and at least one bank reference. Other information that may be required is your marital
status, your spouse's name and occupation, and the names of
both your employers.

Depending on the firm and the types of investments you
are making, you may have to fill out (1) a *trading authorization* (if
someone other than yourself will be giving orders in the account); (2) a *client agreement* (that allows the designated AE to
act as your broker); and (3) a *limited trading authorization* (that
allows the AE to exercise trading discretion over your account,
but not to withdraw securities and funds).

If you are opening a *joint account*; an account for a child; are
buying options or futures; are part of a corporation or sole
proprietorship; or want the securities you buy held in your
broker's name (*street name*), then each situation requires your
signature on an appropriate form. These forms are for your
protection as well as the firm's. Any changes in your situation
or specifications must be documented and endorsed.

Margin Account

Margin accounts can be opened instead of or in addition to
regular cash accounts. In a margin account, you may buy or sell
securities by paying only part of their cost—the broker pays the
rest by loaning you the money. Buying on margin can be a
tempting way to increase your holdings, but can also be
dangerous if the securities you bought go down in price. Never
make an investment by depending on a margin account; you
may get in over your head.

To open a margin account, you must complete the same
forms as for a cash account, as well as some additional
agreements, including: (1) a *margin agreement* or *hypothecation
agreement* that explains the terms and conditions under which a
brokerage firm will finance your transaction (see Figure 7-2); (2)
a *loan consent agreement* (that allows the broker to use your securities as collateral for loans from banks); and (3) a *credit agreement* (that specifies how and when interest is charged on your
account).

Figure 7-2a. *A Typical Customer Margin Agreement/Loan Consent Form (front).*

Stone, Forrest & Rivers
INCORPORATED

Customer Margin Agreement / Loan Consent

Name of Customer | Office Number | Account Number

R.R. Number

Gentlemen:

In consideration of your accepting and carrying for the undersigned one or more accounts (whether designated by name, number or otherwise) the undersigned hereby consents and agrees that:

1. Applicable Rules and Statutes

All transactions under this agreement shall be subject to the constitution, rules, regulations, customs and usage of the exchange or market, and its clearing house, if any, where the transactions are executed by you or your agents, applicable provisions of the federal securities laws, and the rules and regulations of the United States Securities and Exchange Commission, and the Board of Governors of the Federal Reserve System.

2. Liens

Any and all monies, securities, or property belonging to the undersigned or in which the undersigned may have an interest held by you or carried in any of my accounts (either individually or jointly with others) shall be subject to a general lien for the discharge of all of the undersigned's debts and obligations to you, wherever or however arising and without regard to whether or not you have made advances with respect to such property, and irrespective of the number of such accounts you shall have the right to transfer, and you are hereby authorized to sell and/or purchase any and all property in any such accounts without notice to satisfy such general lien. You shall have the right to transfer monies, securities, and other property so held by you from or to any other of the accounts of the undersigned whenever in your judgment you consider such a transfer necessary for your protection. In enforcing your lien, you shall have the discretion to determine which securities and property are to be sold and which contracts are to be closed.

3. Authority to Pledge

Any or all securities or any other property, now or hereafter held by you, or carried by you for the undersigned (either individually or jointly with others), or deposited to secure the same, may from time to time and without notice to me, be carried in your general loans and may be pledged, repledged, hypothecated or re-hypothecated, separately or in common with other securities or any other property, for the sum due to you thereon or for a greater sum, and without retaining in your possession and control for delivery a like amount of similar securities.

4. Authority to Borrow

In case of the sale of any security or other property by you at the direction of the undersigned and your inability to deliver the same to the purchaser by reason of failure of the undersigned to supply you therewith, then and in such event, the undersigned authorizes you to borrow any security or other property necessary to make delivery thereof, and the undersigned hereby agrees to be responsible for any loss which you may sustain thereby and any premiums which you may be required to pay thereof, and for any loss which you may sustain by reason for your inability to borrow the security or other property sold.

5. Maintenance of Margin

The undersigned will at all times maintain margins for said accounts, as required by you from time to time.

6. Payment of Indebtedness upon Demand

The undersigned shall at all times be liable for the payment upon demand of any debit balance or other obligations owing in any of the accounts of the undersigned with you and the undersigned shall be liable to you for any deficiency remaining in any such accounts in the event of the liquidation thereof, in whole or in part, by you or by the undersigned; and, the undersigned shall make payment of such obligations and indebtedness upon demand.

The reasonable costs and expenses of collection of the debit balance and any unpaid deficiency in the accounts of the undersigned with you, including, but not limited to, attorney's fees, incurred and payable or paid by you shall be payable to you by the undersigned.

7. Designation of Orders

It is understood and agreed that the undersigned, when placing with you any sell order for short account, will designate it as such and hereby authorizes you to mark such order as being "short," and when placing with you any order for long account, will designate it as such and hereby authorizes you to mark such orders as being "long." Any sell order which the undersigned shall designate as being for long account as above provided, is for securities then owned by the undersigned and, if such securities are not then deliverable by you from any account of the undersigned, the placing of such order shall constitute a representation by the undersigned that it is impracticable for him then to deliver such securities to you but that he will deliver them as soon as it is possible for him to do so. It is understood that such delivery is due on or before the settlement date of the transaction.

8. Capacity

In all transactions between you and the undersigned, the undersigned understands that you are acting as the brokers of the undersigned, except when you disclose to the undersigned in the confirmation that you are acting as dealers for your own account or as brokers for some other person.

9. Presumption of Receipt of Communications

Communications may be sent to the undersigned at the address of the undersigned or at such other address as the undersigned may hereafter give you in writing, and all communications so sent, whether by mail, telegraph, messenger or otherwise, shall be deemed given to the undersigned personally, whether actually received or not.

10. Reports and Statements

Reports of executions of orders and statements of the account of the undersigned shall be conclusive if not objected to in writing, the former within five (5) days, the latter within ten (10) days, of the date on which such material was forwarded by you or your agents to the undersigned, by mail or otherwise.

11. Free Credit Balances

It is understood and agreed that any free credit balance in any account in which I have an interest is maintained in such account solely for the purpose of investment or reinvestment in securities or other investment instruments.

12. Margin Interest Charges

The undersigned acknowledges receipt of Truth-in-Lending Disclosure Statement. It is understood that interest will be charged on debit balances in accordance with the methods and procedures described in this statement or in any amendment or revision thereto which may be provided to me. Unless otherwise noted hereon, or unless I am provided notice to the contrary in accordance with the relevant provisions of this agreement, the following schedule shall set forth the maximum charges to be made on debit balances in the undersigned's accounts:

Average Debit Balance for Interest Period	Interest Charge Above Broker Call Loan Rate
$ 0–15,000	2.0%
15,001–50,000	1.5%
50,001–and over	1.0%

13. Agreement to Arbitrate Controversies

It is agreed that any controversy between us arising out of your business or this agreement shall be submitted to arbitration conducted under the provisions of the Constitution and Rules of the Board of Governors of the New York Stock Exchange or pursuant to the Code of Arbitration of the National Association of Securities Dealers, as the undersigned may elect.

Figure 7-2b. *Customer Margin Agreement/Loan Consent Form (back).*

Arbitration must be commenced upon service of either a written demand for arbitration or a written notice of intention to arbitrate, therein electing the arbitration tribunal. In the event the undersigned does not make such designation within five (5) days of such demand or notice, then the undersigned authorizes you to do so on behalf of the undersigned.

14. Extraordinary Events

You shall not be liable for any loss caused directly or indirectly by government restrictions, exchange or market rulings, suspension of trading, war, strikes or other conditions beyond your control.

15. Representation as to Capacity to Enter into Agreement

The undersigned, if an individual, represents that the undersigned is of full age, that the undersigned is not an employee of any exchange, or of any corporation of which any exchange owns a majority of the capital stock, or of a member of any exchange, or of a member firm or member corporation registered on any exchange or of a bank, trust company, insurance company or of any corporation, firm or individual engaged in the business of dealing either as broker or as principal in securities, bills of exchange, bankers' acceptances or commercial paper or other forms of credit securities or instruments. The undersigned further represents that no one except the undersigned has an interest in the account or accounts of the undersigned with you.

16. Joint and Several Liability

If the undersigned shall consist of more than one individual, their obligations under this agreement shall be joint and several.

17. Rights under Agreement

Your failure to insist at any time upon strict compliance with this agreement or with any of its terms or any continued course of such conduct on your part shall in no event constitute or be considered a waiver by you of any of your rights or privileges. The undersigned hereby expressly agrees that you shall not be bound by any representation or agreement heretofore or hereafter made by any of your employees or agents which in any way purports to modify, affect or diminish your rights under this agreement, and that no representation or advice by you or your employees or agents regarding the purchase or sale by the undersigned of any securities, or other property bought or sold on the undersigned's order or carried or held in any manner for the undersigned's account shall be deemed to be a representation with respect to the future value or performance of such securities, or other property.

18. Continuity of Agreement

This agreement shall inure to the benefit of your successors and assigns, by merger, consolidation or otherwise, and you may transfer the account of the undersigned to any such successors or assigns.

This agreement and all the terms thereof shall be binding upon the undersigned's heirs, executors, administrators, personal representatives and assigns. In the event of the undersigned's death, incompetency, or disability, whether or not executors, administrators, committee or conservators of my estate and property shall have qualified or been appointed, you may cancel any open orders for the purchase or sale of any property, you may place orders for the sale of the property which you may be carrying for me and for which payment has not been made or buy any property of which my accounts may be short, or any part thereof, under the same terms and conditions as hereinabove stated, as though the undersigned were alive and competent without prior notice to the undersigned's heirs, executors, administrators, personal representatives, assigns, committee or conservators, without prior demand or call of any kind upon them or any of them.

19. Headings are Descriptive

The heading of each provision hereof is for descriptive purposes only and shall not be deemed to modify or qualify any of the rights or obligations set forth in each provision.

20. Separability

If any provision or condition of this agreement shall be held to be invalid or unenforceable by any court, or regulatory or self-regulatory agency or body, such invalidity or unenforceability shall attach only to such provision or condition. The validity of the remaining provisions and conditions shall not be affected thereby and this agreement shall be carried out as if such invalid or unenforceable provision or condition were not contained herein.

21. Written Authority Required for Waiver or Modification

Except as herein otherwise expressly provided, no provision of this agreement shall in any respect be waived, altered, modified or amended unless such waiver, alteration, modification or amendment is committed to writing and signed by an officer of your organization.

22. The Laws of the State of New York Govern

This agreement and its enforcement shall be governed by the laws of the State of New York, shall cover individually and collectively all accounts which the undersigned may open or reopen with you, and shall inure to the benefit of your successors and assigns whether by merger, consolidation or otherwise, and you may transfer the accounts of the undersigned to your successors and assigns.

23. Acknowledgement of Receipt of Agreement

The undersigned has read this agreement in its entirety before signing, and acknowledges receipt of a copy of this agreement.

Dated _____

_____

INDIVIDUAL OR JOINT ACCOUNT SIGNATURE

_____

(Second Party, If Joint Account)

_____

PARTNERSHIP SIGNATURE

(Name of Partnership)

By _____
    (A Partner)

_____

CORPORATION SIGNATURE

(Name of Corporation)

By _____

Title _____

Lending Agreement

You are hereby specifically authorized to lend to yourselves, as principal or otherwise, or to others, any securities held by you on margin for any accounts of the undersigned or as collateral therefore, either separately or with other securities.

This agreement shall inure to the benefit of your successors and assigns, by merger, consolidation or otherwise, and you may transfer the account of the undersigned to any such successors or assigns.

Dated _____

_____

INDIVIDUAL OR JOINT ACCOUNT SIGNATURE

_____

(Second Party, If Joint Account)

_____

PARTNERSHIP SIGNATURE

(Name of Partnership)

By _____
    (A Partner)

_____

CORPORATION SIGNATURE

(Name of Corporation)

By _____

Title _____

Special Miscellaneous (Memorandum) Account (SMA)

A *special miscellaneous account* is established to allow you to make use of *paper profits* or excess deposits without disturbing the security position in your margin account. This account can be viewed as a credit line that costs nothing if unused and, if used, increases your *debit balance*.

Cash Management Account (CMA)

A *cash management account*, also called an umbrella account, an active assets account, a financial management account, and other names, provides a variety of different services depending on the firm you deal with. This type of account requires a minimum deposit ranging from $1,000 to $20,000. Some of the services it provides include: checking privileges, automatic reinvestment of interest or dividends, interest on credit balance, and a credit card. A money market fund account is similar to this type of brokerage account except that a money market account requires a smaller minimum deposit and excludes a credit card. Appropriate forms are need to open this type of account.

8

Entering an Order

How An Order Is Executed

When you contact your brokerage firm to buy or sell a listed security, your AE or broker places the information on an order form, or *office ticket* and it is entered on a computer in the *order department*. The order is then sent to the floor of the exchange via telephone, teletype, or computer, where clerks transfer some of the information onto a *floor ticket*. Federal law and exchange rules determine the information required on both kinds of tickets. Only members of the exchange are permitted to execute orders, so the clerk on the exchange floor contacts an available *commission house broker* or *two-dollar broker* to actually execute the order.

When the execution is completed, the trade information is sent back to the firm's order department. From there, the pertinent information is sent to the *purchase and sales department* (P&S) for recording the order, figuring the monies due, comparing the order with the broker on the other side of the transaction, and confirming the trade with the customer. The cashiering, accounting, and stock record departments are also notified of the trade. (Generally, the broker on the floor will not notify you to confirm the execution of your order. Instead, the

AE will notify you by telephone that the trade took place, and at what price the stock was bought or sold. If you do not get a call from the AE by the end of the day, call him or her for verbal confirmation.

A couple of days after the execution, you should receive written confirmation of your transaction in the mail. The confirmation usually shows the following information:

1) *trade date*
2) *settlement date*
3) quantity
4) price
5) point of execution
6) method of execution
7) customer name and address
8) commission charges
9) applicable taxes and fees
10) money required (if any)

Figure 8-1. *An Illustrative Confirmation Notice.*

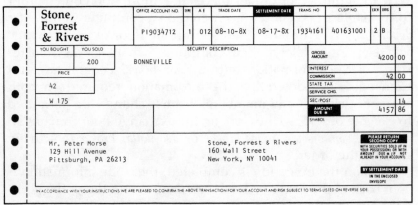

Units of Trading

Most stocks trading on the NYSE are bought and sold in 100-share units called *round lots*. A trading unit less than a round lot (e.g., 1 to 99 shares) is called an *odd lot*. In some cases, orders for a combination of an odd lot and a round lot (e.g., buying 150 shares of a stock), require two order tickets.

Types of Orders

Three major type of orders are: market, limit, and stop orders.

Market Order

A *market order* is an order to buy or sell at the best available price as soon as the order reaches the floor. Usually, this type of order is executed at a price reasonably close to the quote obtained before the order was taken. A broker who fails to follow such instructions due to negligence, is responsible for *missing the market*, and reimburses the customer for any loss. Missing the market rarely occurs but can happen if an order is misplaced, or if the broker accepts too many orders for different securities at the same time.

Limit Order

A *limit order* is entered when you or the broker sets a maximum price you will pay as a buyer or a minimum price you will accept as a seller. Your order must not be executed until the established price is reached. Such a price limitation includes an understood "or better" instruction. Therefore, to avoid missing the market, the broker should execute the order immediately if the limit or better is obtainable.

Stop Order

A *stop order* is an order that is temporarily suspended. In effect, a stop order is a memorandum that will become a buy order or a sell order if and when the market price equals or passes through the price stated in the memorandum. For example, if you bought a stock at $30 and it is currently selling at $28, you might want to place a *sell stop order* at $25. If trading in the stock touches or drops below $25, your order is activated and becomes an order to sell *at-the-market*, limiting your loss to $5 per share plus commissions.

Special Instructions

Market, limit, and stop orders can be supplemented with time instructions, such as a *good-til-cancelled* (GTC) order. This instruction keeps a buy or sell order valid until it is executed or cancelled by the customer (unlike day orders, which are effective only for the trading day on which they are entered).

Other instructions are also used to supplement market, limit, and stop orders, such as not held (NH), all or none (AON), fill or kill (FOK), and immediate or cancel (IOC).

Selling Short

Usually, investors buy securities before they sell them. (Such positions are said to be *long*.) In a *short* sale, however, investors sell securities that they do *not* own and incur the obligation to buy the securities sometime in the future to "cover" the short position. Investors sell short because they anticipate a decline in price. Fundamentally, selling short is an inversion of the buy-low/sell-high principle: sell high (now, without delivering right away) and buy low (later, to repay the shares borrowed). (See Figure 8-2.)

Payment of Dividends

When you invest in common or preferred stock (as discussed in Chapter 2), you are entitled to *dividend* returns on the stock you purchased. (Dividends are that portion of the after-tax earnings that the corporation's directors declare and pay to the shareholders.)

Several key dates apply to dividend payment; as an investor, you should understand their importance. For example,

Figure 8-2. *How a Short Sale Works.*

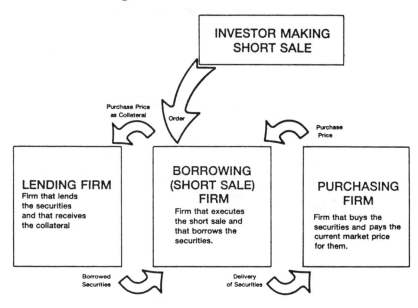

suppose investor Bill Brown knows that his dividends on a particular stock arrive around August 3 or 4. He buys 100 additional shares, but gets no extra dividend. When he calls his broker for an explanation, Bill discovers that he must have owned the newer shares of stock on July 1 to be eligible to receive the August dividend on them.

Susan Ryan sells 100 shares of the same stock on July 24, but still expects to receive the dividend. She is surprised when no dividend arrives because she owned the stock when the dividend was declared.

These and similar situations occur frequently because many investors are confused about the different dividend dates. Therefore we explain here some of the important dividend dates involved in a transaction.

- *Trade date:* the day on which the trade is executed.
- *Settlement date:* the day on which money is due the broker for a purchase, or the certificate is due the broker for a sale.

- *Declaration date:* the day on which a corporation's board of directors meets, decides on the amount of the dividend, and makes the public announcement.

- *Ex-Dividend date:* the day on which a security begins to trade without the value of the dividend belonging to the purchaser. Because almost all securities contracts are settled *regular way* (this means the settlement date is five business days after the trade date), the ex-dividend date is usually the fourth business day before the record date.

- *Record date:* the day on which a corporation closes its register of securities holders to determine the recipients of a previously announced distribution. This date is set by the directors of the issuing corporation.

- *Payment date:* the day on which the corporation makes payment of the dividend to previously determined holders of record.

Whether or not you are entitled to a dividend payment depends largely on the date you purchased or sold your stock and its relation to the record date. Since the record date is set by the corporation's directors, it may seem that you have little control over your dividend acquisition. The concepts behind dividend dates can be very confusing to the novice investor; the knowledge and experience of your AE will probably come in handy at this time. However, a good rule to remember is this: If the settlement date is any day up to and including the record date, the buyer is entitled to the dividend. If settlement date falls after the record date, the dividend belongs to the seller.

Payment of Accrued Interest

Accrued interest is the interest on a bond from the last payment date to settlement date. Accrued interest is paid by the buyer to the seller; but the buyer's expense is only temporary. When the corporation next pays interest on its debt, the purchaser collects the entire amount accumulated during the normal six-month period. Part of this amount is reimbursement for the earlier payment to the previous bondholder. The other part of the interest payment is due because the buyer now has the status of a creditor of that concern.

Your Monthly Statement

Whether you are an active investor, or one who only periodically enhances or changes your holdings, the accounting department of most brokerage firms handles the maintenance of your account, and sends you a statement of your transactions. Under federal law, if there has been any transaction activity, security position, or money balance in an account within the preceding calendar quarter, the customer must be given a statement of account. Many firms comply by sending their customers (particularly margin account customers), monthly statements instead of the mandatory quarterly report.

Whether monthly or quarterly, the statement summarizes all that has occurred in your account during the period. All purchase expenses are debited to the account, and sales proceeds are credited. However, each purchase and/or sales transaction is posted on contract settlement date, whereas all other activities are posted on the day they occur.

For example, a check received from a customer is credited to the account on the day it is received, and money delivered out of the account is debited on the actual day of reimbursement. But a regular-way trade of a corporate security on June 26 is not posted until July 3, five business days later. This difference is often a point of confusion for customers, especially toward the end of the month when they receive their statements of account without the trade posted on it.

Despite the best efforts and intentions of the accounting department, mistakes do occur. Perhaps an issue is not carried forward to the following month's position listing, or duplicate entries are processed accidentally and both items are posted in the account. A typical customer statement therefore contains a self-protective legend, "E & OE," which means, *errors and omis-*

sions excepted. This statement allows the brokerage firm an opportunity to correct the mistake without legal liability.

The statement may also carry a legend advising customers of financial protection afforded them under *SEC Rule 15c3-3*. Free credit balances must be maintained in a "special reserve bank account for the exclusive benefit of customers," a rule that denies the brokerage firm the right to use those funds in the speculative conduct of its own business. The accounting department, employing a formula approved by stock exchange or NASD authority, supervises firm compliance with this rule and ensures that customer money is used only for customer purposes.

Entering an order is perhaps the easiest part of investing, but it can be a source of many a misunderstanding between you and your brokerage firm. To minimize such problems, make certain that you are communicating clearly. State the details of your order slowly and distinctly, and even have the account executive repeat them to you. When you get the call-back confirming the execution of the order, *listen* carefully. Even if there was an error in execution, the damage can be held down by correcting the error promptly.

9
Fundamental Analysis

If you're like most individual investors, you sense an aura of mystery surrounding the world of security analysis. For many investors, security analysts and the tools and techniques of the trade seem remote, complex, and difficult to comprehend. In this chapter, we try to show you that security analysis is simply the application of common sense, in conjunction with certain key mathematical ratios, to decisions to buy, hold, or sell particular stocks.

Many individual investors like yourself hesitate to venture into this area for a number of reasons. First, the practitioners (security analysts themselves) have developed their own jargon as a way of fostering professionalism and discouraging amateur investors. Second, many people are reluctant to deal with the mathematics aspects of security analysis—"number crunching" as professional analysts call it. In the course of this chapter we hope to help you understand the jargon of security analysis and to see the mathematics and its application in a clearer and more comfortable light.

If you plan to hire professionals to direct and advise you

about your investments, you might wonder why you need an understanding of security analysis at all. The reasons are twofold. First, to know whether your investment advisors are doing a good job for you, and presenting you with good ideas and suggestions, you must have some grasp of security analysis and understand what the advisors are talking about. You may discover that their research is of poor quality or that they simply follow the pack rather than offer truly creative suggestions. Second, you may find that you enjoy doing your own research. In fact, in recent years, so many individuals have chosen this route that the National Association of Individual Investors was founded and has grown to over 100,000 members, the vast majority of whom view security analysis and investments as their hobby and/or part-time business.

Fundamental versus Technical Analysis

At the outset, you need to understand the distinction between the two principal schools of thought that dominate security analysis—fundamental and technical analysis. *Fundamental analysis* looks to the fundamentals of a company—its earnings, sales, assets, liabilities, cash flow, and rate of return on equity, to name just a few. Fundamental security analysts believe that these factors are important in deciding whether a particular stock represents a buy, sell, or hold position. Most professional security analysts believe in and practice fundamental analysis, although different analysts place differing amounts of emphasis on particular ratios and factors.

Technical analysts, on the other hand, focus less on the fundamentals of a particular company's stock, and more on what the market action tells them is occurring. Technical analysts spend their time studying price and volume movements and from these studies determine the direction a particular company's stock is going—up, down, or sideways.

Because a substantial number of investors subscribe to technical theories and follow the advice of technical analysts, technical analysis does indeed have an impact on the marketplace. As a final step in analyzing a company, many fundamental analysts consult the brokerage firm's technical analysts to learn their feelings about a particular stock's trading pattern and price prognosis. Fundamental analysis is generally used to discover an appropriate stock; technical analysis is used to determine the right *time* to invest in that stock.

To introduce you to fundamental analysis, we divide the universe of public companies into two categories—asset plays and growth situations. (There are also hybrids of these forms.) This breakdown into categories helps determine whether more emphasis should be placed on analyzing the company's balance sheet or its income statement, and which numerical ratios have the most significance for the company.

Asset Plays

What is an asset play? An asset play is simply a company whose assets significantly exceed its liabilities. In the case of a pure asset play, the company's current assets (cash, cash equivalents, marketable securities, inventories, and receivables) may be many times more than the company's current liabilities. A particular company may also have hidden assets, including such items as undervalued real estate, marketable securities carried at cost rather than current value, valuable consumer franchises and brand names, saleable subsidiaries and divisions, and/or excess funding in a pension plan.

How do you analyze an asset play situation? To analyze an asset play situation, you should concentrate your attention and effort on the company's *balance sheet*. Try to determine if the parts are worth more than the whole. You then apply certain key ratios to the particular company's balance sheet to determine if its stock does, in fact, represent an asset play. The following discussion begins by describing the balance sheet and then explains the key ratios and how to calculate them. Finally, we show you some things to look for when making an analysis of an asset-play company. Figure 9-1 can be used for this exercise.

Figure 9-1. *Income Statement and Balance Sheet.*

Income Statement
for the Year Ended December 31, 19X1
($000)

Net Sales		200
Cost of Goods Sold	150	
Depreciation	10	
Selling, General, and Administrative Expenses	20	
		180
Net Operating Profit		20
Other Expenses	3	
Interest Expense	3	
Income Taxes	4	
		10
Net Income		10

Balance Sheet
of XYZ Corporation December 31, 19X1

Assets		Liabilities	
Cash/Cash Equivalents	80	Accounts/Notes Payable	40
Accounts Receivable	40	Accrued Liabilities	30
Inventory	40	Current Portion,	
Current Assets	160	Long-Term Debt	10
Fixed Assets (Plant &		Current Liabilities	80
Equipment)	100		
Less: Depreciation	(70)	Long-Term Liabilities	
Net Fixed Assets	30	(Funded Debt)	40
Other Assets	10	Total Liabilities	120
Total Assets	200		
		Shareholders' Equity	
		Capital Stock	20
		Retained Earnings	60
		Net Worth—	
		Stockholders' Equity	80
		Total Liabilities & Net Worth	200

The Balance Sheet

A balance sheet presents a company's accounts on a specific date, usually the final business day of the quarter or the year. One side of the balance sheet describes the company's *assets*—the funds the company has—in order of liquidity, from liquid assets (cash and cash equivalents) to illiquid assets (plant and equipment—assets that cannot readily be converted to cash). The other side of the balance sheet lists the company's liabilities and net worth. The *liabilities*—the funds the company owes—are presented in the order in which they come due. *Net worth*—the funds *owned* by the company in excess of the funds *owed* by the company—is displayed as a balancing figure below liabilities. The two sides of a balance sheet must always equal even if a company is insolvent (liabilities exceed assets), the equalization is expressed as a negative net worth. At this point, you should refer to Figure 9-1 to familiarize yourself with a sample balance sheet.

Key Ratios

What key ratios are used to determine if a particular company and its stock represent an asset play? The key ratios in making this determination are referred to as liquidity ratios and include the current ratio and the quick ratio. The *current ratio* is defined as current assets divided by current *liabilities*. (Current assets are those that can be converted into cash within one year or less and current liabilities are those that must be paid within one year.) The current ratio is essentially a measure of liquidity and should be compared to the company's past pattern as well as to the pattern of the industry in which the company operates. A 2:1 ratio is the norm for most companies and industries, while a current asset ratio of 5:1 or more may signal that the company represents an asset play. The higher the current asset ratio the more appealing a company becomes to companies and individual investors seeking to make an acquisition. Refer to the balance sheet in Table 9-1; the *current ratio* would be calculated as follows:

$$\text{Current ratio} = \frac{\text{Current assets}}{\text{Current liabilities}}$$

$$= \frac{160}{80} = 2:1$$

Norm: 2:1

Another ratio used to determine whether a company represents an asset play is the quick ratio, also referred to as the acid-test ratio. This ratio represents an even more stringent measure of liquidity. The *quick ratio* is calculated by adding cash, cash equivalents (for example, marketable securities), and accounts receivable, and then dividing by current liabilities. (The ratio can also be arrived at by subtracting inventory from current assets and dividing by current liabilities as shown here.) Refer to the balance sheet in Figure 9-1; the quick ratio would be calculated as follows:

$$\text{Quick ratio} = \frac{\text{Cash} + \text{Cash equivalents} + \text{Receivables}}{\text{Current liabilities}}$$

$$\text{or, Quick ratio} = \frac{\text{Current assets} - \text{Inventory}}{\text{Current liabilities}}$$

$$\text{Quick ratio} = \frac{120}{80} = 1.5{:}1$$

Norm: 1:1

Note that inventory is excluded from the asset calculation because it is considered the least liquid asset and the most subject to manipulation by corporate management. A ratio of 1:1 is acceptable for most companies, assuming that year-to-year comparisons reveal positive trends.

Calculating the quick ratio (acid-test ratio) brings into focus those companies that represent asset plays. To the professional analyst or the merger and acquisition specialist, a high quick ratio means that the company should be examined more closely. Thus, the quick ratio serves as a *screening device* that a professional analyst can use to rapidly identify those companies worth more of the analyst's time and effort.

Analyzing Current Assets

When examining a company's current assets, pay special attention to the category referred to as marketable securities.

Marketable securities represent stocks or bonds the company is holding for investment purposes. This category is frequently a "burying place" for hidden assets, so whenever you see marketable securities carried on a company's balance sheet, you should determine whether the number shown represents *cost or market value*. In many instances, companies show on their balance sheet the cost value for securities purchased years ago. In such cases, the true worth of the company—the value of the parts as opposed to the whole—may be masked unless the analyst considers the *current value* of the marketable securities owned by the company.

The question of cost versus market value in the case of maketable securities brings home the importance of examining the footnotes to a company's Annual Report. Most professional securities analysts read a company's Annual Report from the back to the front, because most analysts feel that any problems the company has will be buried in the footnotes. The number of footnotes attached to a company's Annual Report may also give an analyst a feeling about the quality of the particular company's sales and earnings figures. Did the company make use of every accounting rule to improve its earnings picture? Generally, the more footnotes attached to an Annual Report, the more closely the numbers—and management's management of these numbers—must be examined. The analyst also needs to know whether the outside accountants who prepared the annual report issued a *qualified opinion*, that is, an opinion based on certain assumptions and representations. If the opinion issued by the accountants is a qualified one, what is the significance of these qualifications? Finally, as an individual investor, you should look to the company's 10K for a complete picture. The 10K is the financial report that the corporation must file with the SEC. The Annual Report released to stockholders is a shortened form of the 10K.

Receivables and inventory are not heavily emphasized when analyzing asset plays. We discuss them here, however, because receivables and inventory have considerable significance as tools for gauging the health of a company.

Receivables represent the money owed to the company by its customers. Receivables are self-liquidating because a company's customers will pay the money they owe to the company within a short period of time—sixty to ninety days. The following key ratios are utilized in analyzing receivables:

$$\text{Receivables turnover} = \frac{\text{Net annual sales}}{\text{Average receivables}}$$

The average receivable is the figure at the beginning of the year plus the figure at year end, divided by two. For purposes of this example, assume that at year end December 31, 19X1 receivables amounted to 45.

$$\text{Receivables turnover} = \frac{200}{(40 + 45)/2} = \frac{200}{85/2} = \frac{200}{42.5} = 4.71$$

$$\text{Average turnover period} = \frac{\text{Number of days in the year}}{\text{Receivable turnover}}$$
$$= \frac{365}{4.71} = 77.49$$

These calculations indicate that receivables are generally collected in about 77 days.

What information about the health and viability of a particular company can you as an individual investor determine from the average turnover period of receivables? Before you can draw any conclusion about the significance of this number, you must first compare it with the prior year's number. Look for the *trend* in receivables, that is, whether the company collects the money owed it by its customers in a progressively longer or shorter period of time. Second, compare the pattern of the particular company's average turnover period with that of other companies in the same industry. Finally, look at who the company's customers are, that is, the *quality* of a company's receivables.

After you have considered all of the foregoing factors, you should be able to determine if the company is having difficulty collecting its receivables. Problems in the area of accounts receivable are usually the first signal of imminent financial and liquidity problems. In this case, you should make an effort to determine how serious or significant the problem is.

Inventories are another area that should be examined when determining the health of a company.

The key ratio in this area is as follows:

$$\text{Inventory turnover} = \frac{\text{Net sales}}{\text{Average inventory}}$$

For the purposes of this example, assume that at year ended December 31, 19X1, inventory amounted to 50.

$$\text{Inventory turnover} = \frac{200}{(40 + 50)/2} = \frac{200}{90/2} = \frac{200}{45} = 4.44$$

As with receivables, you must look at the year-to-year trend to gauge the significance of this ratio. In addition, this number has significance only when compared with the ratios of other companies in the same industry. What might be a normal inventory turnover figure for one industry may be extremely high or low for another. You should consider the range the figure falls into: Too low a figure may mean that the inventory is dated or obsolete (for example, a garment manufacturer with an inventory of double knits); too high a figure could mean that the company is not maintaining an adequate inventory to meet the growth in sales and may be losing sales because it is unable to meet demand.

In summary, the importance of inventory and receivable figures depends on the nature of the industry in which the company engages. Both figures should be used to gauge a company's health.

Analyzing Noncurrent and Hidden Assets

Besides identifying asset-play companies by the cash or cash equivalents on their balance sheets, you can also identify such companies on the basis of their noncurrent or "below-the-line" assets.

What specific noncurrent assets should you concentrate on? Real estate is probably the most important item in this category. When looking at the real estate a company owns, you should consider a number of factors. First, to what degree is the property the company owns fully depreciated on its balance sheet? If a company's plant and offices are fully depreciated, then they were purchased years ago, at prices that today would represent a bargain. The same analysis can apply to department store chains and other retail operations that may have very lucrative lease arrangements in effect. The presence of such fully depreciated real estate on a company's balance sheet warrants further research.

How do you research the value of a company's real estate? The first thing to do is to identify the location of the real estate. Such information is typically contained in the company's Annual Report or Form 10K. Further, the footnotes to the Annual Report or Form 10K identify the cost basis at which the real estate is carried on the company's books. If you are familiar with the prevailing market value of the real estate in the area where the company owns its real estate, you should be able to determine whether the company-owned real estate is "under the market" and, if so, by how much.

Alternative uses for the real estate is another factor to consider when assessing its value. Perhaps a company's real estate would be worth more if it were put to some other use. For example, a company that rents parking spaces might find that the land it owns or has under long-term lease would be more valuable if commercial or residential properties were developed on the parking lot site. Likewise, special interest should be paid to any company that has substantial holdings of undeveloped land on its books. (Many of the smaller railroad and real estate investment trusts fit into this category.) Such holdings may indeed represent hidden assets.

What other types of hidden assets should you look for? Other items that can be categorized as "below-the-line" or hidden assets include undervalued divisions or subsidiaries, trade names or consumer franchises, excess funding in a pension plan, and treasury stock and/or repurchase programs.

In looking for companies that represent asset plays you should consider the real worth of a company's business. For example, in recent years the value of many publishing and printing companies has appreciated at a rapid rate. In some instances—particularly in the smaller newspaper and communication companies—the real worth of such businesses is not reflected on the company's balance sheet. Similarly, many companies have very profitable and valuable subsidiaries whose real value is not reflected in the price of the company's stock. Consumer recognition of a company's products is also worth money to a potential buyer of the company. Finally, many companies have excess funding in their pension plans. Such a buildup of assets may result from either conservative management practices or from a miscalculation of the company's potential pension liabilities. Many companies have moved on their own to eliminate such excess funding and to channel money into other areas of the business.

One important signal to help the individual investor to identify an asset play is the existence of *treasury stock* and/or a stock *repurchase program*. Treasury stock and stock repurchase programs represent a two-edged sword. On the one hand, a company may repurchase its own stock because management feels the stock is undervalued in the marketplace and/or the price does not reflect the real worth of the company. On the other hand, treasury stock or a stock repurchase program makes it difficult, if not impossible, for an outsider to gain control of the company.

Analyzing Proxy Statements

Once you have identified a potential asset play via an examination of the company's current and noncurrent assets, the final step to take before purchasing the stock is to examine the company's proxy statement. Determining management's intentions in relation to the company is the cornerstone of the decision to buy a particular asset play or not. Obviously, the older the management, the more likely it is that the company will soon be sold or liquidated. However, the presence of a chain of succession (a son, daughter, cousin, niece, or nephew in the business) and the absence of professional management, make it less likely that the business will be sold. Obviously, as the company's management and affiliated parties own more stock, they increase their say in the future destiny of the company. For these reasons, the hardest job for investors in asset plays is "crystal balling" what future developments will occur for such companies, and what the timing of such developments will be. Attending the company's Annual Meeting and establishing personal contact with someone inside the company may be the best route to follow when forecasting a particular situation.

Now that you have learned to identify a company that represents an asset play, you're probably asking yourself a couple of questions. First, which industries have the greatest number of companies that meet the criteria for an asset play? Second, what reference sources can you consult to locate asset plays? And last, is there a checklist to use in connection with identifying asset plays?

In answer to the first question, asset plays are typically found off the beaten track in the so-called smoke-stack industries. Because they are in dull, uninteresting, or mature industries, few of the major brokerage firms' analysts take the time to identify and follow asset plays. Many asset plays are found among small companies with few shares outstanding. A major brokerage firm, such as Merrill Lynch, is unlikely to recommend such a stock to its customers, because only a small number of shares are available in the marketplace. For these reasons, many asset plays represent real bargains and sell at ridiculously low prices in light of their assets and earnings. Typically, an asset play remains cheap until it is discovered by an analyst or portfolio manager or until some development—a restructuring of the business, a merger, or a leverage buy-out—makes the public aware of the real worth of the company. In the area of asset plays, the individual investor with the time and the interest to perform the necessary research has a distinct advantage over the professional analyst who confines himself to researching large, well-capitalized, household-name companies.

What sources can be used to identify asset plays? The *Graham-*

Rea Report is an advisory service published on a monthly basis. This report highlights companies that fit the criteria of asset plays. Information provided includes the net cash assets behind each share as well as other relevant figures and ratios. A second approach to identifying asset plays requires you to find out which brokerage firms specialize in identifying undervalued stocks. You can then follow in the *pink sheets* the stocks in which those firms are making a market. In the same vein, you might want to subscribe to a service called *Spectrum*, published on a quarterly basis, that lists the holdings of all mutual funds and investment advisors, including the positions held by limited partnerships. By following what professional asset analysts are doing, you can learn about their techniques and come up with ideas about companies to research further.

Growth Situations

With an asset play you concentrate on analyzing a company's balance sheet, whereas growth situations require you to take apart the company's income statement. Before proceeding further, familiarize yourself with Figure 9-1, concentrating on the items comprising the *Income Statement for the Year Ended December 31, 19X1.*

Characteristics of Growth Situations

Unlike asset plays, in which the emphasis is placed on what the company owns—its assets—the analysis of growth situations is more difficult because you are attempting to look into the future. You must discern *trends in earnings and sales* and, based on past performance, forecast what the future will bring for a particular company. In analyzing growth situations you must get a "reading" on *management's ability to achieve its defined goals* rather than simply analyze balance sheet items such as cash, marketable securities, and real estate. To complicate matters, many growth companies are characterized by weak or poor balance sheets simply because the company is straining its asset base to meet the demand for its products or services. To decide whether a particular growth company is an appropriate investment you must calculate the return on equity and total assets, the growth rate in dividends and earnings (g), and the price-to-earnings ratio.

Techniques for Analyzing Sales, Earnings, & General Expenses

The trend in a company's sales, earnings, and expenses is a crucial factor in deciding whether the company and its stock represent a growth situation. The emphasis is placed on the word *trend*: A sharp rise in sales and/or earnings between one year and the next does not confirm such a conclusion; there must be a *pattern* of such year-to-year growth. Most professional analysts look for the *five-year trend* to confirm that the company does indeed represent a growth situation.

Another area to concentrate on is what professional analysts call the *bottom line*. A yearly increase in sales is significant only if it is reflected as growth in the company's earnings; that is, sales increases should be reflected in the bottom line or earnings figures. In examining a company's earnings figures, look behind the numbers to determine if the improvement is the result of some unusual event or of an accounting change. Because changes in accounting methods can create certain appearances, most professional analysts read an annual report from the back to the front, concentrating their attention on the number and complexity of the footnotes incorporated into the report. Generally, a large number of footnotes indicates that you should examine the company's figures more closely. The footnotes to the annual report can also indicate the quality of a company's sales and earnings figures. If a company makes frequent changes of its outside accountants—referred to as opinion shopping—you should scrutinize its numbers more intensely.

Beyond the sales and earnings figures, you should look to the pattern of the company's general and administrative expenses. In many instances, a company is able to grow at a rapid pace until it reaches a plateau in earnings and sales. Such a plateau frequently occurs when companies lose control of their general and administrative expenses. The purchase of a corporate jet and other perks often spell problems for a growth company, particularly one in the start-up stage when every dollar of capital is needed in the business. Therefore, you should keep track of the trend of such expenses.

A listing of some of the key ratios applicable to the area of sales, earnings, and expenses and a description of their significance follows.

1. Gross profit margin $= \dfrac{\text{Gross profit}}{\text{Net sales}}$

An examination of a company's gross profit margin over time tells you how able the company is to maintain and hopefully expand its position in its industry. The gross profit margin should be compared to industry figures to determine how the company's margin compares to those of other companies in the same industry.

2. Operating profit margin $= \dfrac{\text{Operating profit}}{\text{Net sales}}$

Radical swings in a company's operating profit margin are generally a good indication of the volatility of a particular industry.

3. Net profit margin $= \dfrac{\text{Net Income}}{\text{Net sales}}$

The net profit margin tells you how well a company keeps its tax liabilities down. This number, too, should be compared to the industry norm to determine whether the company is more or less profitable than other companies in the industry.

Management

This factor is perhaps the most crucial and difficult to analyze in any growth situation, because management capability (or the lack of it) does not lend itself to numerical analysis.

Unlike an asset play situation, in which management may simply function in the role of a caretaker preserving corporate assets, most companies in a growth situation are made or broken on the capabilities of their managements. This is particularly true in high-tech industries, where management must react almost daily to changes and new developments.

How can an individual investor evaluate a company's management? The best way is to have a personal and working knowledge of the industry in which the company engages. For this reason some of the best investment selections are made by individuals working in the industry. Many computer programmers and engineers, for example, have invested successfully in computer and software companies with which they are familiar and with which they deal on a daily basis. If you don't have this familiarity with an industry, you should read whatever is available that describes the company's management, goals, objectives, and track record. Attending a company's Annual Meeting of Shareholders can also help you formulate an opinion about management's overall capabilities and its attitude toward shareholders. While the numbers may indicate that a particular company represents a growth situation, attending the company's Annual Meeting may convince you that management lacks the depth and ability to lead the company to further growth or that the numbers are not true and accurate.

Return on Stockholders' Equity

Beyond sales and earnings figures and management capability, you should look at the return on stockholders' equity (total assets) to determine if the company indeed represents a growth situation. The following equation is used to calculate return on equity (ROE):

$$ROE = \frac{Sales}{Total\ assets} \times \frac{Total\ assets}{Equity} \times \frac{Income}{Sales}$$

$$ROE = \frac{Total\ asset\ turnover \times Financial\ leverage}{\times\ Net\ profit\ margin}$$

To understand what return on equity is all about, consider each component of the preceding equation. The three components of a company's return on equity are: (1) total asset turnover, (2) financial leverage, and (3) net profit margin. This clearly brings home the point that ROE can be improved by greater asset efficiency (turning assets over more rapidly), by altering the company's capital structure (increasing the amount of money borrowed), and/or by increasing the company's net profit margin (increasing productivity and/or changing the company's product mix). By determining the significance of each of these factors when figuring a particular company's ROE, you are now able to answer a number of questions: where the company's growth is coming from (asset turnover, leverage, or profit margin), how the company's ROE compares with that of other companies in the same or similar industries, whether this pattern of growth will continue in the future, and what steps the company can take to improve its ROE.

Because the return on equity (ROE) is so significant in determining the merits of a growth situation, we present an actual example of how ROE is calculated for a particular company. Refer to Figure 9-1 and to the items comprising the Income Statement for the Year Ended December 31, 19X1.

From the Income Statement, you can obtain the following information:

```
Sales         = 200
Total assets  = 200
Equity        =  80
Income        =  10
```

Fitting the given factors into the ROE equation, the ROE for this particular company is as follows:

$$ROE = \frac{200}{200} \times \frac{200}{80} = \frac{10}{200}$$

$$ROE = \frac{10}{80} = 12.50$$

Now that you have calculated the ROE, you are probably asking yourself what significance it has for your investment decisions. The ROE tells you how much a company is earning on the equity, that is, the capital, available to it. For a company (and the stock that represents it) to be considered a growth situation, it must have a high ROE compared with other companies, and the trend of its ROE should be stable and rising.

The Growth Rate (g)

The growth rate of a company and hence the market price of its stock depends on two factors: *The rate of return (ROE)* that is earned on the equity retained in the business and *the amount of earnings retained in the business*. This second factor is frequently referred to as th *retention rate* or RR.

What does the retention rate represent and what does it tell you about a particular company's growth track? A company's board of directors decides how much of a company's earnings is retained in the business. For example, the company described in Figure 9-1 had earnings of 10. In a true growth situation, management might decide to retain the full amount (10) and hence the retention rate would be 100%. Retaining all or nearly all (80 to 90%) of a company's earnings indicates that management believes it can earn the most money for its shareholders by investing in the company itself.

The growth rate (g) of our sample company would be calculated as follows:

$$g = ROE \times RR$$
$$g = 12.50 \times 1.00$$
$$g = 12.50$$

Again, you should consider the five-year trend in g rather than a single year's results.

Price/Earnings (P/E) Ratio

The *price-to-earnings (P/E) ratio* is calculated as follows:

$$P/E = \frac{\text{Market price of the stock}}{\text{Latest 12 months' earnings per share}}$$

In our example, the company earned 10 in its latest 12 months. Let us assume that the company has 10 shares outstanding and that the market price of the stock is $40 per share. Therefore, the P/E ratio would be calculated as follows:

$$P/E = \frac{40}{1} = 40$$

What does a P/E ratio of 40 tell you about a particular stock? The P/E ratio tells you something only when it is compared with the P/E ratios of companies in the same or similar industries and with the P/E ratio of the overall market. Second, the P/E ratio of a particular stock has significance only when it is compared with its own P/E ratios for the past few years. You should consider the P/E ratio simply an expression of market sentiment toward a particular company and its stock—in no way as important as ROE or g in measuring the worth of a company.

Recent studies have been made comparing the market performance of high vs. low P/E stocks. These studies found that, on the whole, low P/E stocks (those typically selling at 10 or below) performed better in the marketplace than high P/E stocks (those selling at 30 and above). A number of reasons were given for these findings. First, high P/E stocks typically have a high proportion of institutional ownership and consequently are more volatile because institutions tend to move more rapidly in and out of individual stocks. Second, a high P/E ratio may mean that the market has already discounted future growth; that is, the price of the stock already reflects future growth in sales and earnings. The results of these studies show that the individual investor should be careful when investing in high P/E stocks because they are more volatile and may already discount future growth.

Some Conclusions About Asset Plays
and Growth Stocks

Now that we have explained some of the tools and techniques utilized by security analysts, it seems appropriate to touch on some differences and similarities between asset plays and growth stocks. Asset situations concentrate on a company's balance sheet, whereas growth situations emphasize the income statement. Asset situations are easier to analyze because they call for more objective judgments and rely on numbers and "number crunching" rather than on the evaluation of a company's management and the inherent subjective aspect of any such appraisal. What both asset plays and growth situations have in common is that they require investors to be consistent and logical in their approach to investing. Should you choose to rely on professional advice for selecting your investments, you now at least have the capability to question your advisor and evaluate the credentials presented.

Hybrid Forms

This area requires just a few comments. While most companies can be classified as either asset plays or growth situations, you may conclude after analyzing a company's balance sheet and income statement that it fits neither of these categories. In fact, the company may appear to possess traits of both categories. In this case, determine which of the two categories the company most nearly fits and apply those specific analytical tools in evaluating the investment merits of the company. The utilization of the tools discussed in this chapter should assist you in deciding whether the company warrants your investment.

10

PlatingCo: A Case Study in Securities Analysis

A Brief Recap

In the preceding chapter we discussed the overall concept of security analysis, particularly the mathematics of number crunching. As with most professions—accounting, law, medicine, and so on—the practitioners have developed a jargon that often acts as a barrier to amateur participation. Hopefully, the chapter eliminated some of the mystery surrounding security analysis, and made you aware of some important points. We review them here before you examine an actual case study.

First, security analysis combines elements of an art with those of a skilled profession. While number crunching simply requires you to develop some basic mathematical skills of an objective nature, security analysis demands you make a number of subjective judgments. Evaluating the capabilities of management and the future prospects for a particular industry or company requires you to make subjective judgments because such evaluations include a large amount of guesswork, luck, or "crystal balling" of future economic trends and developments. For this reason growth situations are more difficult to analyze than asset plays because in a growth situation you must look into the future rather than analyze the present.

Second, although professional security analysts may be more familiar with the tools of the profession and have greater access to raw data and computers for analyzing that data, you should not assume that the judgments of such individuals are any better than your own. Don't be overly impressed with professional credentials; rather look to the track record of such investment professionals. If nothing else, the preceding chapter should have furnished you with sufficient knowledge to ask the right questions and to distinguish a skilled investment professional from one who is not. Finally, you should have the feeling that the stock market is the great equalizer. No matter how skilled the investment professional may be, the market still contains an element of randomness or luck. Security analysis seeks to reduce your reliance on luck or guesswork in making investment decisions and, consequently, to reduce the likelihood of your making disastrous investment decisions. Thus we say that security analysis combines the elements of an art with those of a skilled profession.

Approaching the Case Study

At this point, you should be familiar with the concepts behind security analysis and with its mathematical techniques. The real test of your knowledge of any subject area, however, is its application to a real-life situation. Therefore, in this chapter we "walk you through" the analysis of a company selected at random. Utilizing the number crunching techniques learned in the preceding chapter, we explain the logic on which our conclusions and observations are based. You may disagree with our conclusion, but you should realize that the application of logic and reasoning is the cornerstone of security analysis, much as in a game of chess or in putting together a jigsaw puzzle.

Our starting point is the presentation of a sample company's annual report and proxy statement. Let's call the corporation "PlatingCo." You should spend some time reading and reviewing the annual report and proxy statement because most of this chapter deals with this material. See Figures 10-1, 10-2, and 10-3.

(Text resumes on page 197.)

Figure 10-1. *PlatingCo's Proxy Statement.*

PlatingCo

NOTICE OF ANNUAL MEETING OF STOCKHOLDERS
OF
Plating Co.
227 Plain Boulevard
Freemantle, New York 12580

Notice is hereby given that the Annual Meeting of Stockholders of Plating Co, Inc. (hereinafter called the "Corporation") will be held at the Auditorium of the National Bank, on the 9th Floor at 200 Fifth Avenue, New York, New York 10027, on Tuesday, July 16, 19X5 at 10:00 A.M. (Eastern Daylight Savings Time), for the following purposes:

(1) To elect nine directors to serve in accordance with the By-Laws of the Corporation until the next Annual Meeting of Stockholders, and until their successors are elected and qualified;

(2) To ratify the appointment of Harris & Whitney as auditors of the Corporation for the current fiscal year; and

(3) To act on such other matters as may properly come before the meeting or at any adjournments thereof.

The Board of Directors has fixed the close of business on June 14, 19X5 as the record date for the determination of stockholders entitled to notice of and to vote at the meeting. The transfer books will not be closed.

By Order of the Board of Directors
Frank Nopf
Secretary

Dated: Freemantle, New York
June 24, 19X5

YOUR VOTE IS IMPORTANT. If you cannot attend the meeting, you are urged to complete, date, sign and return the enclosed proxy at your earliest convenience. A postpaid return envelope is enclosed for this purpose.

Figure 10-1. *(cont.)*

PLATINGCO, INC.
227 PLAIN BOULEVARD
FREEMANTLE, NEW YORK 12580

PROXY STATEMENT
for the Annual Meeting of Stockholders
to be held July 16, 19X5

This Proxy Statement is submitted to stockholders in connection with the solicitation by the Board of Directors of PlatingCo, Inc. (the "Corporation") of proxies for the 19X5 Annual Meeting of Stockholders to be held on July 16, 19X5, and at any adjournment thereof. If a proxy in the accompanying form is property executed and returned, the shares represented thereby will be voted as instructed in the proxy. Any proxy may be revoked by a stockholder prior to its exercise upon written notice to the Secretary of the Corporation, or by a stockholder's vote in person at the meeting. This Proxy Statement and the enclosed form of proxy is intended to be mailed on or about June 24, 19X5.

The purposes of the meeting are (1) to elect nine directors to serve in accordance with the By-Laws until the next Annual Meeting of Stockholders and until their successors are elected and qualified; (2) to ratify the appointment of Harris & Whitney as auditors of the Corporation for the current fiscal year; and (3) to act in their discretion on such matters as may properly come before the meeting or any adjournments thereof.

The cost of this solicitation will be paid by the Corporation. Such costs include preparation, printing and mailing of the Notice of Annual Meeting, Proxy Statement and the enclosed Proxy. The solicitation will be conducted principally by mail, although directors, officers and regular employees of the Corporation and its subsidiariesmay solicit proxies personally or by telephone or telegram. Arrangements will be made with brokerage houses and other custodians, nominees and fiduciaries for proxy material to be sent to their principals and the Corporation will reimburse such persons for their expense in so doing.

The shares represented by all properly executed and returned proxies will be voted, if received in time for the meeting, in accordance with the instructions, if any, given thereon. Unless otherwise indicated, or if no instructions are given, in respect to any proposal, the shares represented by such proxies will be voted **FOR** such proposal. A proxy is revocable at any time prior to being voted.

The Corporation had outstanding and entitled to vote on June 14, 19X5, the record date for the meeting, 6,016,224 shares of Common Stock, which is its only voting security. Each share is entitled to one vote. The only stockholders known to the Corporation to own of record or beneficially more than 5% of the outstanding shares of Common Stock are Baxter Olsen, Frank Nopf, and Sal Banza. Information with respect to such ownership is set forth in the table under "Election of Directors." By a schedule 13G Filing with the Securities and Exchange Commission, Investment Advisory Corp., 44 Third Avenue, New York, NY 10019 has reported that it is the beneficial owner of 356,725 shares of common stock of the Corporation or 5.93% of the outstanding shares with sole voting power and sole disposition power with respect thereto; it is an Investment Adviser registered under Section 203 of the Investment Advisers Act of 1940.

Figure 10-1. *(cont.)*

STOCKHOLDER PROPOSALS

If a stockholder intends to present a proposal at the Corporation's 19X6 Annual Meeting, the proposal must be received by the Corporation by March 24, 19X6, for inclusion in the Proxy Statement and form of proxy relating to that meeting.

ELECTION OF DIRECTORS

The nine nominees for election to the Board of Directors are presently serving in such capacity. The nominees, constituting the entire Board of Directors, are to be elected at the Annual Meeting for a term of one year, and until the election and qualification of their respective successors. If no contrary instructions are indicated, the proxies will be voted for the election of directors of the nominees named below. The Board of Directors has no reason to believe that any of the nominees will be unable to serve as a director. If any nominee shall be unable, for any reason, to accept nomination or election, it is the intention of the persons named in the enclosed form of proxy to vote the proxy for the nomination and election of such other person or persons as the Board of Directors may designate.

The following table sets forth the name of each nominee, his principal occupation for the last five years, the date he first became a director and the number and percentage of shares of Common Stock owned beneficially as of June 14, 19X5. The information as to ownership of the Corporation's Common Stock is based upon information received from the directors and officers.

Name and Age; Principal Occupation for Last Five Years	Has Been Director for	Amount and Nature of Beneficial Ownership of Common Shares and Percent of Class as of June 14, 19X5	
		Number	Percent
Baxter Olsen; 71 Chairman of the Board of Directors and past President of the Corporation (2)(3)	32 years	603,696	10.03
Frank Nopf; 68 Vice Chairman of the Board and Secretary and past Executive Vice President of the Corporation (3)(4)(5)	32 years	644,875	10.72
Reginald Olsen; President of the Corporation and past Vice President-Administration and past Assistant Secretary of the Corporation(2)(7)	10 years	165,024	2.74
David Greenbaugh; 56 Vice President-Finance and Treasurer of the Corporation(2)(6)	15 years	19,530	0.32

Figure 10-1. *(cont.)*

Name and Age; Principal Occupation for Last Five Years	Has Been Director for	Amount and Nature of Beneficial Ownership of Common Shares and Percent of Class as of June 14, 19X5	
Melvin Nessman; 70 Past Vice President-Sales of the Corporation; Presi- dent of Electro Corp. an affiliate of the Cor- poration	15 years	5,000	0.08
Marvin Gilhouley; 73 Attorney; partner of Gilhouley & Stern, General Counsel to the Corporation (4)	15 years	18,015 97,773	0.30 1.63
Sal Banza; 60 Investments(3)(5)	13 years	344,322	5.72
Ike Lovett; 46 Chief Investment Officer and founder of World Finance Corp.(8)	5 years	250	—
Alfred Wilson; 41 Financial Analyst with Luck House & Co. since November 1984; pre- viously Managing Direc- tor of Warrel Pilton & Co.(9)(10)	5 years	2,997	0.05
All present directors and officers as a group (12) persons; including directors named above . . .		1,925,434	32.00

(1) Named directors and all present directors and officers as a group have a sole investment and voting power over shares listed, except as indicated in specific footnotes.

(2) Mr. Greenbaugh is a brother-in-law and Reginald Olsen is a son of Baxter Olsen. Reginald Olsen is a nephew of Mr. Greenbaugh. No other family relationship exists between any of the above-named directors and executive officers.

(3) The indicated individuals may be deemed to be "controlled persons" of the Corporation by reason of share ownership. The address of Messrs. Baxter Olsen and Frank Knopf is c/o PlatingCo, Inc., 227 Plainview Boulevard, Freemantle, New York 12580 and the address of Mr. Sal Banza is 1300 Park Avenue, New York, New York 10017.

(4) Mr. Marvin Gilhouley owns 16,415 shares and 1,600 shares as his allocated interest in a partnership. Mr. Gilhouley is a trustee of trusts for the benefit of the children of Frank Nopf which hold an aggregate of 97,773 shares. As one of two trustees of such trusts, Mr. Gilhouley has shared voting and investment power with respect to such shares but has no other interest therein. Such shares are not listed as being owned by Frank Nopf.

Figure 10-1. *(cont.)*

(5) Frank Nopf and Sal Banza are co-trustees of trusts for the benefit of Mr. Banza's children which hold an aggregate of 26,660 shares. As co-trustees of such trusts, Frank Nopf and Sal Banza have shared voting and investment power with respect to such shares. Such shares are included in the amounts listed for Frank Nopf and Sal Banza.

(6) Does not include an aggregate of 47,287 shares owned by Vera Greenbaugh, wife of David Greenbaugh, which are held in trust for the benefit of Mr. Greenbaugh's children; Mr. Greenbaugh disclaims beneficial ownership of such shares.

(7) Includes 112,500 shares held in trust for the benefit of Reginald Olsen, as to which Reginald Olsen is one of two trustees and has shared voting and investment power. Also includes 37,104 shares held for Reginald Olsen's children, of which Reginal Olsen or his wife, Barbara Olsen, is custodian.

(8) World Finance Corporation is a registered investment advisory firm.

(9) Luck House & Co. is an investment management company and Warrel Pilton & Co., Inc. is an investment advisory and venture capital firm.

(10) Includes an aggregate of 1,665 shares held for Mr. Wilson's children, of which Mr. Wilson is custodian.

During the fiscal year ended February 28, 1985, the Board of Directors held four meetings, of which Mr. Banza attended seventy-five percent.

Committees of the Board of Directors

The Audit Committee consists of Messrs. Lovett and Wilson. The Committee meets periodically to review the auditors's reports to the Board of Directors, financial statements and internal accounting controls. It also monitors the independence and fees of the independent auditors and recommends further appointments thereof.

The Investment Committee consists of Messrs. Greenbaugh and Lovett. The Committee meets as necessary to review and report on any investments in excess of $250,000 to be made by the Corporation.

The Executive Compensation Committee consists of Messrs. Berg and Gilhouley. Both of them attended its three meetings.

The Corporation does not have a standing nominating committee.

REMUNERATION

The following table sets forth the aggregate remuneration for services in all capacities paid by the Corporation in respect of the fiscal year ended February 28, 19X5 to each of the seven highest paid executive officers of the Corporation whose aggregate remuneration exceeded $60,000 and to all officers and directors as a group:

Messrs. Berg, Lovett and Wilson each receive $1,000 for each meeting attended while serving as a director of the Corporation. No other director receives compensation for serving as a director.

The term of separate employment agreements entered into between the Corporation and Messrs. Baxter Olsen, Frank Nopf, David Greenbaugh, and Melvin Nessman, each dated as of March1, 19X6 and as amended on October 31, 19X8, continued for the term ended February 29, 19X4. Pursuant to the arrangements made in the foregoing

Figure 10-1. *(cont.)*

Name of Individual or Number of Persons in Group; Capacities in Which Served	Cash Compensation	
	Salaries, Fees Directors' Fees Commissions Bonuses	Insurance Benefits or Reimbursement Personal Benefits(1)
Baxter Olsen Chairman of the Board and Chief Executive Officer	$ 90,000	$ 5,214
Frank Nopf Vice Chairman of the Board and Secretary	84,000	1,523
Reginald Olsen President and Chief Operating Officer	190,000	7,297
David Greenbaugh Vice President-Finance and Treasurer	78,000	4,451
Robert Kinder Vice President-Market Technology and Assistant Secretary	132,061	1,147
Dillard Tollan Assistant Vice President	95,060	1,192
Donald Reston Assistant Treasurer and Controller	89,462	468
All directors and officers as a group (12) persons, including those listed above	831,583	21,619

(1) Officers of the Corporation receive certain executive perquisites which are directly related to job performance and are, therefore, excluded from remuneration. Executive officers did not receive any significant personal benefits during the past fiscal year which may be deemed non-job-related.

agreements to continue the availability of these senior officers, supplements to each of such agreements, dated February 15, 19X4, were entered into with them, whereby for a period of five years, commencing March 1, 19X4, their services as consultants were enlisqed until February 28, 1989, for which they are to receive the following annual sums: Baxter Olsen—$75,000; Frank Nopf—$70,000; David Greenbaugh—$65,000; and Melvin Nessman—$50,000 less any compensation received by him from any affiliated company. The consultants were all called upon for extra services for which they were paid the additions reflected in the above table. In addition, the agreement with Melvin Nessman—provides for payment of deferred compensation for an aggregate of $60,000 payable over a period of sixty months commencing March 1, 19X4. For the fiscal year he received an additional $12,000 for extra services. If any of the foregoing persons dies during the term aforesaid, the widow of such person, if living, otherwise his estate, shall receive the foregoing sums until the end of the consulting period.

Figure 10-1. *(cont.)*

INCENTIVE STOCK OPTIONS

At the Annual Meeting of the Shareholders of the Corporation held on July 20, 19X2, the Shareholders approved the 19X2 PlatingCo, Inc. Incentive Stock Option Plan, adopted by the Board of Directors on January 14, 19X2. Under the terms thereof, 100,000 shares of the Corporation's authorized common stock, par value, $1, were reserved for future issuance thereunder (increased to 125,000 shares by virtue of the stock split of 25% distributed on March 1, 19X3 to stockholders of record on February 15, 19X3).

On August 4, 19X2, options thereunder were granted to employees to purchase 19,316 shares at a base price of $10.40 per share. On September 28, 19X2, additional options were granted to employees to purchase 30,566 shares at a base price of $11.20 per share. The numbers of options and option price per share have been adjusted to reflect the stock changes affected by the foregoing stock split as provided in the Plan including the foregoing options and those referred to thereafter. In addition, options for 23,600 shares were granted on July 31, 19X4 at a price of $14 per share.

Of the above, the following options were granted to officers: to Reginald Olsen, for 6,250 shares on September 28, 19X2 and 5,000 shares on July 31, 19X4; to Robert Kinder, for 3,125 shares on August 4, 19X2, 3,125 shares on September 28, 19X2 and 2,500 shares on July 31, 19X4; to Dillard Tollan, for 2,500 shares on August 4, 19X2, 2,500 shares on September 28, 19X2 and 1,000 shares on July 31, 19X4; to Donald Reston, for 1,875 shares on August 4, 19X2, 2,625 shares on September 28, 19X2 and 1,500 shares on July 31, 19X4.

No options were exercised by offices during the fiscal year ended February 28, 19X5.

SELECTION OF AUDITORS

Subject to the approval of the stockholders at the Annual Meeting, the Board of Directors of the Corporation has engaged the firm of Harris & Whitney to audit the books, records and accounts of the Corporation for the current fiscal year. Harris & Whitney has acted in that capacity for several years. A representative of Harris & Whitney is expected to be present at the Annual Meeting of the Stockholders.

OTHER MATTERS

The Corporation has no knowledge of any other matters to be presented to the meeting. If, however, other matters are presented to the Meeting, it is the intention of the persons named in the closed proxy to act in their discretion on such other matters as may property come before the Meeting and any adjournment thereof.

The Annual Report to Stockholders for the fiscal year ended February 28, 19X5 is being forwarded contemporaneously herewith to all stockholders of record on June 14, 19X5. Such Annual Report is not incorporated herein by reference and is not to be deemed part of this Proxy Statement.

By Order of the Board of Directors
Frank Nopf
Secretary

Dated: Freemantle, New York
    June 24, 19X5

Figure 10-2. *PlatingCo's Annual Report.*

PlatingCo: A story about product proliferation

Our product list of chemical specialties for the electronics, industrial and finishing industries has grown from the one product we started with in 1953—"Plateshine"—to over one hundred. Even as you read this, more new products are in the making. New processes for plating, new inks and solder masks for printed circuit boards, and new chemical specialties for commercial and electronic applications. And PlatingCo's 335 people, worldwide, are committed to meet each change in today's technology with innovative, quality products.

PlatingCo has been a public company since 1967, and its shares are traded on the New York Stock Exchange under the symbol of PLC. The corporate entrepreneurial incentive remains strong as insiders own almost one-third of all the outstanding shares.

Both in the U.S. and abroad, our management teams and technical staffs are "nationals," citizens of each of the counties in which the Company operates. And all products are either made or stocked locally. Our newly built facility in Freemantle, N.Y., is now in full production, along with other locations throughout the U.S., Europe, and the Far East, including new constructions or expanded facilities in England and Switzerland. All reflect the PlatingCo dedication to play a worldwide leadership role in the many exciting changes in technology that lie ahead.

Contents

PlatingCo, Inc. and Subsidiaries
Selected Financial Data

Figure 10-2. *(cont.)*

	Year Ended February 28 or 29				
	19X5	19X4	19X3	19X2	19X1
Net Sales	$130,536,000	$163,326,000	$142,812,000	$172,243,000	$234,205,000
Net Income (c)	$ 8,077,000	$ 6,918,000	$ 6,602,000	$ 7,892,000	$ 8,038,000
Per share (a)(b)(c)	$ 1.34	$ 1.15	$ 1.10	$ 1.31	$ 1.33
Total assets	$ 55,894,000	$ 54,564,000	$ 46,308,000	$ 44,767,000	$ 41,413,000
Working Capital	$ 37,473,000	$ 35,560,000	$ 32,918,000	$ 30,145,000	$ 25,751,000
Property, plant & equipment—net	$ 9,278,000	$ 8,579,000	$ 7,113,000	$ 5,887,000	$ 5,392,000
Long-term debt, less current portion	$ 2,057,000	$ 2,546,000	$ 2,168,000	$ 419,000	$ 540,000
Stockholders' equity	$ 45,547,000	$ 42,565,000	$ 35,249,000	$ 35,249,000	$ 29,434,000
Cash dividends declared per share (a)	$ .37	$ .36	$ .33	$ .32	$ .26
Average number of common shares outstanding (a)	6,013,036	6,014,392	6,018,625	6,030,561	6,055,930
Return on average Stockholders' Equity	18%	17%	18%	24%	30%

(a) Adjusted for all stock splits and stock dividends.
(b) Net income per share is based on the average number of shares of Common Stock outstanding.
(c) Effective March 1, 19X2, the Company changed its method of accounting for foreign currency translation by electing early adoption of Financial Accounting Standards Board Statement No. 52 "Foreign Currency Translation." Prior years' data shown above has not been restated for the change. Pro forma data as if this change has been made as of the beginning of fiscal 1981 follows:

	19X2	19X1
Net Income	$8,619,000	$8,414,000
Per Share	$ 1.43	$ 1.39

(d) This selection consolidated financial data should be read in conjunction with the Consolidated Financial Statements and the notes thereto.

173

Figure 10-2. *(cont.)*

Price Range of Common Stock and Dividends Per Share by Fiscal Quarters

The Company's Common Stock, $1.00 par value, is listed on the New York Stock Exchange and its symbol is PLC. The following tables indicates the quarterly high and low sale prices for PlatingCo Common Stock on the New York Stock Exchange and cash dividends declared for the past two years:

| | Year Ended February 28 or 29 | | | | | |
| | 19X5 | | | 19X4 | | |
Quarter Ended	Sales Price High	Low	Cash Dividends Declared	Sale Price High	Low	Cash Dividends Declared
May 31	$18⅝	$15⅜	9¢	$20⅞	$18½	9¢
August 31	$18½	$14	9¢	$25⅛	$19	9¢
November 30	$17⅝	$15	9¢	$21¼	$16½	9¢
February 28 or 29	$20⅞	$15	10¢	$19⅛	$15⅝	9¢

Approximate number of record holders of Common Stock on May 8, 19X5: 2,600.

Letter to Our Shareholders

Dear Shareholder:

The fiscal year ended February 28, 19X5, was the best in our history. Net income was $8,077,000 or $1.34 per share as compared with $6,918,000 or $1.15 per share for the corresponding previous fiscal year. An accurate reflection of PlatingCo's performance are sales of our patented and proprietary additives, called process sales. Sales of these proprietary chemical specialties to the electronics and metal finishing industries clearly provide value added to our customers in their manufacturing of end use products. For the fiscal year ended February 28, 19X5, these sales were $30,035,000 compared with $24,495,000 for the prior year.

The growth of our process sales clearly demonstrates the impact and influence tha PlatingCo's technology exerts in our markets.

WHO AND WHAT IS LRI?

PlatingCo is a worldwide supplier of specialty chemicals to the electronics and metal finishing industries. Through the years, we have made a smooth transition from a one-product, one-market company with few direct sales personnel and limited research and development expenditures to an

Figure 10-2. *(cont.)*

internationally recognized corporation with an aggressive, solid, young field sales and service team complemented by a fully staffed research and development group. We are a special, specialty chemical company because we have demonstrated the ability to adjust successfully to changing technical and market conditions. From a single-product company serving only the automotive industry, we have dramatically expanded the products we have developed and the end use markets we serve to clearly establish Plating Co as a leadin supplier of electronic and metal finishing chemicals.

Record sales of proprietary chemicals and record net income were achieved by anticipating market requirements and market changes. We have overcome recessionary conditions, changes in requirements of the semi-conductor industry and connector markets and still attained our goals.

Our Company has grown because of our creativity, our flexibility and our informal management style. New technology and increased marketing aggressiveness are a "given" at Plating Co.

NEW TECHNOLOGY—A STATUS REPORT

During the past fiscal year we further progressed in the development of our WeldTo process technology. We now offer a family of fluoborate-free, pollution-free, tin-lead processes for funishing connectors, semi-conductors, wire, and printed circuit boards. Patents have been issued for the proprietary chemistry utilized to make our WeldTo systems the recognized standard for fluoborate-free, tin-lead process technology in the industry.

Growing market acceptance of PlatingCo's screen inks and solder masks utilized when manufacturing printed circuit boards, has stimulated continued technological breakthroughs for these products. Our latest, a solder mask cured by ultraviolet light passes the most stringent UL Class III testing methods. With the addition of three marketing specialists to our staff during the past year, industry recognition of the technical benefits of PlatingCo's materials versus others in the marketplace has become increasingly evident.

During the past year we further enhanced the technological advantages of our gold process technology. These systems are either nickel or cobalt hardened gold alloy processes for plating connectors or printed circuit boards either at high speeds or in barrel applications. Product differentiation between our conventional gold systems becomes apparent when comparing the amount of gold utilized in the bath, the alloy stability and the plating speeds obtained with low metal concentrations.

We have continued introduction of additional chemical specialties utilizes in

Figure 10-2. *(cont.)*

the manufacture of printed circuit boards. We are now able to offer all the chemistry required to manufacture a circuit board from start to finish.

There also have been bright spots in the general metal finishing area, and we are adding additional field sales and service staff to help promote sales. Our newly introduced bright acid zinc plating process has been well received and we look for significant sales with this pollution-free process technology.

FINANCIAL HIGHLIGHTS

PlatingCo continues to build on its strong financial foundation.

The following financial highlights clearly indicate the strength of our Company and the recognition that we have attained in the marketplace.

1. Current assets at year end were $43,152,000 and current liabiities were $5,679,000. The long-term debt of $2,057,000 was minimum in related to stockholders' equity of $45,457,000. Our cash and short-term investments were $18,016,000.

2. The return on average stockholders' equity was 18 percent for the fiscal year ended February 28, 19X5.

3. The Board of Directors voted to increase the quarterly dividend to 10 cents per share an increase of 11 percent.

FOREIGN BUSINESS

Net income from foreign operations was $2,449,000 compared with $1,809,000 for the prior fiscal year. Each of our subsidiaries or jont ventures participated in the economic recovery, both in Europe and in Asia. Despite the fact that assets valuation declined as a result of the appreciation of the dollar, our respective businesses continue to increase in real terms. During the past fiscal year we commenced on a limited scale, the marketing of PlatingCo screen inks and solder masks in Europe. A new manufacturing facility to blend and mill these materials is being constructed at PlatingCo U.K.

To help us meet the increased demand for our products in the Swiss, German and Asian markets, PlatingCo Switzerland completed construction of a new fully integrated lab and manufacturing plant. The name of our French subsidiary was changed to PlatingCo France in order to take advantage of the worldwide recognition of the name in the industries we serve.

In the Far East, an accelerated program of technological and commercial exchanges has taken place between Japan Co. and PlatingCo, Inc. The close cooepration between our Companies has contributed to a significant increase in proprietary process sales and the corporate value of Japan Co. which is generating substantial royalty income for PlatingCo, Inc.

Figure 10-2. *(cont.)*

KEEPING US UNIQUE

We are confident that the steps we take can continue to further distinguish PlatingCo in the marketplace. Utilizing our strong financial condition we intend to further broaden our market coverage by continued expansion of our product line. We will expand our field sales and service staff to enable us to respond efficiently and effectively to customers needs and demands. In addition:

    1. We have implemented the most up to date and efficient quality control procedures in all of our manufacturing plants to that we "get it right the first time" when manufacturing our chemical specialty additives. These new procedures have been developed in concert with many of our large world renowned customers as part of a close interaction to develop mutually efficient technologies.

    2. A new data processing center at our Freemantle, New York headquarters has been designed and will be in operation by the middle of the new fiscal year. Additional data processing power will enable us to further control a growing and more complex integrated worldwide business. Greater access and faster response to changes, whether they be financial or commercial, can be more readily recognized through this sophisticated data processing capability.

    3. Additional state of the art analytical and developmental equipment has been ordered for our research laboratories as part of our renovation and expansion of the 277 Plain Boulevard facility. These sophisticated tools will further assist the research and development team to provide our customer base with the most advanced, easy to operate, easy to control, chemical specialty process technology.

    We will do all of the above without sacrificing the principles, concepts and commitment to being the best in what we do. For that, we have to thank our employees for their efforts during the past year and thank our shareholders for the confidence they have shown in PlatingCo. Our goal for fiscal 19X6 is another record performance.

PlatingCo, Inc.
Baxter Olsen   Reginald Olsen
Chairman of the Board   President and Chief
and Chief Executive Officer   Operating Officer

Figure 10-2. *(cont.)*

Management's Discussion and Analysis of Financial Condition and Results of Operations

Net sales decreased in fiscal 19X5 by $32,790,000 or 20% from fiscal 19X4. Net sales increased in fiscal 19X4 by $20,514,000 or 14% from fiscal 19X3. The significant differences in reported sales from year to year are primarily due to fluctuations in the average price of gold bullion which is included in many of the proprietary and patented additives sold, the volume of such previoius metal contained sales and the effect of foreign currency exchange rates. The average gold bullion price per troy ounce for fiscal 19X5, 19X4, and 19X3 was $348, $406 and $393, respectively. A major component of the change from year to year sales was a decrease in lower margin sales from the Company's United Kingdom refinery operation to $5,932,000 in fiscal 19X5 ($29,412,000 in fiscal 19X4). A better measure of sales levels is "process sales," sales of proprietary and patented additives, which do not include the distortions created by fluctuating prices of precious metals sold in conjunction with the additives. Process sales for fiscal 19X5, 19X4, and 19X3 were $30,035,000, $24,495,000 and $20,766,000, respectively. Previous metal process sales increased by 19% and non-precious metal process sales increased by 24% in fiscal 19X5. Precious metal process sales increased by 5% and non-precious metal process sales increased by 25% in fiscal 19X4. The significant increase in process sales has come from increased sales volume to the electronics market with major contributions from new products for printed circuits, reel-to-reel plating of connectors, semiconductors, and wire for the telecommunications industry.

Cost of sales decreased by 24% in fiscal 19X5 and increased by 15% in fiscal 19X4, principally as a result of the aforementioned factors affecting sales. Gross profits continued to increase in fiscal 19X5 due to the significant increase in process sales.

Selling, general and administrative expenses continued to increase in fiscal 19X5 and fiscal 19X4 as a result of increased technical service and sales personnel in the field and costs related to the promotion of new product developments. Research and development expenditures increased by 12% in fiscal 19X5 and 9% in fiscal 19X4, resulting from the Company's commitment to improving its existing technology and the development of new processes and systems for the plating of connectors and printed circuit boards.

Interest income and other income varied significantly over the three years ended February 28, 19X5. The components of these accounts have been influenced by the Company adjusting its investment portfolio to changing market and economic conditions during the periods. The Company's general investment policy is to realize a reasonable rate of return with a limited amount of risk of principal. In fiscal 19X5, the Company's Swiss subsidiary recognized foreign currency exchange gains of approximately $893,000 primarily on its investments in U.S. dollar denominated certificates of deposit.

During fiscal 1985, the Company made provisions for losses on loans and advances to its former equipment affiliate which ceased operations in July 19X4 and is currently in bankruptcy proceedings. Additionally, the Company reduced the carrying value of its investment in a company in the information storage industry to its estimated current market value.

Figure 10-2. *(cont.)*

The effective income tax rates changed during the periods as a result of certain non-recurring income tax benefits and the increased portion of income from foreign operations which is taxed at lower tax rates. In fiscal 19X3 deferred income taxes were reduces by $550,000, representing the reversal of U.S. taxes previously provided on undistributed earnings of the Company's Swiss subsidiary, which are considered to be permanently reinvested.

Net income increased by 17% in fiscal 19X5 as a result of increased process sales, interest and other income. Net income increased by 5% in fiscal 19X4 as a result of increased process sales, net of the reduced deferred tax benefits realized during the period as compared to fiscal 19X3.

Inflation has been a significant factor in our economy and the Company is continually seeking ways to cope with its impact. Where competitive conditions permit, the Company has increased prices of its products to offset inflationary pressures. The Company uses the LIFO method of accounting for its domestic gold and silver inventories. Under this method, the cost of products sold reported in the financial statements approximates current costs and thus reduces distortion in reported net income due to increasing costs. A major indirect effect that inflation has had on the Company's business is the relationship between the rate of inflation and the prices of precioius metals and other commodities. Demand for precious metals historically has increased significantly during periods of inflation, uncertainty and tension. The past three years have seen relatively lower inflation rates, a continuation of high "real" interest rates and a weakening of industrial demand for precious metal products resulting in lower precious metal prices compared to previous periods.

At February 28, 19X5, the Company has working capital of $37,473,000 and current assets of $43,152,000, including $18,016,000 in cash and short-term investments. The Company's immediate capital expansion requirements of approximately $2,100,000 ($1,100,000 for purchase of the building which it is currently leasing for its California operation and $1,000,000 for other operations) will be funded by working capital and cash flow from operations. The Company has sufficient lines of credit with banks available should any additional funds be required for possible acquisitions or other circumstances.

Figure 10-2. *(cont.)*

PlatingCo, Inc. and Subsidiaries

Consolidated Statements of Income

	Year Ended February 28 19X5	Year Ended February 29 19X4	Year Ended February 28 19X3
Net sales	$130,536,000	$136,326,000	$142,812,000
Interest income	1,223,000	978,000	1,859,000
Other income—Note I	1,757,000	891,000	416,000
	133,516,000	165,195,000	145,087,000
Costs and expenses:			
Cost of sales	108,689,000	143,527,000	125,095,000
Selling, general and administrative	8,780,000	8,153,000	7,085,000
Research and development	1,605,000	1,435,000	1,316,000
Minority interests	187,000	149,000	119,000
Interest	288,000	151,000	68,000
	119,549,000	153,415,000	133,683,000
Income before income taxes	13,967,000	11,780,000	11,404,000
Income taxes—Note C			
Federal	3,970,000	3,298,000	3,450,000
Foreign	814,000	244,000	1,107,000
State and local	454,000	492,000	582,000
Deferred	652,000	828,000	(337,000)
	5,890,000	4,862,000	4,802,000
Net income	$ 8,077,000	$ 6,918,000	$ 6,602,000
Net income per share of Common Stock—Note A	$1.34	$1.15	$1.10

See notes to consolidated financial statements.

Figure 10-2. *(cont.)*

PlatingCo, Inc. and Subsidiaries

Consolidated Balance Sheets

Assets	February 28 19X5	February 29 19X4
Current assets		
Cash	$ 1,551,000	$ 2,842,000
Short-term investments—Note A	16,465,000	12,689,000
Receivables, less allowance for doubtful accounts—		
$440,000—1985 and $545,000—1984	15,141,000	17,437,000
Inventories—Note A		
Finished products	3,594,000	2,851,000
Materials and supplies	5,625,000	6,360,000
	9,219,000	9,211,000
Deferred income taxes	362,000	125,000
Other current assets	362,000	125,000
Other current assets	414,000	330,000
Total current assets	43,152,000	42,634,000
Other assets—Note E	3,228,000	3,091,000
Property, plant and equipment—on the basis of cost— Note E		
Land and buildings	6,845,000	6,203,000
Machinery and equipment	6,611,000	6,050,000
Automotive and other	1,061,000	1,048,000
Allowance for depreciation and amortization		
(deduction)	(5,239,000)	(4,722,000)
	9,278,000	8,579,000
Patients—at cost, less amortization	326,000	260,000
	$55,984,000	$54,564,000

Financial Highlights
(unaudited)

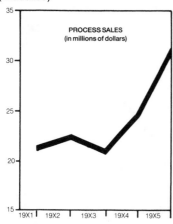

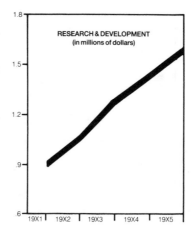

181

Figure 10-2. *(cont.)*

Liabilities and Stockholders' Equity	February 28 19X5	February 29 19X4
Current liabilities		
Short-term debt—Note H	$ 62,000	$ 918,000
Accounts payable	2,873,000	3,728,000
Payroll and related items	727,000	711,000
Accrued expenses and other liabilities	550,000	519,000
Income taxes	1,178,000	566,000
Current portion of long-term debt—Note E	289,000	652,000
Total current liabilities	5,679,000	7,074,000
Long-Term Debt, less current portion—Note E	2,057,000	2,546,000
Deferred income taxes—Note C	1,992,000	1,523,000
Minority interests	799,000	856,000

Stockholders' Equity—Note G

	February 28 19X5	February 29 19X4
Common stock, par value $1 per share— authorized 15,000,000 shares: issued 6,014,439 shares in 19X5 and 6,019,851 shares in 19X4, including 7,969 shares in 19X4 held in treasury	6,014,000	6,020,000
Additional paid-in capital	8,998,000	8,972,000
Retained earnings	35,219,000	29,496,000
Cost of common stock in treasury (deduction)		(137,000)
Equity adjustment from foreign currency translation	(4,774,000)	(1,786,000)
	45,457,000	42,565,000
	$55,984,000	$54,564,000

See notes to consolidated financial statements.

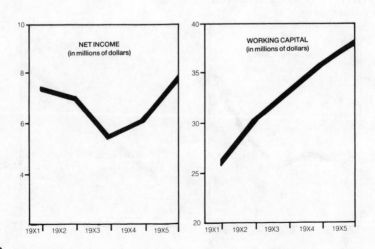

Figure 10-2. *(cont.)*

PlatingCo, Inc. and Subsidiaries

Consolidated Statements of Changes in Financial Position

	Year Ended February 28 19X5	Year Ended February 29 19X4	Year Ended February 28 19X3
Source of Funds			
From operations:			
Net income for the year	**$ 8,077,000**	$6,918,000	$6,602,000
Charges (credits to income not requiring current outlay of working capital:			
Mepreciation and amortization	**1,314,000**	1,092,000	1,011,000
Amortization of patents	**9,000**	8,000	11,000
Deferred income taxes,			
noncurrent	**832,000**	775,000	119,000
Other			8,000
Total from operations	**10,419,000**	8,942,000	7,252,000
Decrease in other assets			60,000
Exercise of stock options	**28,000**	36,000	
Increase in long-term debt		604,000	2,000,000
Reduction (increase) in noncurrent assets resulting from exchange rate changes:			
Property, plant and equipment	**504,000**	96,000	272,000
Other assets	431,000	(13,000)	23,000
	11,382,000	9,665,000	9,607,000
Application of Funds			
Portion of equity adjustment from foreign currency translation affecting working capital as of March 1, 1982			38,000
Purchases of property, plant and equipment (net) and patents	**2,592,000**	2,719,000	2,937,000
Cost of treasury stock		137,000	166,000
Cash dividends	**2,225,000**	2,166,000	1,985,000
Decrease in long-term debt	**290,000**	149,000	232,000
Investments in and advances to unconsolidated domestic investees	**(534,000)**	295,000	31,000
Increase in other assets	**1,102,000**	1,160,000	

Figure 10-2. *(cont.)*

PlatingCo, Inc. and Subsidiaries

Consolidated Statements of Changes in Financial Position—Continued

	Year Ended February 28 19X5	Year Ended February 29 19X4	Year Ended February 28 19X3
Reduction in noncurrent liabilities and stockholders' equity resulting from exchange rate changes:			
Long-term debt	199,000	77,000	19,000
Deferred income taxes	363,000	9,000	114,000
Minority interests	244,000	41,000	107,000
Stockholders' equity	2,988,000	270,000	1,205,000
	9,469,000	7,203,000	6,834,000
Increase in working capital	$ 1,913,000	$2,642,000	$2,773,000

Changes in Components of Working Capital			
Increase (decrease in current assets:			
Cash	$(1,291,000)	$ (450,000)	$ (936,000)
Short-term investments	3,776,000	2,055,000	(528,000)
Receivables	(2,296,000)	4,676,000	361,000
Inventories	8,000	(828,000)	1,555,000
Deferred income taxes	237,000	(52,000)	(163,000)
Other current assets	84,000	(136,000)	165,000
	518,000	5,265,000	454,000
Decrease (increase) in current liabilities:			
Short-term debt	856,000	(144,000)	(623,000)
Accounts payable	855,000	(2,410,000)	1,215,000
Accrued expenses, payroll and other liabilities	(47,000)	(189,000)	533,000
Dividends payable		542,000	(60,000)
Income taxes	(612,000)	12,000	1,385,000
Current portion of long-term debt	343,000	(434,000)	(131,000)
	1,395,000	(2,623,000)	2,319,000
Increase in working capital	$ 1,913,000	$ 2,642,000	$ 2,773,000

See notes to consolidated financial statements.

PlatingCo, Inc. and Subsidiaries

Consolidated Statements of Changes in Stockholders' Equity

Figure 10-2. *(cont.)*

	Total Stockholders' Equity	Par Value of Shares of Stock Issued	Common Stock to be Distributed	Additional Paid-In Capital	Retained Earnings	Cost of Common Stock in Treasury	Equity Adjustment from Foreign Currency Translation
Balance at February 28, 19X2	$35,249,000	$4,830,000		$8,940,000	$21,627,000	$(148,000)	
Adjustment from restating foreign assets and liabilities as of March 1, 19X2 to apply current rate method of translation	(311,000)						$ (311,000)
Net income for the year	6,602,000				6,602,000		
Common shares to be distributed for five for four (25%) stock split—Note G			$ 1,203,000	(1,203,000)			
Cost of 9,730 shares of common stock purchased for treasury	(166,000)					(166,000)	
Cash dividends—$.33 per share	(1,985,000)				(1,985,000)		
Retirement of 16,800 shares of common stock held in treasury		(17,000)			(297,000)	314,000	
Translation of adjustment for the year	(1,205,000)						(1,205,000)

Figure 10-2. (*cont.*)

Balance at February 28, 19X3	38,184,000	4,813,000	1,203,000	8,940,000	24,744,000		(1,516,000)
Net income for the year	6,918,000				6,918,000		
Common shares distributed for five for four stock split—Note G		1,203,000	(1,203,000)				
Cost of 7,969 shares of common stock purchased for treasury	(137,000)					(137,000)	
Cash dividends—$.36 per share	(2,166,000)				(2,166,000)		
Proceeds from issuance of 3,326 shares of common stock upon exercise of stock options	36,000	4,000		32,000			
Translation adjustment for the year	(270,000)						(270,000)
Balance at February 29, 19X4	42,565,000	6,020,000		8,972,000	29,496,000	(137,000)	(1,786,000)
Net income for the year	8,077,000				8,077,000		
Cash dividends—$.37 per share	(2,225,000)				(2,225,000)		
Translation adjustment for the year	(2,988,000)						(2,988,000)
Retirement of 7,969 shares of common stock held in treasury		(8,000)			(129,000)	137,000	
Proceeds from issuance of 2,557 shares of common stock upon exercise of stock options	28,000	2,000		26,000			
Balance at February 28, 19X5	$45,457,000	$6,014,000	$ —	$8,998,000	$35,219,000	$ —	$(4,774,000)

See notes to consolidated financial statements.

Figure 10-2. *(cont.)*

Report of Independent Accountants

Shareholders and Board of Directors
PlatingCo, Inc.
Freemantle, New York

We have examined the consolidated balance sheets of PlatingCo, Inc. and subsidiaries as of February 28, 19X5 and February 29, 19X4, and the related consolidated statements of income, changes in stockholders' equity and changes in financial position for each of the threeyears in the period ended February 28, 19X5. Our examinations were made in accordance with generally accepted auditing standards and, accordingly, included such tests of the accounting records and such other auditing procedures as we considered necessary in the circumstances.

In our opinion, the financial statements referred to above present fairly the consolidated financial position of PlatingCo, Inc. and subsidiaries at February 28, 19X5 and February 29, 19X4 and the consolidated results of their operations and changes in their financial position for each of the three years in the period ended February 28, 19X5, in conformity with generally accepted accounting principles applied on a consistent basis during the period.

Melville, New York
May 8, 19X5

PlatingCo, Inc. and Subsidiaries
Notes to Consolidated Financial Statements
February 28, 19X5

Note A—Summary of Accounting Policies

Principles of Consolidation: The consolidated financial statements include the accounts of the Company, its wholly-owned domestic subsidiaries and its foreign subsidiaries, PlatingCo (U.K.) plc (93%), PlatingCo AG (93%), PlatingCo France (65%) and PlatingCo GmbH (100%). The financial statements of the Company's affiliates are included in the consolidated financial statements from the time the Company acquires an interest in excess of 50%. All significant intercompany accounts and transactions have been eliminated. Investments in the common stock of 20% to 50% owned affiliates are accounted for by the equity method and are not significant.

Property, Plant and Equipment and Patents: Depreciation is computed on the straight-line and declining balance methods at rates calculated to amortize the cost of the depreciable assets over the related estimated useful lives. Upon sale or retirement, the cost of the assets and related allowances for depreciation are removed from the accounts and

Figure 10-2. *(cont.)*

PlatingCo, Inc. and Subsidiaries

Notes to Consolidated Statements—Continued

the resulting gains or losses included in operations. Patents are being amortized over their estimated useful lives.

Short-term Investments: These investments are carried at the lower of cost or market and include marketable securities totalling $9,375,000 (19X5) and $6,605,000 (1984) and bank certificates of deposit, time deposits and repurchase agreements totalling $7,090,000 (19X5) and $6,084,000 (19X4).

Inventories: Domestic gold and silver inventories are carried at the lower of cost (last-in, first-out (LIFO) method) or market. All other inventories are carried at the lower of cost (first-in, first-out (FIFO) method) or market. If the FIFO method of accounting had been used by the Company, domestic gold and silver inventories at February 28, 19X5 and February 29, 19X4 would have been $2,143,000 and $4,208,000 higher, respectively.

Income Taxes and Investment Credit: Provisions for income taxes are based on the earnings for each year and recognize the effect of timing differences (deferred taxes) between book and tax treatment of certain items of income and expense (principally inventories, direct financing leases, depreciation, doubtful accounts and income not currently reportable of a foreign subsidiary).

Investment tax credits, not material in amount, are recorded on the flow-through method, thereby reducing the income tax provision in the year in which the credits are available to offset income taxes payable.

Per Share Data: Net income per share of common stock has been computed based on the weighted average number of shares outstanding during each period, after giving effect to all stock splits and stock dividends distributed through March 1, 19X3, as follows: 6,013,036—19X5; 6,014,392—19X4; 6,018,625—19X3.

Note B—Domestic and Foreign Operations

The Company and its consolidated subsidiaries are in the business of development, production, sale and distribution of a varied group of electroplating processes and chemical additives to industrial users throughout the United States (Domestic) and Europe (Foreign).

Information as to the Company's operations by geographic area for the three years ended February 28, 19X5 is summarized below:

	Domestic	Foreign	Elimination	Combined
Fiscal 19X5				
Revenue	$101,557,000	$32,324,000	$(701,000)	$133,180,000
Operating profit	9,791,000	4,314,000		14,105,000
Identifiable assets	39,619,000	15,546,000	(297,000)	54,868,000

Figure 10-2. *(cont.)*

PlatingCo, Inc. and Subsidiaries

Notes to Consolidated Financial
Statements—Continued

Fiscal 19X4				
Revenue	$115,141,000	$50,678,000	$(809,000)	$165,010,000
Operating profit	8,836,000	3,059,000		11,895,000
Identifiable asses	38,162,000	15,753,000	(301,000)	53,614,000
Fiscal 19X3				
Revenue	$118,767,000	$27,046,000	$(704,000)	$145,109,000
Operating profit	8,959,000	2,654,000		11,613,000
Identifiable assets	32,700,000	13,304,000	(472,000)	45,532,000

Transfers between geographic areas are accounted for at prices comparable to unaffiliated customer sales. Revenue is net sales and other income less equity in the earnings of unconsolidated affiliates. Operating profit is revenue less operating expenses, excluding interest expense and minority interest. Identifiable assets are total assets less investment in unconsolidated affiliates.

Domestic operations include export sales to unaffiliated customers of $2,679,000 in fiscal 19X5, $3,590,000 in fiscal 19X4, and $6,284,000 in fiscal 19X3. Net sales include sales to a distributor of $13,857,000 or 11% of net sales in fiscal 19X5. In fiscal 19X4, here were no sales to any one customer in excess of 10% of net sales. Net sales include sales to a customer of $20,172,000 or 14% of net sales in fiscal 19X3.

Note C—Income Taxes

The components of income before income taxes consist of the following:

	19X5	19X4	19X3
Domestic	$ 9,644,000	$ 8,769,000	$ 8,834,000
Foreign	4,323,000	3,011,000	2,570,000
	$13,967,000	$11,780,000	$11,404,000

The reconciliation of the difference between total income tax expense and the amount computed by applying the statutory federal income tax rate to income before income taxes is as follows:

	19X5	19X4	19X3
Computed tax expense	$6,425,000	$5,419,000	$5,246,000
State and local taxes, net of federal tax benefits	245,000	266,000	314,000
Reversal of deferred taxes provided in prior years on the income of domestic sales corporation	(94,000)		

Figure 10-2. *(cont.)*

	19X5	19X4	19X3
Tax-exempt interest income and U.S. dividend income subject to 85% exclusion	**(157,000)**	(382,000)	(125,000)
Reveral of U.S. taxes on undistributed earnings of Swiss subsidiary			(550,000)
Effect of lower foreign tax rates	**(347,000)**	(328,000)	(65,000)
Other	**(182,000)**	(113,000)	(18,000)
	$5,890,000	$4,862,000	$4,802,000

The major components of deferred income tax expense are as follows:

	19X5	19X4	19X3
U.S. tax effect of adjustment of carrying value of silver inventory	**$(178,000)**	$ (61,000)	$ 137,000
Reversal of U.S. taxes provided on undistributed earnings of Swiss subsidiary			(550,000)
U.K. taxes provided on income from direct financing leases	**523,000**	675,000	
ACRS depreciation for U.S. tax purposes	**136,000**	105,000	
Reversal of deferred taxes provided in prior years on the income of domestic sales corporation	**(94,000)**		
Increase in foreign taxes not currently payable by a foreign subsidiary	**206,000**	150,000	12,000
Other	**$ 652,000**	$ 828,000	$(337,000)

During fiscal 19X3, the Company's Swiss subsidiary completed negotiations and plans for the purchase of land and building to replace its then existing manufacturing facility in Switzerland. This project was completed in fiscal 19X5 at an approximate cost of $1,200,000. As a result of this investment, the Company reversed in fiscal 19X3 $550,000 of U.S. taxes previously provided on undistributed earnings of its Swiss subsidiary which are now considered to be permanently reinvested.

Note D—Foreign Subsidiaries

Certain combined financial information of the foreign subsidiaries is included in the accompanying financial statements as follows:

	19X5	19X4	19X3
Total current assets	**$11,000,000**	$12,529,000	$11,422,000
Total assets	**15,744,000**	15,940,000	13,436,000
Total current liabilities	**3,171,000**	2,881,000	3,247,000

Figure 10-2. *(cont.)*

PlatingCo, Inc. and Subsidiaries

Notes to Consolidated Financial Statements—
Continued

	19X5	19X4	19X3
Long-term debt	**454,000**	792,000	265,000
Undistributed earnings	**$13,625,000**	11,175,000	9,366,000
Cumulative translation adjustment	**(4,673,000)**	(1,786,000)	(1,516,000)
Revenues	**32,311,000**	50,527,000	27,058,000
Net income	**2,449,000**	1,809,000	1,358,000

U.S. taxes have not been provided on the undistributed earnings of foreign subsidiaries at February 28, 19X5, February 29, 19X4 and February 28, 19X3 as they are considered to be permanently reinvested.

Note E—Long-Term Debt

Long-term debt at February 28, 19X5 and February 29, 19X4 consists of the following:

	19X5	19X4
I.D.A. Loan	**$1,700,000**	$1,834,000
Loan payable to a U.S. bank	**439,000**	1,042,000
Mortgage note payable	**54,000**	70,000
Loans payable to a foreign bank	**153,000**	232,000
	2,346,000	3,178,000
Less: current portion	**289,000**	632,000
	$2,057,000	$2,546,000

In February 19X4, the Company's U.K. subsidiary received the proceeds of a 735,000 U.K. pound loan (approximately $1,094,000) from a U.S. bank to be repaid in quarterly installments with interest at 12½% per annum through November 19X8. The loan was used to finance the purchase of machinery and equipment which was leased to unaffiliated companies for periods of up to five years under direct financing leases, which are guaranteed by a foreign bank. The loan is collateralized by the assignment of the proceeds of the aforementioned leases. The noncurrent portion of the net investment in such leases of $528,000 is included in other assets in the accompanying balance sheet.

In fiscal 19X3, the Company received the proceeds of a loan for the purchase of land and construction of a building in Freemantle, N.Y. The loan was provided by the issuance of a $2,000,000 Industrial Development Bond by the Nassau County Industrial Development Agency (I.D.A.). The loan is payable in quarterly installments of $33,333 for 12 years with interest at 65% of the prime rate of Chemical Bank. The Bond is guaranteed by the

Figure 10-2. *(cont.)*

Company and its domestic subsidiaries. The loan agreements require the Company to maintain certain amounts of consolidated tangible net worth, consolidated working capital and limit consolidated unsubordinated liabilities, as defined in the agreements. In addition the loan is collateralized by land and building included in property, plant and equipment with a carrying value of $2,381,000 at February 28, 19X5.

The Company's German subsidiary has a loan from a foreign bank to be repaid in equal semiannual installments through June 30, 19X9 with interest at up to 8% per annum. The loan is collaterlized by land and buildings with a net carrying value of approximately $287,000 at February 28, 19X5.

The mortgage note payable is due in monthly installments through maturity in December 19X7 with interest at 6% per annum.

Maturities of long-term debt during the next five fiscal years amount to $289,000—19X6; $304,000—19X7; $319,000—19X8; $256,000—19X9; $145,000—19X0 and $1,033,000 thereafter.

Note F—Summary of Quarterly Results of Operations—Unaudited

The following is a summary of the unaudited quarterly resuls of operations for the two years ended February 28, 19X5:

Three Months Ended	Net Sales	Cost of Sales	Net Income	Net Income Per Share of Common Stock (See Note A)
Fiscal 19X5				
May 31	$ 35,775,000	$ 30,185,000	$1,871,000	$ .31
August 31	37,359,000	31,916,000	2,038,000	.34
November 30	30,005,000	24,654,000	2,052,000	.34
February 28	27,397,000	21,934,000	2,116,000	.35
	$130,536,000	$108,689,000	$8,077,000	$1.34
Fiscal 19X4				
May 31	$ 47,682,000	$ 43,040,000	$1,503,000	$ .25
August 31	36,040,000	31,112,000	1,764,000	.29
November 30	36,232,000	31,361,000	1,663,000	.28
February 29	43,372,000	38,014,000	1,988,000	.33
	$163,326,000	$143,527,000	$6,918,000	$1.15

Note G—Stockholders' Equity

In January 19X2, the Board of Directors of the Company adopted an Incentive Stock Option Plan covering key employees of the Company and its subsidiaries. The plan provides for the granting of options to key employees to purchase up to a total of 125,000 shares of the Company's common stock over a ten-year period from date of grant at

Figure 10-2. *(cont.)*

PlatingCo, Inc. and Subsidiaries

Notes to Consolidated Financial Statements—Continued

prices not less than the stock's fair market value on the date of grant. Options become exercisable one year from the date of grant.

Option activity during the three years ended February 28, 19X5 is summarized as follows:

	Shares Under Option	
	Option Price Per Share (at Dates of Grant)	Number of Shares
Balance at March 1, 19X2		-0-
Granted	$10.40	19,316
Granted	$11.20	30,566
Balance at February 28, 19X3		49,882
Exercised	$10.40 to $11.20	(3,326)
Balance at February 29, 19X4		46,556
Granted	$14.00	23,600
Exercised	$10.40 to $11.20	(2,557)
Cancelled	$10.40 to $11.20	(626)
Balance at February 28, 19X5		66,973

At February 28, 19X5, there were 52,144 shares available for the granting of future options (75,118 shares at February 29, 19X4). The number of shares exercisable at February 28, 19X5 and February 29, 19X4 are 43,999 and 46,556, respectively.

On January 13, 19X3, the Board of Directors declared a five for four (25%) stock split in the form of a stock distribution paid on March 1, 19X3 to shareholders of record on February 15, 1983.

Dividends per share, stock options and prices at which options are exercisable have been computed giving retroactive effect, where applicable, to the aforesaid stock split.

Note H—Short-Term Debt and Lines of Credit

Short-term debt at February 28, 19X5 and February 29, 19X4 consists of foreign bank advances of $62,000 and $918,000, respectively.

The Company has unsecured line of credit arrangements (reviewed annually) with domestic banks under which it may borrow, at the option of the banks, up to $14,000,000 at the bank's prime interest rate. The foreign bank advances are payable in foreign currencies by the Company's foreign subsidiaries under unsecured lines of credit of 3,000,000 United Kingdom (U.K.) pounds (including a maximum of 1,500,000 U.K. pounds guaranteed by the Company) and 300,000 German marks, at up to 1¼% over the bank's prime interest rate.

Figure 10-2. *(cont.)*

Note I—Other Income

Other income for the three years ended February 28, 19X5 consists of the following:

	19X5	19X4	19X3
Royalty income	$ 547,000	$460,000	$277,000
Dividend income	90,000	623,000	36,000
Foreign currency exchange gains	952,000	24,000	75,000
Gains (losses) and provisions for losses on investment transactions	(154,000)	(323,000)	22,000
Equity in earnings (losses) of unconsolidated affiliates	337,000	185,000	(22,000)
Other, net	(15,000)	(78,000)	28,000
	$1,757,000	$891,000	$416,000

In fiscal 19X5, the Company's Swiss subsidiary recognized foreign currency exchange gains of $893,000 primarily on its investments in U.S. dollar denominated certificates of deposit.

Corporate Data

Officers and Directors

MR. BAXTER OLSEN
    Chairman of the Board
    and Chief Executive Officer
MR. FRED NOPF
    Vice Chairman of the Board
    and Secretary
MR. REGINALD OLSEN
    President and Chief Operating
    Officer and Director
MR. DAVID GREENBAUGH
    Financial Vice President and
    Treasurer and Director
MR. MELVIN NESSMAN
    President—GenRon Division
    and Director

MR. ROBERT KINDER
    Vice President—Market Technology
    and Assistant Secretary
MR. DILLARD TOLLAN
    Assistant Vice President,
    Prod. Dev. Mgr., Precious Metals
MR. DONALD RESTON
    Assistant Treasurer
MR. SAL BANZA
    Private Investments, Director
MR. MARVIN GILHOULEY
    Gilhouley & Stern, Director
MR. ALFRED WILSON
    Luck House & Co., Director
MR. IKE LOVETT
    World Finance Corporation, Director

Figure 10-2. *(cont.)*

Corporate Offices
227 Plain Boulevard
Freemantle, New York 12580

Regional and Subsidiary Offices
PLATINGCO, CHICAGO
  Sales Mgr., Lyle Lipper
PLATINGCO, ORANGE, CA.
  General Mgr., John Rex
PLATINGCO, U.K. plc.
  Buxton, England
  Mgr. Director, Richard Hall
PLATINGCO, AG
  Lucerne, Switzerland
  Mgr. Director, Fredy W. Hunziker
PLATINGCO, GMBH
  Birkenfeld, W. Germany
  Mgr. Director, Gerhardt Wünnerlich
PLATINGCO, FRANCE
  Lyon, France
  Mgr. Director, Alain Menard
JAPAN CO., INC.
  Tokyo, Japan
  Mgr. Director, Oyia Murito
  Mgr. Matsui Kimota

Independent Auditors
Harris & Whitney
One Harrington Plaza
Melville, New York 11747

Registrar and Transfer Agent
Harris Trust Company of New York
110 William Street
New York, New York 10038

10-K Available
The annual report of PlatingCo, Inc.
to the Securities and Exchange
Commission on Form 10-K is
available upon written request.
Please direct requests to:
PlatingCo, Inc.
227 Plain Bouelvard
Freemantle, New York 12580

General Counsel
Gilhouley & Stern
1300 Park Avenue
New York, New York 10017

Figure 10-3. *The Standard & Poor's Corp. Report on PlatingCo.*

PlatingCo.

NYSE Symbol PLC

Price		ange	P-E Ratio	Dividend	Yield
S&P Ranking					
Mar. 21 'X5	19X5				
18½	20⅞-15	14	0.40	2.2%	A

Summary

This company develops and markets a varied group of electroplating processes with many industrial applications; gold plating is the most important of these processes. Process sales were up significantly in the first nine months of fiscal 19X4-X5, benefiting from new products and from increased volume for higher technology processes. In January, 19X5 directors raised the quarterly dividend 11%.

Business Summary

PlatingCo develops and produces a varied group of electroplating processes, chemical specialty additives and related equipment for industrial concerns in the U.S., Canada, Europe, South America and Asia.

Gold plating is the most important of the company's precious metal electroplating processes, accounting for between 87% and 93% of sales (including the value of the gold content) in the five years through fiscal 19X3-X4, and between 40% and 50% of pretax income. PlatingCo also produces and markets about 96 other processes, and additives relating to the plating of other metals, including nickel, tin, copper, zinc, brass, and other metals.

Gold electroplating processes are marketed to about 500 customers. More than 85% of the gold process sales are made to the electronic and electrical industries. PlatingCo has developed several processes for gold plating, used in the production of semiconductors, printed circuit boards and electrical contacts, all of which are essential components of missile guidance systems, telephone switching equipment, data processing equipment, consumer appliances, electrical equipment, and electronic games.

Non-gold processes are sold to about 1,400 customers in a wide range of industries, including automotive, appliances, garden tools, electronic parts, plastics, handbag frames, furniture and toys.

In addition to electroplating processes, PlatingCo sells a variety of additives useful in various plating operations, anti-tarnish materials and specialized equipment used in gold electroplating operations.

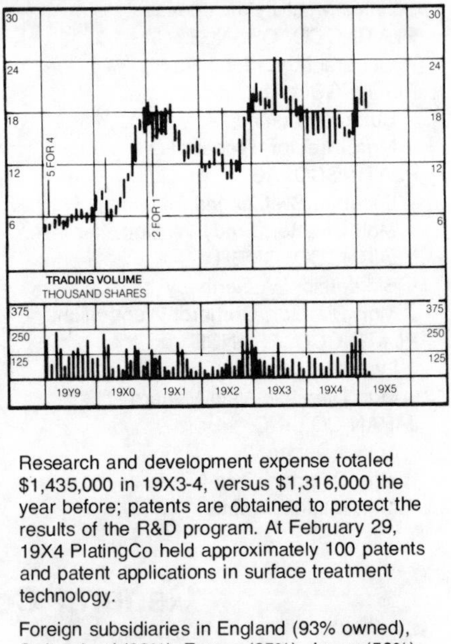

Research and development expense totaled $1,435,000 in 19X3-4, versus $1,316,000 the year before; patents are obtained to protect the results of the R&D program. At February 29, 19X4 PlatingCo held approximately 100 patents and patent applications in surface treatment technology.

Foreign subsidiaries in England (93% owned), Switzerland (93%), France (65%), Japan (50%), and Germany (100%) accounted for 31% of revenues and 26% of net income in 19X3-4.

Important Developments

Jan. 'X5—Directors raised the quarterly dividend 11%, to $0.10 from $0.09, in keeping with PLC's stated 25%-30% payout policy. PLC estimated that, based on growth in process sales, it should achieve record earnings for fiscal 1985.

Per Share Data ($)

Yr. End Feb. 28[1]	19X4	19X3	19X2	19X1	19X0	19X9	19X8	19X7	19X6	19X5
Book Value	**NA**	7.04	6.31	5.81	4.85	3.82	3.06	2.54	2.19	1.91
Earnings	**NA**	1.15	1.10	1.31	1.33	0.99	0.70	0.46	0.38	0.26
Dividends	**0.37**	0.36	0.33	[3]0.40	0.24	0.19½	0.19	0.07¼	0.08½	0.10⅛
Payout Ratio	**NA**	31%	30%	30%	18%	20%	27%	16%	23%	40%
Prices[2]—High	**19⅛**	25⅛	19¼	19⅝	18⅞	7¼	5⅛	2⅞	2½	2¼
Low	**14**	16⅛	10¼	12¼	5¾	4½	2⅝	2⅛	1⅝	1¼
P/E Ratio—	**NA**	22-14	18-9	15-9	14-4	7-4	7-4	6-5	7-4	9-5

Figure 10-3. *(cont.)*

PlatingCo.

Income Data (Million $)

Year Ended Feb. 28[1]	Oper. Revs.	Oper. Inc.	% Oper. Inc. of Revs.	Cap. Exp.	Depr.	Int. Exp.	Net Bef. Taxes	Eff. Tax Rate	Net Inc.	% Net Inc. of Revs.
19X3	163	11.3	6.9%	2.72	1.10	0.15	[2]11.9	40.8%	6.92	4.2%
19X2	143	10.3	7.2%	[4]2.94	1.02	0.07	[2]11.5	41.7%	6.60	4.6%
19X1	172	13.1	7.6%	[4]1.58	1.04	0.27	[2]14.2	44.0%	7.89	4.6%
19X0	234	16.1	6.9%	2.10	0.80	0.37	[2]16.1	49.6%	8.04	3.4%
19X9	199	12.2	6.1%	1.40	0.59	0.25	[2]12.3	49.7%	[3]6.06	3.0%
19X8	114	8.1	7.1%	0.83	0.47	0.07	[2] 8.5	48.3%	4.31	3.8%
19X7	77	4.9	6.4%	0.67	0.42	0.01	[2] 5.5	46.6%	2.85	3.7%
19X6	61	4.9	7.9%	1.08	0.28	0.01	4.9	51.5%	2.36	3.8%
19X5	55	3.6	6.4%	0.49	0.31	0.01	3.5	52.0%	1.63	3.0%
19X4	67	3.7	5.6%	0.85	0.27	0.03	3.9	47.9%	1.98	3.0%

Balance Sheet Data (Million $)

Feb. 28[1]	Cash	—Current— Assets	Liab.	Ratio	Total Assets	Ret. on Assets	Long Term Debt	Com- mon Equity	Total Cap.	% LT Debt of Cap.	Ret. on Equity
19X3	15.5	42.6	7.1	6.0	54.6	13.7%	2.55	42.6	47.5	5.4%	17.1%
19X2	13.9	37.4	4.5	8.4	46.3	14.5%	2.17	38.2	41.9	5.2%	18.0%
19X1	15.4	36.9	6.8	5.5	44.8	18.3%	0.42	35.2	38.0	1.1%	24.4%
19X0	8.6	35.0	9.2	3.8	41.4	20.9%	0.54	29.4	32.2	1.7%	30.5%
19X9	2.6	30.8	11.2	2.7	35.9	19.6%	0.11	23.4	24.7	0.5%	28.8%
19X8	3.9	22.0	6.2	3.5	26.1	18.1%	0.12	18.9	19.9	0.6%	25.0%
19X7	3.6	17.7	4.9	3.6	21.5	14.6%	0.14	15.7	16.6	0.8%	19.5%
19X6	2.6	14.7	3.2	4.6	18.0	14.5%	0.15	14.0	14.8	1.0%	18.1%
19X5	1.8	12.3	1.6	7.6	14.7	10.6%	0.16	12.3	13.1	1.2%	14.0%
19X4	3.2	14.0	4.4	3.2	16.1	12.6%	0.17	11.1	11.7	1.4%	19.1%

Data as orig. reptd. **1.** Of fol. cal. yr. **2.** Incl. equity in earns. of nonconsol. subs. **3.** Reflects acctg. change. **4.** Net of curr. yr. retirement and disposals.

Net Sales (Million $)

Quarter:	19X4-5	19X3-4	19X2-3	19X1-2
May	35.8	47.7	32.7	43.9
Aug.	37.4	36.0	34.5	42.6
Nov.	30.0	36.2	39.8	48.3
Feb.		43.4	35.8	37.4
	163.3	142.8	172.2

Sales for the nine months ended November 30, 19X4 fell 14%, year to year. Lower gold prices, the loss of a gold process customer that switched to supplying its own bullion, and lower refining sales from the U.K. outweighed higher process sales stemming from increased volume from the electronics market. Total costs fell at a faster pace, and pretax income rose 18%. After taxes at 42.6%, versus 44.2%, net income advanced 21%, to $0.99 a share from $0.82.

Common Share Earnings ($)

Quarter:	19X4-5	19X3-4	19X2-3	19X1-2
May	0.31	0.25	0.29	0.33
Aug.	0.34	0.29	0.34	0.38
Nov.	0.34	0.28	0.24	0.35
Feb.		0.33	0.23	0.25
		1.15	1.10	1.31

Figure 10-3. *(cont.)*

Dividend Data

Cash has been paid each year for 22 years.

Amt. of Divd. $	Date Decl.	Ex-divd. Date	Stock of Record	Payment Date
0.09 26'X84	May 22	Jun. 6	Jun. 12	Jun.
0.09	Jul. 17	Aug. 6	Aug. 10	Aug. 31'X4
0.09	Oct. 16	Oct. 30	Nov. 6	Nov. 27'X4
0.10	Jan. 22	Jan. 30	Feb. 5	Feb. 26'X5

Next dividend meeting: late May 'X5.

Finances

At February 29, 19X4 the company had a line of credit amounting to $10 million, with interest at prime.

Capitalization

Long Term Debt: $2,183,000.

Minority Interests: $808,000.

Common Stock: 6,013, 195 shs. ($1 par).
Officers and directors control about 32%.
Institutions hold about 34%.
Shareholders of record: 2,500.

The Company's Background

Most professional security analysts begin by reading the company's annual report, to try to get a "feel" for a particular company, its products, and its management. If the annual report keeps the analyst's interest, the next step is to review the company's 10K from which the annual report is drawn. Only when thoroughly familiar with the available financial data does the analyst consider speaking to management. Thus, as a starting point we direct your attention to certain key characteristics of PlatingCo so you can get a feel for it.

If you were to consult the standard financial reference sources (Standard & Poor's, Moody's, or Value Line Investment Survey) that are available in any public library, you would discover that PlatingCo came into existence in the early 1950s. The financial statements indicate that, from sales of a few million dollars and earnings in the hundred-thousand-dollar range, the company has reached sales of $130 million and earnings of $6 million. From a one-product company, it has developed into one that controls more than one hundred patents; thus it enjoys a dominant position in its industry niche. PlatingCo's annual report shows the company to be a specialty chemical company and therefore the margins on the products it sells are higher than those of the bulk chemical companies (such as fertilizer companies), which historically have had much lower margins and have been more subject to competition and cyclical factors. (Value Line Investment Survey is a good source for a comprehensive overview of many industries and is particularly useful in getting a feel for an industry. Industry trade associations are also good sources of this type of information.)

Footnotes to the Annual Report

You can obtain much useful information from the footnotes to a company's annual report. Because corporate secrets are often hidden in the footnotes, most security analysts spend time reading and evaluating the footnotes before they look at the textual material in an annual report. As a rule, if the footnotes contained in an Annual Report are complex, you should spend more time understanding them and considering their impact on your evaluation of the company.

starting point in examining the footnotes to a company's annual report. In the case of PlatingCo, the opinion is *clean*, meaning that the independent (outside) accountants did not qualify their opinion about the completeness and accuracy of the company's financial statements when they compared them to the company's books. Any such qualification is considered significant and you should take time to analyze and understand it. Likewise, you should consider the quality of a company's figures if the company frequently changes outside accountants. The company may be *opinion shopping*—seeking accountants who will produce the best figures for assets, sales, and earnings.

In PlatingCo's annual report, Note A—Summary of Accounting Policies—is of primary importance. This footnote explains which accounting principles the company relied on to

(Text resumes on page 204.)

Figure 10-4. *PlatingCo.*

Summary of Key Characteristics. The company develops and markets various electroplating processes with numerous industrial applications; gold plating is the most important of these processes. Process sales were up significantly for the first nine months of fiscal 19X4–5, benefiting from new products and from increased volume for higher technology processes. Research and development expense totaled $1,435,000 in 19X3–4, versus $1,316,000 the year before; patents are obtained to protect the results of the R&D program. Foreign subsidiaries in England, Switzerland, France, Japan, and Germany accounted for 31% of revenues and 26% of net income in 19X3–4. Insiders dominate the board of directors and collectively own 32% of PlatingCo's common stock; institutions (29) own approximately 38% of PlatingCo's common stock.

Ratio Analysis. In ratio analysis, key concepts are *quality* of figures and *trends*. For the purpose of this exercise, we will deal with two years' figures; a more detailed approach would involve a five-year analysis.

1. Current Ratio

$$\text{Current ratio} = \frac{\text{Current assets}}{\text{Current liabilities}}$$

$$\text{19X5 CR} = \frac{43,152,000}{5,679,000} = 7.6$$

$$\text{19X4 CR} = \frac{42,634,000}{7,074,000} = 6.0$$

2. $$\text{Quick ratio} = \frac{\text{Cash} + \text{Receivables}}{\text{Current liabilities}}$$

$$\text{19X5 QR} = \frac{33,157,000}{5,679,000} = 5.8$$

$$\text{19X4 QR} = \frac{32,968,000}{7,074,000} = 4.7$$

3. $$\text{Receivables turnover} = \frac{\text{Net annual sales}}{\text{Average receivables}}$$

$$\text{RT} = \frac{130,536,000}{(15,141,000 + 17,437,000)/2}$$

$$\frac{130,536,000}{(32,578,000)/2}$$

$$\frac{130,536,000}{16,289,000} = 8.01$$

Figure 10-4. *(cont.)*

4. Inventory turnover $= \dfrac{\text{Net sales}}{\text{Average receivables}}$.

$$\text{19X5 IT} = \frac{130,536,000}{(9,219,000 + 9,211,000)/2}$$

$$\frac{130,536,000}{(18,430,000)/2}$$

$$\frac{130,536,000}{9,215,000}$$

14.17

Bear in mind the impact of gold being a component of total inventory.

5. Equity turnover $= \dfrac{\text{Net sales}}{\text{Average equity}}$

Equity includes common stock, paid-in capital, and total retained earnings. The purpose of the ratio is to determine the dollars of sales generated per dollar of equity capital

$$\text{ET} = \frac{130,536,000}{(50,231,000 + 44,488,000)/2}$$

$$\frac{130,536,000}{(94,719,000)/2}$$

$$\frac{130,536,000}{47,359,500} = 2.76$$

6. *Analysis of Profitability*
Gross profit is equal to net sales minus the cost of goods sold.

$$\begin{array}{r} \text{19X5 Gross profit} = 130,536,000 \\ - 108,689,000 \\ \hline 21,847,000 \end{array}$$

$$\text{GPM} = \frac{\text{Gross profit}}{\text{Net sales}}$$

$$\text{19X5 Gross profit margin} = \frac{21,847,000}{130,536,000}$$

$$= .1674 = 16.74\%$$

Figure 10-4. *(cont.)*

19X4 Gross profit $= 163,326,000$
$$\underline{- 143,527,000}$$
$$19,799,000$$

$$= \frac{19,799,000}{163,326,000}$$

$$= .1212 = 12.12\%$$

7. *Operating Profit Margin*
Operating profit margin is gross profit minus sales, general administrative expenses

$$\text{Operating profit margin} = \frac{\text{Operating profit}}{\text{Net sales}}$$

$$19X5 \text{ OPM} = \frac{21,847,000 - 8,780,000}{130,536,000}$$

$$= \frac{13,067,000}{130,536,000} = .1001 = 10.01\%$$

$$19X4 \text{ OPM} = \frac{19,799,000 - 8,153,000}{163,326,000}$$

$$= \frac{11,646,000}{163,326,000} = .0713 = 7.13\%$$

8. *Net Profit Margin*
Net income is earnings after taxes but before dividends on preferred and common stock.

$$\text{Net profit margin} = \frac{\text{Net income}}{\text{Net sales}}$$

$$19X5 \text{ NPM} = \frac{8,077,000}{130,536,000}$$

$$= .0619 = 6.19\%$$

$$19X4 \text{ NPM} = \frac{6,918,000}{163,326,000}$$

$$= .0423 = 4.23\%$$

9. *Common Size Income Statement*
Return on Owners' Equity

Figure 10-4. *(cont.)*

$$\text{Return on total equity} = \frac{\text{Net income}}{\text{Average total equity}}$$

$$1985 \text{ RTE} = \frac{8,077,000}{(45,457,000 + 42,565,000)/2}$$

$$= .1875 = 18.75\%$$

10. *Return on Common Equity*

$$\text{RTE} = \frac{\text{Net income} - \text{Preferred D.}}{\text{Average common equity}}$$

$$= \frac{8,077,000}{(50,231,000 + 44,488,000/2}$$

$$= \frac{8,077,000}{(94,719,000)/2}$$

$$= \frac{8,077,000}{47,359,500} = .1705 = 17.05\%$$

11. *Financial/Risk Ratio*

$$\text{Debt-to-equity ratio} = \frac{\text{Total long-term debt}}{\text{Total equity}}$$

$$19X5 \text{ DER} = \frac{2,057,000}{45,457,000}$$

$$= .045$$

$$19X4 \text{ DER} = \frac{2,546,000}{42,565,000} = .060$$

12. *Determinants of Growth*

$$\text{ROE} = \frac{\text{Sales}}{\text{Total assets}} \times \frac{\text{Total assets}}{\text{Equity}} \times \frac{\text{Income}}{\text{Sales}}$$

ROE = (Total asset × (Financial × (Net profit
      turnover)   leverage)   margin)

ROE can be increased by greater *asset* efficiency (total asset turnover), by changing capital structure (increasing financial leverage), or by increasing profitability (raising the profit margin).

arrive at the final figures contained in the annual report. Of particular interest is the method used for inventory valuation and depreciation. In the case of PlatingCo, note A indicates that the company adheres to standard practice. However, if the company were to utilize accounting practices substantially different from the norm, you should question the reason for such standards. This footnote also brings out the fact that the raw materials utilized in the company's manufacturing process include gold and silver, and for this reason, commodity prices may have an impact on sales and earnings figures.

Other footnotes to PlatingCo's annual report discuss the treatment of income taxes, debt structure, stockholders' equity, and domestic and foreign operations. In the case of PlatingCo, the treatment of these area conforms to the standard practices of the accounting profession. Note that footnotes B and D deal with the company's treatment of its domestic and foreign subsidiaries. The fact that two footnotes deal with this area highlights the point that PlatingCo gets a significant portion of its income from the international licensing of its patents. Because the company does significant overseas business, pay special attention to how the company protects itself from devaluations of foreign currencies, and from changes in the political and international business climates in which it operates overseas. For any company, you should use the footnotes to discover if the company has any lines of business in addition to its core business, and to discover who the company's dominant customers and suppliers are.

Looking At The Pictures–The Annual Report Itself

At this point, you should "look at the pictures"—that is, read the textual parts of the annual report, look at the pictures of the company's products, and evaluate the comments and observations made by the company's president. At the same time, take time to read and understand the section entitled, "Management's Discussion and Analysis of Financial Condition and Results of Operations." Despite its long title, this section of the typical annual report serves a simple purpose: It gives management a forum in which to explain why the numbers came out the way they did. Even though your own analysis may lead you to disagree with management's arguments, it is useful to see their point of view, and should provide a clue to which areas of the balance sheet and income statement demand special attention.

The Proxy Statement–Evaluating Management

What information can you obtain from reading XYZ Company's Proxy Statement? The first conclusion you might reach is that the management and principal stockholders, who have been in place since the founding of the company approximately thirty years ago, might be expected to retire soon. On the surface, such a situation suggests that the company might be sold or liquidated. However, on further examination the Proxy Statement shows that the company has a chain of succession in place, with younger family members holding senior management positions ready to take the places of the company founders. Typically, family-controlled companies are sold or liquidated only when family members decide such an event is in their best interests, and such companies do not normally lend themselves to hostile takeovers because so much of the stock is controlled by insiders.

The Proxy Statement also gives you some information about the number and affiliations of outside board members. The presence of outside board members is generally viewed as a positive factor because they prevent a company from becoming too inbred and narrow in its perspective. In the case of PlatingCo, the absence of outside board members should be viewed as a negative factor, although it is not of paramount importance.

Evaluating the Company's Ownership

Now you should consider a third key aspect in analyzing a company's stock: the matter of institutional ownership. Most security analysts emphasize the question of who owns the company's stock. Owners fit into any of three categories: insiders (corporate officers and directors), institutions (mutual funds, pension plans, and bank trust accounts), and individual investors.

To determine who are the major holders or "players," you should calculate the stock's float. The *float* focuses on individuals who have significant holdings of the stock in question. For PlatingCo, the float equals the number of shares outstanding (6,014,439—determined from the balance sheet) less the number of shares held by insiders (1,925,434—determined from the proxy statement) less the number of shares held by institutions (2,012,000—obtained from Standard & Poor's, Monthly Stock Guide, or from Vickers, or from any of a number of other financial publications that list institutional holdings). What is left represents the float—the number of shares held by individual investors.

Analyzing the float of PlatingCo's common stock tells you to what extent insiders and institutions control this stock. Together they own 3,937,434 shares (1,925,434 plus 2,012,000) of the 6,014,439 shares outstanding. This represents 65.5% of the outstanding shares—a statistic that would definitely have an impact on an analyst's evaluation of the company. Because so much of the stock is closely held, a takeover without management's cooperation appears unlikely. Also, institutions have historically proved to be more fickle than the average investor, liquidating positions at the first sign of a downturn in quarterly earnings. Stocks discovered by institutional investors tend to sell at high price-to-earnings ratios (P/Es), making them more vulnerable to shifts in investor sentiment. In the case of PlatingCo, the dominant position held by insiders and institutions probably should be viewed negatively with regard to the performance of the stock.

Examining the Financial Statements

After you have gotten a feel for the company's business and its management and ownership, you are ready to apply the mathematical techniques learned in Chapter 9 to the company's balance sheet and income statement. First, *does PlatingCo represent an asset play, growth situation, or a combination of both?* To obtain an answer to this question, you must calculate certain key ratios. Once you have answered this question, you know whether to concentrate your attention and effort on analyzing the company's balance sheet or income statement, or to divide your time between both. The calculation of certain other key ratios helps you determine the direction the company is headed in terms of earnings and sales, how much risk is attached to the projected return, and, hopefully, what the strengths and weaknesses of the company are.

Balance Sheet Ratios

For the purposes of this case study, we use two years' figures for PlatingCo. (Most analysts prefer to use five years' figures to get a better reading on the trend.) Refer to the ratios calculated in Figure 10-4.

Current Ratio. Examining the current ratio shows that the company seems to have one key characteristic of an asset play: a high current asset ratio. To confirm this conclusion, you must calculate additional balance sheet ratios.

Quick Ratio. The quick ratio of 4.7 shows that the corporation's current assets are concentrated in cash, cash equivalents, and receivables—another key characteristic of an asset play.

Receivables Turnover. To calculate earlier/comparative data, refer to the company's 10K.

Inventory Turnover. (To calculate earlier/comparative data, refer to the company's 10K.) The receivables and inventory turnover ratios—indicators of operating performance—show that the PlatingCo is not an asset play because the ratios are those of an *operating* company rather than a passive holder of assets. Therefore you should not devote your time solely to an analysis of the company's balance sheet, but move on to examine the income statement to see if PlatingCo represents a growth situation or a combination of the growth and asset-play categories.

Income Statement Ratios

You should now direct your attention towards analyzing PlatingCo's Income Statement.

Gross Profit. The figures show an average growth pattern, at least for the two years we are analyzing. To confirm this pattern, you must calculate the net profit margins for 19X4 and 19X5.

Net Profit Margin. The calculation of the net profit margin confirms what the gross profit margin showed: The growth pattern for PlatingCo has been undramatic for the two years we studied.

Return on Equity. If we want to determine the reasons for this pattern of nongrowth, we must look to the company's Return on Equity (ROE) and its component parts.

$$\text{ROE} = \frac{\text{Sales}}{\text{Total assets}} \times \frac{\text{Total assets}}{\text{Equity}} \times \frac{\text{Income}}{\text{Sales}}$$

ROE = Total Asset Turnover × Financial Leverage
× Net Profit Margin

The PlatingCo has made our work easier: Page 1 of the annual report shows the corporation's return on stockholders'

equity for the period 19X1 through 19X5, thus eliminating the
need to calculate it.

At this point, you're probably wondering, *What does this
data tell me about PlatingCo?* You probably observed that the
company's return on equity declined from a high of 30% in
19X1, to a low of 17% in 19X4, rebounding to 18% in 19X5. You
may also have noticed that sharp swings have occurred in the
company's return on equity from year-to-year. Variations were
as much as 6% for the periods 19X1–19X2 and 19X2–19X3, end-
ing with what should be considered a respectable rate of return
of 18%.

These observations should bring to mind certain questions. *Why has the company's return on equity declined so substantially? Why has the return on equity varied sharply from year to year?*
Most importantly, *Does PlatingCo represent a growth situation?*

To answer the questions about the erratic and downward
trend of the company's return on equity over the past five
years, look at the numbers and the nature of the company's
business. The equation used to calculate return on equity includes three basic components: (1) asset turnover, (2) financial
leverage, and (3) net profit margin. Each of these factors must
be examined separately to determine what causes this pattern.

Because PlatingCo's debts are insignificant (a fact that can
be confirmed by examining the company's balance sheet),
leverage—or the lack of it—has not played a major role in the
erratic and downward pattern of the corporation's return on
equity. Sales and profit margins present a different case: As the
income statement shows, the company's sales ranged from a
high of $234 million in 19X1 to a low of $130 million in 19X5;
with net income hovering around $8 million for most of the
period. The textual material in the annual report explains the
degree to which the company's fortunes are tied to the fortunes
of the semiconductor manufacturers who are its customer. Second, the foreign competition faced by many of these semiconductor manufacturers has resulted in pressure on PlatingCo's
profit margins. Third, because gold and silver are used in
PlatingCo's manufacturing processes, sales and profits have
felt the impact of the swings in the prices of these commodities

over the past five years. Last, the strength of the U.S. dollar has hurt the company's overseas subsidiaries.

We conclude that PlatingCo does not appear to fit the mold of a pure growth situation because its return on equity is erratic and its sales and earnings stagnant. PlatingCo fits the category of a hybrid security; combining elements of an asset play and a growth situation.

The Growth Rate (g). As we mentioned in Chapter 9, the growth rate of a company is a function of two factors: its return on equity and its retention rate. In the case of PlatingCo, ROE has had an erratic and mostly declining pattern over the past five years. But *what has happened to the money management has decided to retain in the business?*

To answer this question, compare the percentage of earnings paid out as dividends in 19X1 with the percentage of earnings paid out as dividends in 19X5. In 19X1 the percentage was 19.5% (.26 divided by $1.33 earnings per share); in 19X5 it was 27.6% (.37 divided by $1.34 earnings per share). The fact that management decided to reward its shareholders with a larger dividend payout probably indicates that management doubts that it can obtain a greater return for its shareholders by keeping the money in the business. PlatingCo is changing from a growth company to a mature company operating within a maturing industry. You might find it worthwhile to determine how much money the company is spending on research and development (R&D) and how 19X5 expenditures compare with those of 19X1, in terms of both dollar amount and use—whether to fund basic or applied research.

Again, the foregoing factors indicate that PlatingCo represents something between an asset play and a growth situation—a hybrid security.

Price-to-Earnings Ratio. For this case study, assume that the stock of PlatingCo is selling at $14 per share at the end of 19X5. With earnings of $1.34 per share, its P/E ratio would be 10.4 ($14 divided by $1.34). To know whether the P/E ratio of 10 is high or low, you should compare it with (1) the P/E ratio of the overall market at the time, and (2) the stock's own historical P/E ratio. In light of what we know about PlatingCo, such a study would tell you whether the stock is cheap or dear at current prices.

What other conclusions can you draw from the company's P/E ratio of 10? A P/E ratio of 10 for the stock is surprising when you consider that so much of the stock is in the hands of institutions. Institutional ownership has probably built up slowly over time rather than through a rapid acquisition program. In the same context, you might wonder *why PlatingCo is such an institutional favorite in view of its erratic ROE over the past five years.* The answer may be that institutional investors have a positive opinion about future prospects for the company's products and developments. By attending annual meetings of the corporation, trade association meetings and shows, and so on, you can determine if this positive opinion is well founded. Your analysis of the stock should give you satisfactory answers to all these questions before you buy a single share.

Conclusions

Your number crunching has brought into focus some important characteristics of the PlatingCo, including:

1. The company has a strong balance sheet and very little debt.
2. The corporation derives the bulk of its income from ongoing operations rather than from asset management; hence it does not fit the category of an asset play.
3. Over the past five years, the corporation has had an erratic and declining ROE, although ROE remains above average at 18%.
4. Over the past five years, the corporation has increased the percentage of earnings it pays out to its shareholders in the form of dividends (reduced its retention rate). Management apparently concluded that the company's rate of growth is slowing down.

5. Because of its erratic and declining ROE and reduced RR, the corporation does not appear to represent a growth situation at the present time.

6. The corporation appears to fit the category of a hybrid security. You should devote equal time to examining and analyzing its balance sheet and income statement rather than concentrate on one or the other.

7. The corporation's price-to-earnings ratio of 10.4 appears low for that of an institutional favorite, indicating that the position was probably built up over a period of time rather than through a short-term acquisition program.

8. The corporation continues to be an institutional favorite despite a declining ROE. Therefore, you should determine what strengths the institutions see in the company's future prospects (whether new products or new markes) that warrant their holdings of the corporation's common stock.

Questions That Need Answers

These conclusions highlight the areas you should concentrate on and the questions you should answer before you buy PlatingCo's common stock. Some of these unanswered questions include: (1) What will be the company's future growth pattern (assuming that the company's family ownership makes sale or liquidation unlikely)? (2) What do institutions see in the company's future prospects that warrants their substantial holdings of its common stock? (3) What price determines whether the stock is cheap compared with future prospects (its risk/reward ratio)?

As you can see, security analysis leaves a number of unanswered questions. You can pursue the answers by attending the annual meeting of shareholders, by consulting your investment advisor, or by reading available research reports. Security analysis focuses your attention on those areas that require further study and enables you to isolate the key questions you must answer, using whatever sources are available to you.

11
Technical Analysis

Fundamental analysis focuses on the supply and demand factors underlying price movements, and this approach is therefore said to study the *causes* of price movements. By contrast, technical analysis studies the *effects* of supply and demand—that is, the price movements themselves. In fact, technical analysis is also called *charting* since it is essentially the charting of actual price changes as they occur. The charting approach reflects the basic assumption of the technician that all influences on market action—from natural catastrophes to trading psychology—are automatically accounted for, or *discounted*, in price activity.

Given this premise, charting can be used for at least three purposes:

1. *Price Forecasting:* The technician can project price movements either in tandem with a fundamental approach or solely on the basis of charted movements.

2. *Market Timing:* Chart analysis is much better suited than the fundamental approach for determining exactly *when* to buy and sell.

3. *Leading Indicator:* If market action discounts all influences on it, then price movement may be considered as a leading indicator, and it may be used in two ways. First, the chartist may—without regard for why prices are moving in one direction or the other—buy or sell. Second, an unusual price movement can be taken as a signal that some influence or another on the market has not been accounted for in the fundamentalist's analysis and that further study is required.

The technician uses two working assumptions: (1) Markets move in trends, and (2) trends persist. The reasoning is that if market action discounts all influences, then prices move not randomly, but in trends. Identifying the trend at an early enough stage enables the trader to take the appropriate positions. The tool used to track price movements and thus to identify trends is the chart.

Two basic types of charts are available to the technician: the bar chart (Figure 11-1) and the point and figure chart (Figure 11-2). Note that the point and figure (P&F) chart does not indicate time or trading volume.

Figure 11-2. *A Point and Figure (P&F) Chart.*

Figure 11-1. *A Bar Chart.*

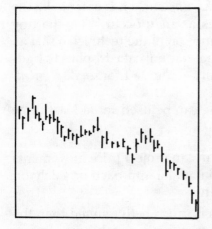

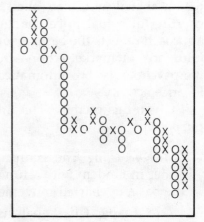

Bar Charts

Constructing a bar chart is simple. At the top of the chart enter the name of the contract. To the vertical axis assign a price scale. On the horizontal axis mark off the calendar time scale—days, weeks, or months. On a daily bar chart, every five-day period (a trading week) is usually marked by a vertical line that is heavier than the others. For each day, the high, low, and closing (or settlement) prices are plotted. See Figure 11-3. A vertical line, or *bar*, connects the high and low prices. A horizontal tic to the right of the bar indicates the closing price.

Figure 11-3. *How a Bar Chart Is Constructed.*

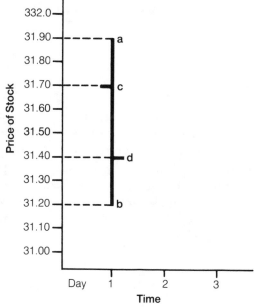

a: The high price for the day, $31.90.

b: The low price for the day, $31.20.

c: The opening price (not always on the bar chart), $31.70.

d: The closing price, $31.40.

(A tic on the left side of the bar marks the opening price for the day.) With so many chart services available, however, plotting one's own charts is often an unnecessary and unprofitable way to spend time.

Trade and Trendlines

A *trend* is a series of price changes that collectively move in one direction or another. An *uptrend* is a series of peaks and troughs that rises on average. See Figure 11-4. A *downtrend* is a series that declines. See Figure 11-5. A series of price fluctuations that neither rises nor falls is *trendless*, and the market is said to be moving *sideways* or *horizontally*. See Figure 11-6.

Trends are commonly classified according to their duration:

- *Secondary* trends last for one to three months.
- *Minor* trends persist for a few weeks or less.

On a bar chart, a trend is identified by drawing a *trendline*, which is a straight line connecting two or more successive high or low points in a series of price movements. An *uptrendline*, which rises from left to right, connects two or more low points so that all of the price activity is above the line. See Figure 11-7. A *downtrendline*, declining from left to right, connects two or more high points so as to keep all the movements below the line. See Figure 11-8.

Figure 11-4. *An Uptrend.*   **Figure 11-5.** *A Downtrend.*

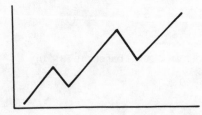   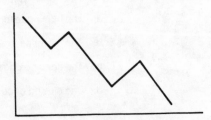

Figure 11-6. *A Sideways, or Horizontal, Trend.*

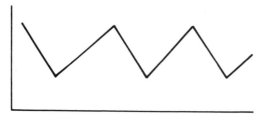

Although either type of trendline can be drawn using only two points, at least one more point is needed to validate the trendline. In Figure 11-7, for example, the major uptrendline is validated at points 1, 3, and 5. In Figure 11-8, the downtrendline is similarly validated.

Channel Lines

Sometimes prices trend within a clearcut range between the main trendline and another parallel line, called a *channel* or *return* line. In an uptrend, the channel runs below the price activity and parallel to the uptrendline. See Figure 11-9. In a declining market, the channel runs above the price activity and parallel to the downtrendline. See Figure 11-11.

Figure 11-7. *An Uptrend and Channel Line.*

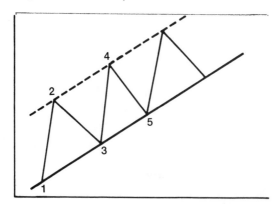

Figure 11-8. *A Downtrend and Channel Line.*

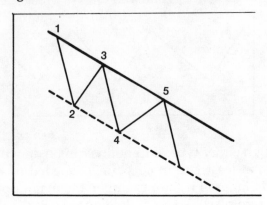

The identification of both a trendline and channel is a po-
tentially profitable piece of information. With it, the technician
has advance notice of turning points in market price. In Figure
11-10, for example, points 2 and 4 would represent good buying prices, while points 1, 3, and 5 are good selling levels. Even
when prices move outside the channel, the chartest can profit,
since once a breakout occurs, prices typically travel a distance

Figure 11-9. *An Uptrend, Channel Line, and Breakout.*

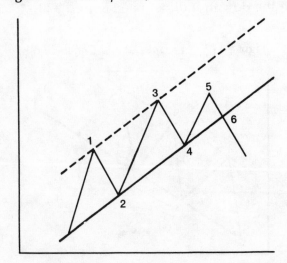

equal to the width of the channel. Once a breakout occurs, the chart user can measure the width of the channel and project that distance from the point of the breakout to calculate a buying or selling point. In Figure 11-10, after an upward breakout, prices are likely to move to point 7 before changing direction.

Trendlines and channel lines are two of the technician's simplest tools.

Retracement

In the course of any trend, prices will *countertrend*; that is, they move back against a portion of the current trend before resuming the original direction. These temporary counter trends are called *retracements*.

Key Reversal Day

Any day on which the market reverses is a potential key reversal day, also known as a *top/bottom reversal day* or *buying/selling climax*. See Figures 11-11 and 11-12. When does a reversal day

Figure 11-10.

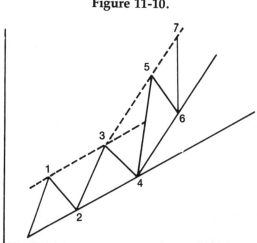

become key? In an uptrend, a *top reversal* is a day on which a new high is established but the market closes lower than on the day before. In a *bottom reversal*, a new low in the downtrend is set but the market closes higher than on the prior day. In either case, volume is usually heavy. Also, if the high and low on the reversal day exceeds the range of the previous day, forming what is known as an outside day, the reversal carries more weight. In many cases, however, a true key reversal day cannot be positively identified until long after prices have moved significantly past it.

Sometimes a reversal takes two days to form and is called, appropriately, a *two-day reversal*.

Price Gaps

A *gap* is an area on chart where no trading takes place. In an uptrend, the present day's low is higher than the previous day's high. The converse applies in a downtrend. See Figures 11-13 and 11-14.

There are four general types of gaps:

1. The *common gap*, the least important in charting, occurs in thinly traded markets or in the middle of horizontal trading

Figure 11-11.   **Figure 11-12.**
A Key Reversal Day in an Uptrend.   *A Key Reversal Day in a Downtrend.*

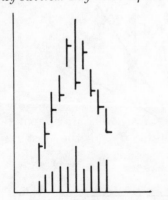

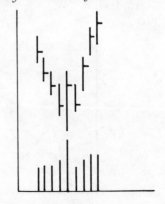

Figure 11-13.
A Gap in an Uptrend.

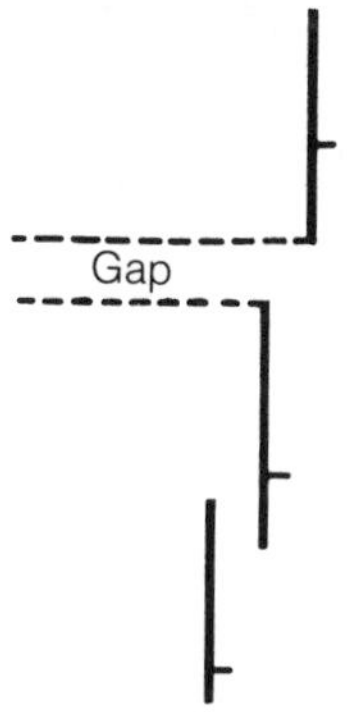

Figure 11-14.
A Gap in a Downtrend.

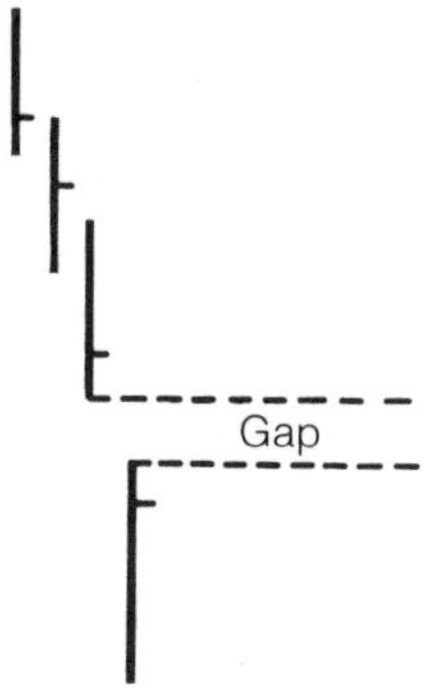

ranges. Generally ignored by technicians, it reflects merely a lack of trading interest.

2. The *breakaway gap* usually occurs at the completion of an important price pattern on heavy volume and may signal the start of a significant market move. This gap is generally not completely filled by trading on ensuing days. In fact, the upper side of the gap often acts as a support level for subsequent trading. ("Support" is explained in the next section.) See Figure 11-15.

3. A *runaway gap* occurs on moderate volume, with the market trending effortlessly. It is a sign of strength in an uptrend but one of weakness in a downtrend. A move below a runaway gap in a uptrend is a negative sign. Like the breakaway, this type of gap is usually not filled.

   This formation is also called a *measuring gap* because it commonly occurs about halfway through a trend. The distance from the beginning of the trend to the gap is the probable extent of the trend from the gap to its completion.

4. The *exhaustion gap* appears near the end of a market move, after all objectives have been achieved and after breakaway and runaway gaps have been identified. It is the "last gasp," so to speak, of the trend. When prices close under the last gap, the chartist can be quite sure that the exhaustion gap has made its appearance.

Figure 11-15. *Various Types of Gaps.*

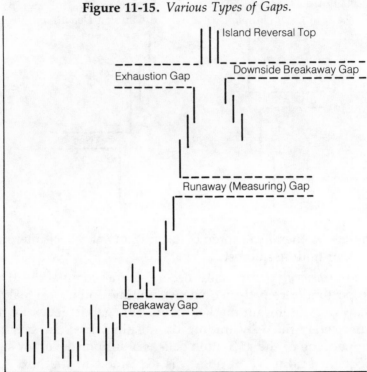

Island Reversal

When a trend reverses sharply, with gaps preceding and following the reversal period, the few days' or weeks' worth of price action between the gaps is referred to as an "island." See Figure 11-15. The significance of such a formation arises from the two gaps, not from the activity within the island itself. While the exhaustion gap signals that the trend is sputtering, the breakaway gap after the island presages a major move in the opposite direction.

Resistance and Support

Prices change direction for many reasons, not all of which can be identified, much less foreseen. Perhaps the greatest influence on price behavior, however, consists of the expectations and desires of the market participants, who fall into three basis categories:

1. The "longs"—those who own stock.
2. The "shorts"—those who have sold stock short.
3. The uncommitted—those who are not "in" the market at the moment. This is known as being *flat*.

Any of these types of participants can affect price movements. For example, with prices in an uptrend, the longs are delighted but wish they had bought more. The shorts are coming to the conclusion that they were wrong and would like to get out without losing too much. Of the uncommitted group, some never opened a position but wish they had, and others liquidated positions and wish they had not. All four of these groups are watching the market for a dip. If prices break downward, they are all liable to become buyers, that is, "buy the dip." As a result, should prices begin to drop for any reason, these would-be buyers respond by buying, thereby creating demand and forcing prices up again.

When declining prices meet with such demand and "bounce back," they are said to have hit *support*. The price dip as plotted on the chart is known as a *trough* or *reaction low*. Support is therefore a level or area below the market where buying interest is strong enough to overcome selling pressure.

Resistance is the opposite of support. It is a level or area, above the market, at which selling pressure overcomes buying interest. In this case, the market is trending downward. The longs are looking for a chance to sell, while the shorts are waiting for the opportunity to increase the size of their positions. The uncommitted are likely to go short. Should the market turn upward, all these participants are pimed to sell, thereby creating supply and eventually causing prices to turn downward again. (The upturn and drop in prices, once charted, are referred to as a *peak* or *reaction high*.)

Support and resistance often reverse their roles once they are significantly penetrated by price movements. Penetrated by

Figure 11-16. *How Resistance Can Become Support.*

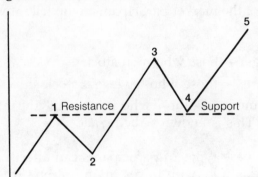

upward movement, resistance becomes support (Figure 11-16). Support, after being penetrated, becomes resistance (Figure 11-17). What constitutes "significant" penetration, however, is arguable. Some chartists say 10%, others 3 to 5%. In practice, each technician must set an individual criterion for a "significant" penetration.

Price Patterns

In addition to trendlines and channel lines, technicians are able to identify a number of *price patterns*. These are price move-

Figure 11-17. *How Support Can Become Resistance.*

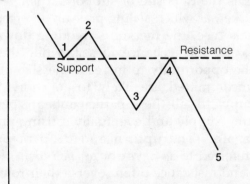

ments that, when charted, describe a predictable pattern. Some price patterns indicate a trend reversal, and they are therefore called *reversal patterns*. Others, called continuation patterns, reflect pauses or temporary reverses in an existing trend and usually form more quickly than reversal patterns.

Since the aim of this guide is only to introduce you to the basics of analysis, we will look at only one or two of each type of pattern. There are many good books available on technical analysis. If you choose to pursue this type of analysis, you should certainly study it further before basing investment decisions on your conclusions.

Reversal Patterns

Head and Shoulders. Perhaps the best known of reversal patterns, the head and shoulders has three clear peaks, with the middle peak (or *head*) higher than the ones before and after it (the *shoulders*). See Figure 11-18. The *neckline* is the trendline drawn to connect the two troughs between the peaks. A close below the neckline signals the completion of the pattern and an important market reversal. A breakaway gap at the point of

Figure 11-18. *A Head and Shoulders Pattern.*

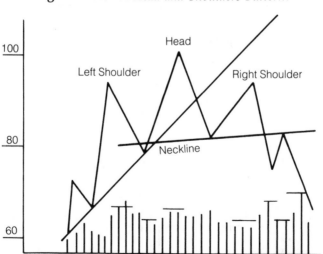

penetration through the neckline lends weight to the probability that a true reversal has taken place. The minimum extent of the reversal can be estimated. To do so, measure the distance from the head to the neckline and project the same distance from the breakthrough point in the neckline. A return move is likely, but it generally does not penetrate the neckline.

There are several variations of this type of pattern.

Saucers. There are many other names for this pattern. In an uptrend, the pattern may be referred to as an *inverted saucer* or *rounding top*. During a downtrend, it can be a *rounding bottom* or *bowl*. See Figures 11-19 and 11-20. Regardless of its name, the pattern consists of a gradual turning of the trend on diminishing volume.

No precise measurement can be made of the extent of the reversal by means of a saucer. The duration and size of the prior trend have some bearing on the new trend, as does the time the saucer takes to form. Other criteria are the previous support and resistance levels, gaps, long-term trendlines, and so on.

Continuation Patterns

As we know, continuation patterns represent not reversals in the making, but rather only pauses in the current trend.

Figure 11-19. *A Saucer Top.*

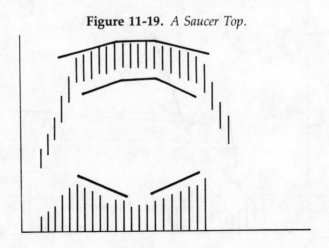

Figure 11-20. *A Saucer Bottom.*

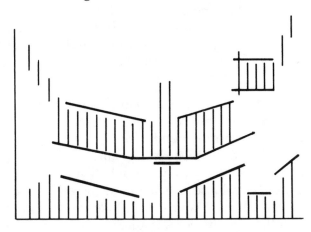

Symmetrical Triangle. Also known as a *coil*, this pattern forms, on diminishing volume, as a triangle that narrows evenly from left to right, with at least four reference points. See Figure 11-21. The trend may be expected to resume, with a closing price outside the triangle, sometime after one-half and three-quarters of the triangle's length is developed. Occasionally, there is a return move on light volume, but the penetrated trendline of the triangle acts as support in an uptrend or as resistance in a downtrend. In either direction, volume generally picks up as the trend resumes. The apex itself can also serve as longer-term support or resistance.

A couple of measuring techniques are associated with

Figure 11-21. *A Triangle.*

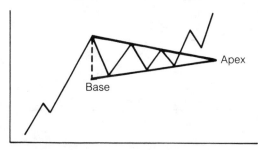

triangles. To project the minimum extent of the resumed trend, measure the height of the base (distance A-B in Figure 11-22) and extend a line of the same length from the breakout point (points C-D). Alternatively, draw a line from the top of the base (point A) that is parallel to the bottom line in the triangle.

Rectangle. Also known as a *trading range* or *congestion area*, this pattern typically reflects a consolidation period before a resumption of the current trend. See Figures 11-23 and 11-24.

Because this formation closely resembles a triple top or bottom, the chartist must rely on volume to distinguish the two. If in an uptrend the volume is heavier on the rallies than on the setback, then a rectangle is probable. In a downtrend, a rectangle is likely if the dips are accompanied by heavier volume than the rallies. Otherwise, a triple top or bottom could be in the making.

After the breakout, the extent of price movement can be gauged by measuring the height of the trading range and extending a line of the same length up or down from the point of breakout.

Figure 11-22. *Measuring the Duration of a Breakout from a Triangle.*

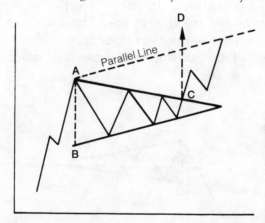

Figure 11-23. *Upside Breakout from a Sideways Market.*

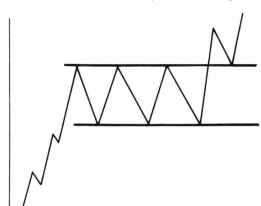

Blowoffs and Selling Climaxes

Sometimes at the end of a long advance or decline, sudden and dramatic market action will lead to a sharp reversal. When this occurs at the end of a prolonged uptrend, it consists of a great deal of buying, which causes prices to rise quickly, and is called a *blowoff*. In the case of a downtrend, it is called a *selling climax*,

Figure 11-24. *A Downside Breakout form a Rectangle.*

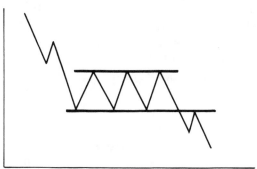

which is accompanied by much selling and, of course, sharp declines in prices. In either case, as volume picks up, open interest drops off. Under these conditions, be on the lookout for an abrupt reversal.

Moving Averages

As you might have concluded by now, the technical approach can be a subjective practice, with two analysts in total disagreement over a pattern. Moving averages represent a step toward making chart analysis more scientific.

A *moving average* is an average of closing prices over a certain number of days. (Midpoint prices might also be used.) For example, a 10-day moving average includes the past 10 days' prices. It is "moving" because as the latest day's prices are included in the average, the oldest day's prices are left out.

The moving average is a trend-tracking tool. Typically represented on a chart as a curving line laid over the price movements, the moving average "smooths out" the trend, enabling analysts to see whether prices are in or out of line. Thus, as a market follower, it signals whether a trend is still in effect or has reversed.

The responsiveness of a moving average to price movements depends on the number of days included in the calculation. Generally, the fewer the days included, the more closely the average tracks the price action. A 5- or 10-day average, for instance, would "hug" the market activity more closely than one of 40 days. See Figure 11-25.

The easily quantified and programmed moving average lends itself readily to today's computerized market-monitoring systems.

Oscillators

An oscillator is a line at the base of a bar chart that is plotted around a midpoint line within a price range, whose boundaries

Figure 11-25. *A Moving Average on a Bar Chart.*

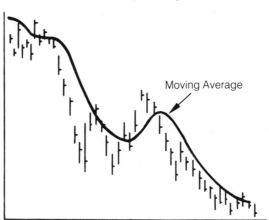

are based on historical extremes. See Figure 11-26. The plotted line is a measure of price *momentum*, that is, how fast prices are changing. As the momentum of price changes increases, the momentum line draws away from the midpoint line and toward one limit of the trading range or the other. As prices go up, the momentum line moves toward the upper, positive boundary; when they go down, the line moves into the nega-

Figure 11-26. *An Oscillator on a Bar Chart.*

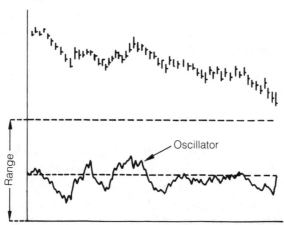

tive range below the midpoint line. Like the moving average, a 5-day oscillator is more sensitive than a 10-day oscillator.

An oscillator tells the analyst whether a market is *over-bought*, if the momentum line touches the lower one. For this reason, oscillators are particularly useful in sideways or horizontal markets. In addition, a divergence between price action and an oscillator in an extreme position is usually a warning that a price correction is imminent; the price has gone "too far, too fast." Some charts even use the crossing of the midpoint (or zero) line as a buy or sell signal—of course, always in conjunction with other technical considerations.

Point and Figure (P&F) Charts

Unlike bar charts, point and figure charts record only price movements; if no price change occurs, the chart remains the same. Time is not reflected on a P&F chart, although time reference points, such as a "10:00" for ten o'clock, are sometimes used. Volume is indicated only by the number of recorded price changes, not as a separate entity. Although traditionally ignored, gaps may be represented by empty boxes.

Nevertheless, point and figure charts have at least two major advantages over bar charts: First, they can be used on an intraday basis to identify support, resistance, and other price-related data—particularly congestion areas—that bar charts can miss completely. Second, P&F charts are more flexible than bar charts in that the analyst can vary the size of the box and the reversal criterion, either of which can drastically change the appearance of the formation.

Box Size

In a P&F chart a rising price change is represented by an X, a declining price movement by an O. Each X or O occupies a box on the chart. One of the first decisions in constructing a P&F chart is therefore how great a price change each box should represent. For example, a gold chart might have a box size of $1. On a less sensitive chart, each box might equal $5; a more sensitive scale would be $.50 a box. Obviously, the smaller the value assigned to a box, the more detailed price action the chart can convey—and the more tedious it becomes to construct.

Reversal Criterion

On a P&F chart, the analyst moves one row of boxes to the right each time the market reverses. The next question is then what constitutes a reversal? Is a one-box change in direction a reversal? Or is it three boxes worth of movement?

A P&F chart constructed with each box equal to one point and a three-box reversal criterion is a "1 × 3"chart. See Figure 11-27. (The columns are numbered only for this illustration; they are not usually numbered in practice.) The chartist can make the same data plot differently—and make the chart less sensitive—by changing either the size of the box or the reversal criterion. For example, Figure 11-28 is the 1 × 3 cotton chart that was started in Figure 11-27, now plotted out for several hours worth of trading. Compare it with Figure 11-29, which reflects the price changes but in a 2 × 3 format; that is, each box now represents two points, and the reversal criterion is still three days.

Figure 11-27. *P&F Chart.*

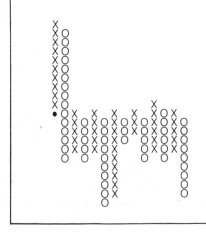

Figure 11-28. *Continuation of the P&F Chart.*

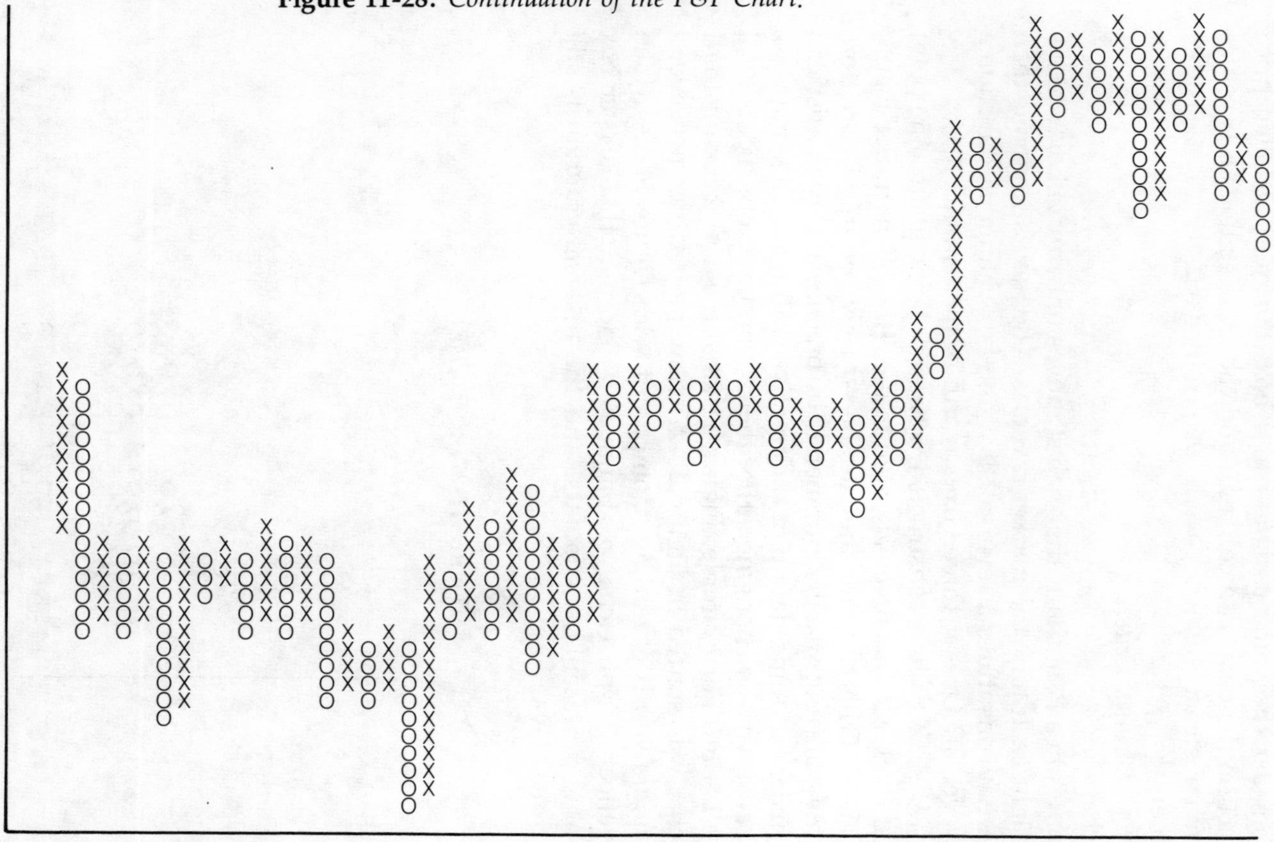

The Horizontal Count

Whereas price objectives are determined by vertical measurements on a bar chart, they are obtained by what is known as a *horizontal count* on a P&F chart. On intra-day, one-box reversal charts, the analyst measures the width of the congestion area and uses that number of boxes to measure the up- or downside target. Usually the column to count from is the one with the greatest number of X's and O's.

The point of a compass is placed at the extreme right of the area, and an arc is projected up- or downward once the width of the area has been measured.

Price Patterns

Although some patterns, such as gaps, flags, or pennants, are not evident on P&F charts, most formations can be seen. Their appearance, however, is sometimes different from the bar chart variety.

Using Long-Term Charts

Technical analysis techniques can be used in any time dimension. They apply not only to daily charts, but also to weekly charts (which contain up to five years of data) and to monthly charts (which can offer up to 20 years of price movements).

In fact, even though this chapter has focused on the daily chart, no analyst could get a broad enough picture of a market without referring first (and often) to longer-term charts. (See Figure 11-30.)

Confirmation and Divergence

Running throughout technical analysis are the two themes of confirmation and divergence. No one pattern, no one indicator

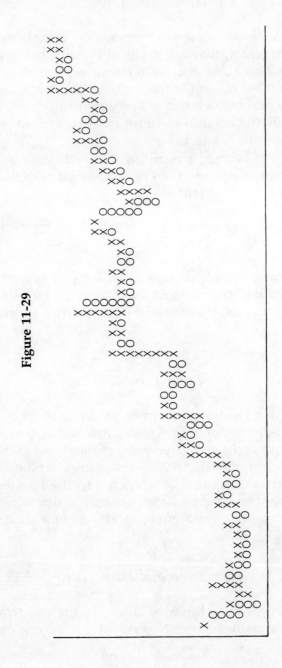

Figure 11-29

Figure 11-30. *A Long-Term Bar Chart.*
Rectangular Base Pattern

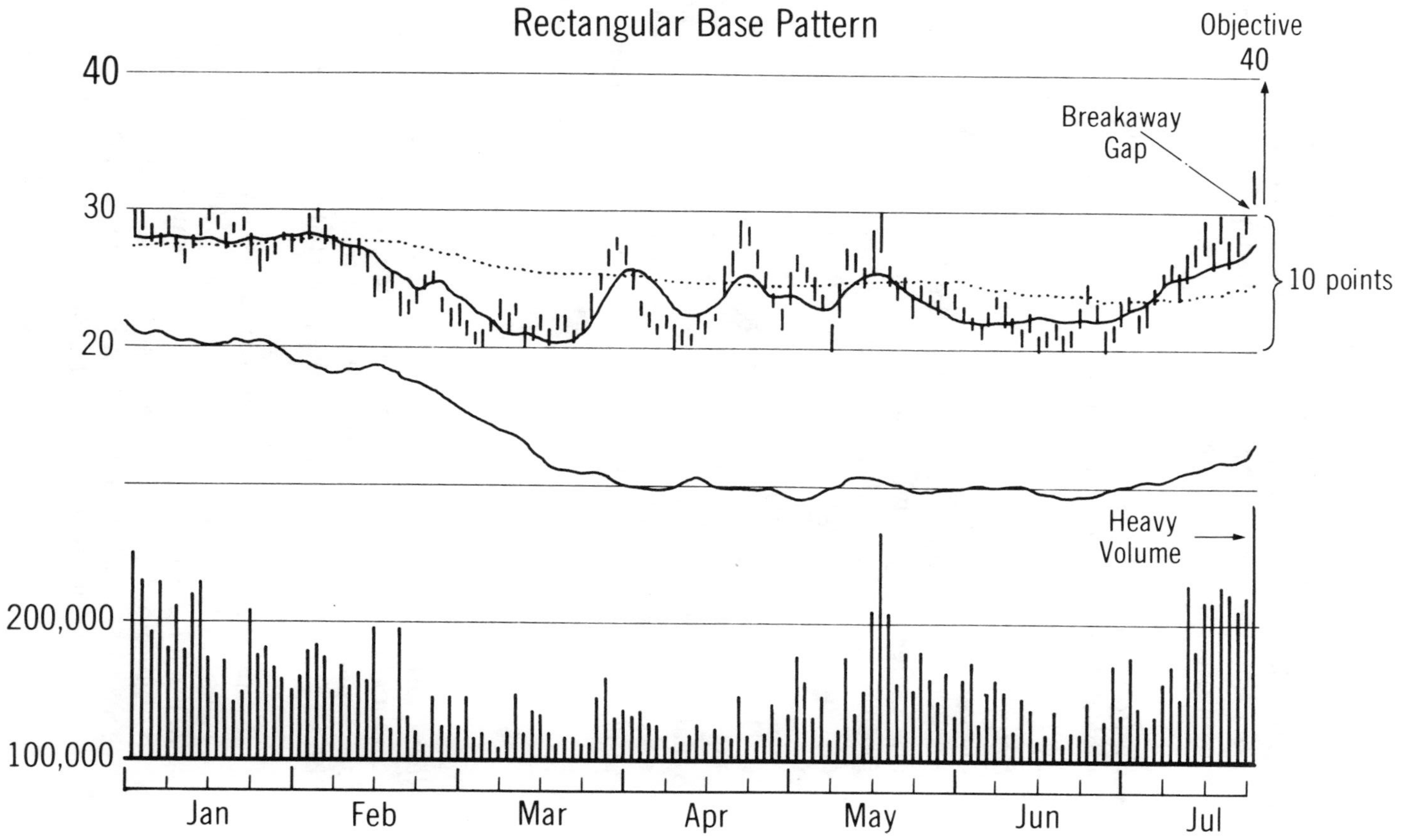

can be used in isolation. Instead, the chartist must take into consideration all the elements of the market, always seeking to test the signals given by the price movements. Two basic tests are confirmation and divergence:

- *Confirmation* is the comparison of all technical signals and indicators to ensure that most of them point to the same conclusion and thereby confirm one another.

- *Divergence* is a situation in which the indicators fail to confirm one another. Perhaps other delivery months or related markets are headed in a different direction than that of the one under study. Divergence is not necessarily a negative finding. It can be a valuable concept in market analysis and an early warning signal of an impending trend reversal.

The essential point is that charting price movements, considered by itself, usually does not provide enough information to make an intelligent investment decision. You must look at the stock itself, the economic conditions, the issuing company, and any other factors that might be influencing the market.

Conclusion

New chartists sometimes mistakenly regard technical analysis techniques as infallible—or nearly so. Their subliminal assumption is sometimes that, by drawing the trendlines associated with a pattern, they can "make" the projected price movement happen.

But perhaps the first rule in chart analysis is that there are no "rules" as such. A pattern will probably develop as anticipated, but it is not certain to do so. That is why chartists use the word "indicator," not "rule" and surely not "guarantee."

That is also why confirmation is so important. Analysts must combine all they know and all they see before taking a position. They must bring to bear the findings of their fundamental studies, their awareness of the market and industry in general, and their willingness to constantly review indicators other than price. Only then can they reasonably expect to profit from their trading—most of the time.

12

Your Rights as an Investor

In the process of investing, several questions may come to your mind. *What rights does ownership of a stock, bond, or any financial asset bring with it? How do I, as an individual investor, protect these rights? If I feel that I have been treated in an unfair or illegal manner, to whom do I turn and what can I expect in the way of compensation for my loss?*

Most public companies—and the brokerage community in general—are fair and equitable in their dealings with the investing public. Scrutiny by the media and fifty-odd years of state and federal regulation have contributed to this practice of fair dealing. This is not to say that individual investors have never been taken advantage of by unscrupulous or incompetent corporate officers, brokers, or financial advisors. As with any industry, the investment business has its share of "bad apples." However, because the securities industry is so closely regulated, such individuals are eventually forced out. In this chapter, we discuss your rights as a shareholder/investor and the mechanisms available for the redress of wrongs.

Shareholder Rights

As a shareholder, whether you own 50 shares or 5,000 shares, you are part-owner of the public company whose shares you own. Bear in mind that the management of a public company "works for you" and is answerable to you as a shareholder.

What are your specific rights as a shareholder? First, the management of a public company is required by law to keep you informed about the progress of and general developments that affect the company. This disclosure requirement is mandated by the federal securities laws enacted by Congress in the mid-1930s and enforced by the U.S. Securities & Exchange Commission (SEC), which oversees the nation's financial markets and the brokerage community.

The concept of disclosure is at the heart of the federal securities laws: A public company must disclose (reveal) all the pertinent facts about itself to its shareholders. (You should understand that disclosure provides no guarantee against loss in an investment The disclosure laws attempt to put every investor on an equal footing in terms of access to relevant information; however, the decision to buy, sell, or hold a particular stock or bond is yours alone.) Disclosure takes several forms. As an investor in a public company you are entitled to receive an annual report, a quarterly report, and a proxy statement, and to be informed of any significant corporate development (such as replacement of a corporate officer, destruction of corporate property, or any offer to buy the company). All such information must be furnished on a timely basis, and filed with the SEC before distribution to shareholders. The SEC reviews the information to determine if it meets disclosure requirements but makes no judgment regarding the information's significance. Information about public companies that is filed with the SEC is kept on microfilm at the SEC regional offices and is available for examination by the public. Many shareholders/investors are not aware of this source of information, but its usefulness is evident from the number of professional securities analysts who review it regularly.

After review by the SEC staff, if no errors, omissions, or

false statements are uncovered, companies mail copies of these reports to their shareholders. (Chapters 9 and 10 explain the techniques you can use to analyze and evaluate the data available in a company's annual and quarterly reports, proxy statement, and other sources. In this section we concentrate on the proxy statement—the document most concerned with your rights as a shareholder.

The Proxy Statement

In addition to receiving information, as part-owner of a public corporation, a shareholder has the right to vote on an annual basis to select the company's officers and directors. The company must hold an annual meeting, at which the shareholders can voice their opinions and meet and speak with management. For the most part, the shareholders' rights with respect to the selection of management and the holding of the annual meeting are governed by the laws of the state in which the company is incorporated. However, all proxy statements must be filed with and reviewed by the SEC.

What is a proxy statement and what information does it contain? A *proxy statement* is simply a ballot sent to the shareholders of a public corporation whereby the corporation requests the shareholders' votes that its officers and directors continue in their positions. A proxy also provides for a negative vote: As a shareholder you are under no obligation to vote for the present management. It is extremely difficult, however, for individual shareholders to oust the existing management of a public corporation unless management has overtly abused its positions. The theft of corporate funds or the acceptance of kickbacks are examples of the instances in which shareholders might vote to throw out the current management. Until the recent trend of mergers and acquisitions, it was not uncommon for a mediocre management to continue running a public corporation for a number of years, particularly if ownership of the company's shares was widely dispersed and fragmented.

A proxy may also be used to secure stockholders' approval of the selection of outside accountants as well as of changes in the corporation's *charter*. Such changes might include the addition of provisions to make a takeover of the company more difficult and expensive, a change in the state of incorporation, or the introduction of stock option plans to compensate management for superior performance.

Theoretically, proxy requirement and, hence, the annual election of officers and directors puts the individual outside stockholder on an equal basis with the institutional holder and with management. In reality, however, some individuals and institutions are "more equal than others." Unless you own a substantial amount of a public company's stock (5% or more), you best route, if you feel that a company's management is incompetent or self-serving, is to "vote with your feet," that is, to sell your shares. Most professional investors and money managers use this strategy.

Although, as an individual shareholder, your ability to influence the company's management is limited, a proxy statement is important to you because it contains information you can use. Chapter 10 discusses the significance of the information contained in a proxy. The following highlights some of the more important information you can glean from a proxy statement.

First and foremost, the proxy provides information about the ages of the company's officers and directors and their business backgrounds. The fact that management is older may mean that the company is a likely candidate for sale or takeover. The proxy statement may also indicate that the company is beyond its growth stage and that management is more interested in preserving the status quo than in expanding and growing. Likewise, the absence of outside directors, that is, directors not directly employed by the corporation, may leave you with the feeling that the corporation is too inbred and its focus and point of view too narrow. The proxy also tells you whether the company is a "family affair." If close relatives are waiting to step into the top positions, you might wonder whether the company is run on the basis of nepotism rather than on sound business judgment. Because such a company is viewed as an extension of the founding family rather than as a business, it is unlikely to be the subject of takeover attempts unless "family squabbles" arise. Finally, the proxy statement furnishes information about the level and nature of management compensation. The compensation management pays itself tells you whether management is interested in seeing the company grow or merely views it as a "cash cow" to be drained of its assets. The level of compensation management pays itself should be compared with the compensation paid by companies of similar size engaged in the same or similar business.

The Annual Meeting

Attending the annual shareholders' meeting is something few investors do although it is one of the basic rights that comes with ownership of stock in a public corporation. Every investor should attend at least one annual meeting, as it gives a real insight into how the affairs of the corporation are conducted. Looking at the pictures in an annual report or the numbers on a balance sheet or income statement never gives you a clear understanding of management's style, goals, or objectives. Particularly if you intend to invest a substantial amount of money in a company, you should make every effort to attend the company's annual meeting and meet management face to face. Your attendance also affords you the opportunity to meet with other shareholders and to appraise their backgrounds, to raise questions you feel are important, and to listen to management's responses to any questions raised. Most professional investors decide to invest in a company only after attending the annual meeting and speaking with senior management. Shareholders who attend annual meetings are generally surprised to find that a company with a thousand or more shareholders may have as few as ten in attendance. The fact that individual shareholders do not attend such meetings may encourage management's abuse of its position.

Priority Claims

In the event that a public company falls on bad times and is liquidated or files for reorganization under the bankruptcy statutes, the common stockholder's rights to share in the remaining assets of the corporation or to have a say in the company's reorganization are subordinate to those of secured creditors, bondholders, and preferred shareholders. Most bankruptcies wipe out the common shareholders, although they may be able to recover something of their investment in certain cases. As a common stockholder you should be aware that most state incorporation laws include a fairness provision, which specifies that a shareholder has the right to petition the state to bring in an outside appraiser if the shareholder believes that the company is being sold (to outsiders or to the company's management) through a *leveraged buy-out* at a price that is out of line with the real worth of the corporation. In today's world, a company's management or outside investors can rarely "steal" a company, because institutional investors react quickly and are likely to sue any company that makes such an attempt. In addition, some law firms specialize in *stockholder derivative suits,* which are class-action suits brought on behalf of all shareholders when it is believed that management is taking advantage of them. Only if there are no institutional stockholders or if stock ownership is fragmented among a number of small and unsophisticated investors, can management get away with this type of abuse of its position. The federal and state regulatory authorities also discourage such practices.

Protecting Yourself Against Fraud

In the preceding section, you learned what your rights are as a shareholder of a public corporation. You also learned how best to utilize these rights to improve your ability to judge the merits of investing in a particular company. In this section, we point out some common "scams"—tricks used to separate investors from their hard-earned money. We discuss where you can turn for help if you feel that you have been wronged by someone in the investment community, or if you have fallen victim to one of these schemes.

About 99% of all scams (frauds) worked on individual investors start with a phone call. The caller most likely claims to be an employee of a major investment firm or a financial advisor with a long history of making clients rich. In most instances, the caller puts the person receiving the call on the defensive and pressures for quick action "before the opportunity of a lifetime passes by." The products offered may range from a tax-shelter offering a 10-to-1 write-off (meaning that for every dollar you invest in the shelter, you can write off ten dollars on your taxes) to schemes involving currency futures and rare metals, participation in "government-sponsored" lotteries of oil and gas leases, and investments in silver and gold coins and gems. What the caller offers for sale varies with what is currently in vogue in the news. These scams are particularly reprehensible because they are most effective with the elderly and with others who are least able to afford the loss. Because scams operate from out-of-town locations that change frequently, (as do the corporate names), it is nearly impossible for small investors to recover any of their money. Trade associations and regulatory bodies, as well as people who work in the securities industry, attempt to weed out con artists from the securities business but individual investors must still be wary.

How can you avoid falling victim to such calls? First, you should always investigate before you invest. Since most fraudulent sales pitches appeal to human greed, you should always ask yourself if the return promised is totally out of proportion to anything you have seen before. Always ask yourself, *"If the deal is so good, why are the promoters not keeping it for themselves?"*

The following checklist includes questions you should ask a caller before you invest any money. As an investor you have the right to ask these questions and to obtain accurate answers.

Investor Checklist

1. *Where did you get my name?* No legitimate salesperson would hesitate to answer such a question; if the caller is vague or reluctant to reply to this question, invest your money elsewhere.

2. *Will I receive a prospectus or offering circular?* You should never commit any money until you have received and read a document that decribes all aspects of your prospective investment.

3. *What are the risks involved?* Some investments are not suitable for particular investors; salespersons should fully explain all risks involved in the investments they recommend.

4. *How much commission must I pay to make this investment?* The level of commission paid to a salesperson tells a lot about the availability of buyers for an investment product.

5. *To what regulatory body or industry association does the firm you are selling for belong?* If the salesperson is vague or unwilling to answer this question, end the conversation. If the information is supplied to you, call the agency or industry body named to determine if the firm is indeed registered or a member.

6. *What happens if I decide to liquidate my investment?* Be sure the salesperson fully explains all the terms and penalties connected with a withdrawal from or liquidation of the investment.

7. *(for a stock or bond) Where is this security traded and who are the market-makers?* If you buy a highly speculative stock (referred to as a penny stock), you should be made aware of the risk it entails and given the opportunity to contact other market-makers in the stock to check that the price quoted to you is in line with the market. You should also be given the opportunity to research the stock before you enter a buy order.

8. *May I have a list of banks and other financial institutions that have dealt with you in the past?* Even when such references are given, you should contact the Better Business Bureau to determine whether the company or the individual has been the subject of complaints, and the nature of any such complaints.

9. *Can I refer you to my accountant or lawyer for any additional questions they might have?* This question is a good one to ask

any cold caller. By all means let your accountant or lawyer speak to the salesperson before you commit any money.

10. *Will I have an opportunity to meet you face-to-face?* If this call or pitch is from a crooked firm, the caller will refuse to meet you because of the time involved and because the sales techniques of such firms work better on the telephone than in person. If the caller agrees to such a meeting, bring your lawer, accountant, or financial advisor with you.

If you use this investor checklist, you should be able to successfully screen out the crooks from the legitimate salespeople. A key point to remember is that any legitimate salesperson will furnish all the information you request and will not put any time pressures on you or urge you to invest before the opportunity disappears. Do your investigating before you invest.

Preventing and Correcting Errors

Most problems investors encounter fall into one of two categories. The first category consists of outright stealing of investor's money through some sort of scam or phony transaction. In the preceding section, we outlined the questions you should ask to protect yourself from being taken in by any of these schemes. If you *are* taken in, it is difficult if not impossible to recover your money. You should, however, contact the regulatory authorities immediately and describe the circumstances. In the case of a nonsecurity transaction, such as the purchase of gems, or gold and silver coins, contact the local district attorney's office. If you were contacted about the investment via a mail solicitation you should notify the postal inspectors. If the investment was related to securities, you should contact the SEC, state securities officials, and the various industry associations. Any hope of recovering your investment depends on the speed with which you act.

The more common problems encountered by individual investors fall into a second category: disputes about the execution of a particular trade or about the way an account is handled. Problems related to a particular transaction may arise when the buy or sell order is entered. For example, you may be surprised to receive a confirmation in the mail for a particular trade because you believe that you never actually gave the order to the account executive (AE). Or a problem may arise if you believe an error was made in the way an order was entered or executed. The practice of placing orders over the telephone rather than in person, increases the likelihood of error. For this reason, more and more brokerage firms—particularly discount brokers—make tape-recordings of all conversations between brokers and customers. The vast majority of individual brokers and firms active in the securities business are honest and fair in their dealings with the public; the errors that occur are simply that—with no intention to cheat the customer.

Select the Right Account Executive For You

How can you prevent such errors from occurring? First, take adequate time to select your account executives (AEs) or brokers before you do any business with them. Chapter 7 discusses this process in detail; we review here some of the more important points.

The key to this selection process is compatibility: your personality, your goals, and your approach to investing must be compatible with those of your AE. Many of the problems that arise between customer and AE stem from incompatibility in these areas. Both you and your AE should understand each other's background and goals before entering into that first trade. Second, check out the brokerage firm that employs the AE. *Does the firm have a good reputation?* Third, ask the AE about previous employment. If an AE has been employed by a number of "marginal firms" (firms you have never heard of or whose principal business is the underwriting and sale of penny stocks), you should seriously consider whether it is appropriate for you, in your particular financial circumstances, to deal with such a person. Likewise, you might also be concerned that an

AE who has frequently switched firms may have been terminated by these firms for any number of reasons.

How can you check out a particular AE and firm? To check out any firm or AE, you can call or write the U.S. Securities & Exchange Commission, the registration sections of the various exchanges, and the National Association of Securities Dealers. (Refer to the Reference section at the end of this book for more information.) Although these agencies and self-regulatory bodies cannot endorse a particular AE or the firm employing such a person, they can tell you whether the AE or firm is, in fact, registered (that is, licensed to conduct a securities business). These organizations can furnish the names of the AE's past employers and can inform you if the AE or the firm has been the subject of disciplinary actions. As in most business dealings, you must judge the character and honesty of the account executive and the brokerage firm before you do business with them.

Even if you take all the necessary precautions and check the credentials of all parties you do business with, the likelihood persists that an error or disagreement will occur in connection with your account. The first step in resolving such a problem is to discuss it directly with your AE. The majority of problems and errors are resolved at this level. However, if you and the AE cannot resolve the problem, the next step is to speak to the firm's office manager. The office manager is responsible to see that the AEs employed by the firm conduct business in an ethical and honest manner. Most brokerage firms require their office managers to review on a daily basis all trades that go through the branch office, looking for errors, questionable or unauthorized transfers of funds, and concentrations of buying or selling in a security that is unfamiliar to the firm. This scrutiny enables the office manager to spot and correct most errors and irregularities before they reach a customer's account. The office manager (through years of experience) is usually able to spot "problem" AEs and warn or fire them if necessary. So if you are unable to resolve a matter directly with your AE, a meeting between yourself, the account executive, and the branch office manager will most likely bring about its resolution.

Deal With the Compliance Department

The majority of brokerage firms have compliance departments, which function as internal auditors. The compliance department is charged with the overall supervision of a firm's branch offices and branch managers and should know if a particular branch is poorly supervised and/or if its employees act in a dishonest manner. If you have a problem, the final level of appeal within a firm is to the compliance and/or legal department.

Where To Turn For Help

Most problems and difficulties between AEs and customers are resolved internally. However, Congress, the various states, and the securities industry itself provide additional means for customers who feel they have been treated unfairly to seek redress. These agencies and legal authorities want to know if the management of a public company uses its position to steal from the company, if individuals profit from using "inside information" about impending corporate developments, and/or if any organized attempt is made to manipulate the price of a company's stock. In this section, we describe the various protections and defenses available to you as an individual investor and how to use them to assert your rights.

One of the first places individual investors consider turning in the event of difficulties with an AE or a brokerage firm is to the *Securities & Exchange Commission* (SEC). The name of the SEC appears almost daily in the financial press in connection with actions against public corporations or brokerage firms. (The number of such actions is small, however, considering how many public companies and securities firms are operating today, and the number of people employed in the business.)

How can the SEC assist the individual investor seeking to redress a wrong? Most problems are presented to the SEC either in the form of a letter or a personal meeting between the investor and the SEC's representative. In many ways a letter is the best approach because it allows you to describe what occurred in your own words and in a logical and coherent manner. When sending such a letter, you should include *copies* of any correspondence, confirmations, or documents in your possession that relate to the transaction in question. (Always keep your originals in a safe place—you may need them.) On receipt of such a letter or after a complaint is presented in person, the SEC must determine if the federal securities laws have been violated. In making this determination, the SEC consults all parties involved in the transaction—the AE as well as the customer. Many disputes between AEs, the firms who employ them, and their customers are resolved at this level. Most complaints involving transaction errors or failure to deliver securities or dividends are also resolved here. If it can be shown that the firm or the particular account executive has a pattern of dishonest and illegal activity, the SEC may bar the individual and/or the firm from the securities business and refer the matter to the U.S. Attorney's office for criminal prosecution.

Can the SEC recover money for an individual investor who has been defrauded? The answer to this question is no. The SEC is not a collection agency. However, an SEC action against an AE, a brokerage firm, or a public corporation can be used as the basis for a civil suit brought by the wronged investor. In instances where well-known brokerae firms are the subject of SEC action, the firms generally seek to make good to the investors, if for no other reason than to reduce the bad publicity that accompanies SEC action.

State authorities play a role similar to that of the SEC. The effectiveness of state securities authorities vaies considerably from one state to another as well as from one administration to another. The state authorities use their power to regulate limited partnerships set up as tax shelters, or for specific purposes (such as to raise money to finance a Broadway show). Many state authorities actively pursue the promoters of con schemes worked on the residents of the particular state or locale. The state and local authorities work closely with the federal authorities in seeking to eliminate the "bad apples" from the securities business. Like the SEC, state authorities are not empowered to represent individual investors nor to recover money on behalf of such investors.

How to Recover Your Money

If federal and state authorities cannot recover money you lost to a con artist or crooked brokerage firm, *what can you do to get your money back?* Two basic mechanisms exist: arbitration and the use of private counsel.

Arbitration

Within the past few years, the securities industry has adopted a simplified uniform procedure for the processing and handling of cases in which investors seek to recover money from brokerage firms. The arbitration procedure comes into play when the claim against the brokerage firm is for $5,000 or less.

What steps must you take to initiate an arbitration procedure? Three steps are involved in starting an arbitration procedure. First, you must file with the arbitration authority a typewritten or printed letter describing the nature of the claim. (Most securities industry organizations such as the NYSE, AMEX, and other regional exchanges have their own arbitration director, to whom you send this letter.) Second, you must deposit with the arbitration authority a check or money order, in an amount prescribed by Section 2(c) of the Uniform Code. This requirement is intended to eliminate frivolous complaints; the final disposition of the deposit is left to the ruling of the arbitrator. Third, the complainant must sign and return to the authorities a submission agreement, stating that the complainant will submit to the jurisdiction of the arbitration authority and will accept the decision it reaches.

The arbitration process itself is relatively straightforward.

The arbitration authority appoints an arbitrator (usually an individual who is not associated with or employed by a brokerage firm or securities industry association) to look into the matter. The arbitrator examines the claim submitted by the individual investor and determines if the matter can be resolved to the satisfaction of all parties involved without going to an actual hearing. The complainant has the right to insist on an actual arbitration hearing; but in many cases the mere presence of an impartial arbitrator results in settlement without a hearing.

If the complainant requests it, or the arbitrator feels that the matter cannot be resolved on the basis of the letter and the submitted documents, a date will be set for a formal arbitration hearing. This hearing is similar to a regular court procedure: The arbitrator and witnesses are sworn in, and each party is given the opportunity to make an opening statement. The individual making the complaint presents a case using the relevant documents and the testimony of live witnesses, and the parties that are the subject of the complaint are allowed to present their side of the case. Counterclaims and closing statements conclude the arbitration proceeding. After all the facts have been presented, the arbitrator reviews the whole matter, reaches a decision, and advises the disputing parties of the decision by mail. The arbitrator is empowered to order a brokerage firm to return money to an individual investor; and any decision is final as provided in the submission agreement.

This arbitration procedure has worked well when it involved a brokerage firm that was registered with the relevant authorities and a member of the Securities Industry Association. However, if the individual or firm is a fly-by-night operation without any fixed location or address, it is virtually impossible to use this procedure to recover money. Therefore, you *must* check out individual salespersons and the firms that employ them before you enter into any transactions.

Private Counsel

If more than $5,000 are involved is a dispute, or if you feel that a court of law would provide a better forum for your case,

you can retain legal counsel and sue the AE and the firm involved in the transaction. In recent years, a number of individual investors have brought such suits successfully and have
been awarded large sums of money. The successful suits have
had certain elements in common: First, the investors involved
were able to show that they were relatively unsophisticated in
the area of investing and that the trades in question were the
first ones they entered into. The investors were also able to
show that the disputed investments were totally inappropriate
or excessive, considering the investors' ages or financial circumstances. For example, a court of law might find high-risk
growth stocks or active option trading using complex strategies
to be inappropriate investments for someone 85-years old.
Many successful suits have shown that the AE used excessive
influence in dealing with an older or infirm customer. But even
in the most blatant instances, the costs of bringing such suits
are high, and the party bringing the suit has no guarantee of
success.

Final Comments

As we noted earlier in the chapter, most disputes investors
have with their account executives and brokerage firms relate
to errors or mistakes in the execution of trades. Many of these
complaints stem from mismatches between the personality and
philosophy of the customer and those of the AE or the brokerage firm. The majority of these complaints, however, can be
easily resolved. If you feel uncomfortable with or distrust a
particular AE, the wise move is to look for another AE with
whom you are more comfortable. Changing AEs (as discussed
in Chapter 7) is an easy process.

Sources for Additional Information on Brokerage Firms

- U.S. Securities and Exchange Commission, Public Reference
  Room, Washington, D.C. 20549, (202) 272-7450. Order a
  copy of a brokerage firm's registration statement (Form BD).

- U.S. Securities and Exchange Commission, Office of Consumer Affairs and Information Services, Washington, D.C. 20549, (202) 272-7440. "Consumers Should Know" booklet, "Investigate Before You Invest" booklet, "How To Proceed With The Arbitration of a Small Claim" booklet.

Regional and Branch Offices

- Region 1
  NEW YORK REGIONAL OFFICE, 26 Federal Plaza, Room 1028, New York, NY 10278, (212) 264-1636. Region: New York and New Jersey.

- Region 2
  BOSTON REGIONAL OFFICE, 150 Causeway St., Boston, MA 02144, (617) 223-2721. Region: Maine, New Hampshire, Vermont, Massachusetts, Rhode Island, Connecticut.

- Region 3
  ATLANTA REGIONAL OFFICE, 1375 Peachtree St., NE, Suite 788, Atlanta, GA 30367. (404) 347-4768, Region: Tennessee, Virgin Islands, Puerto Rico, North Carolina, South Carolina, Georgia, Alabama, Mississippi, Florida, and Louisiana east of the Atchafalaya River.

- MIAMI BRANCH OFFICE, Dupont Plaza Center, 300 Biscayne Blvd. Way, Suite 500, Miami, FL 33131, (305) 350-5765.

- Region 4
  CHICAGO REGIONAL OFFICE, Everett McKinley Dirksen Blvd. 219 South Dearborn St., Room 1204, Chicago, IL 60604, (312) 353-7390. Region: Michigan, Ohio, Kentucky, Wisconsin, Indiana, Iowa, Illinois, Minnesota, and Missouri.

- DETROIT BRANCH OFFICE, 231 W. Lafayette, 438 Federal Bldg. and U.S. Courthouse, Detroit, MI 48226, (313) 226-6070.

- Region 5
  FORT WORTH REGIONAL OFFICE, 411 W. Seventh St., 8th Floor, Forth Worth, TX 76102, (817) 334-3821. Region: Oklahoma, Arkansas, Texas, and Louisiana west of the Atchafalaya River and Kansas.

- HOUSTON BRANCH OFFICE, 7500 San Felipe St., Suite 550, Houston, TX 77063, (713) 266-3671.

- Region 6
  DENVER REGIONAL OFFICE, 410 17th St., Suite 700, Denver, CO 80202, (303) 844-2071. Region: North Dakota, South Dakota, Wyoming, Nebraska, Colorado, New Mexico, and Utah.

- SALT LAKE BRANCH OFFICE, U.S. Post Office and Courthouse, 350 S. Main St., Room 505, Salt Lake City, UT 84101, (801) 524-5796.

- Region 7
  LOS ANGELES REGIONAL OFFICE, 5757 Wilshire Blvd., Suite 500 East, Los Angeles, CA 90036-3648, (213) 468-3098. Region: Nevada, Arizona, California, Hawaii, and Guam.

- SAN FRANCISCO BRANCH OFFICE, 450 Golden Gate Ave., Box 36042, San Francisco, CA 94102, (415) 556-5264.

- Region 8
  SEATTLE REGIONAL OFFICE, 3040 Jackson Federal Building, 915 Second Avenue, Seattle, WA 98174, (206) 442-7990. Region: Montana, Idaho, Washington, Oregon, and Alaska.

- Region 9
  PHILADELPHIA REGIONAL OFFICE, 600 Arch Street, Room 2204, Philadelphia, PA 19106, (215) 597-3100. Region: Pennsylvania, Delaware, Maryland, Virginia, West Virginia and District of Columbia.

- The National Association of Securities Dealers, 1735 K Street, N.W., Washington, D.C. 20006, (202) 728-8000, (for over-the-counter securities).

- Municipal Securities Rulemaking Board, 1150 Connecticut Avenue, N.W., Suite 507, Washington, D.C. 20036. (202) 223-9347, (for municipal bonds).

Glossary

Account Executive (AE)   A brokerage firm employee who advises clients and handles orders for them. The AE must be registered with the National Association of Securities Dealers (NASD) before taking orders from clients. Also known as registered representative (RR) or financial consultant.

Accounting Equation   A formula used in totalling balance sheets:

Total assets = Total liabilities + Shareholder's equity.

The formula may be restated in terms of shareholder's equity or in terms of total liabilities as follows:

Total assets − Total liabilities = Shareholder's equity or Total assets − Shareholder's equity = Total liabilities.

Accounts Receivable   Any money due a business for merchandise or securities that it has sold or for services it has rendered. This is a key determinant in analyzing a company's liquidity.

Accrued Interest   (1) The amount of interest due the seller, from the buyer, on settlement of a bond trade. (2) Prorated interest due since the last interest payment date.

Acid Test Ratio The value of cash, cash equivalents, and accounts receivable (the quick assets) divided by current liabilities. A measurement of corporate liquidity. Also known as quick asset ratio or liquidity ratio.

All-or-None Order An order to buy or sell more than one round lot of stock at one time and at a designated price or better. It must not be executed until both conditions can be satisfied simultaneously.

Alternative (Either/Or) Order An order to do either of two alternatives such as either buy at a limit or buy stop for the same security. Execution of one part of the order automatically cancels the other part.

Annual Report A formal statement issued yearly by a corporation to its shareowners. It shows assets, liabilities, equity, revenues, expenses, and so forth. It is a reflection of the corporation's condition at the close of the business year, and the result of operations for that year.

Arrearage Undeclared and/or unpaid dividends due holders of cumulative preferred stock.

As Agent The role of a broker/dealer firm when it acts as an intermediary, or broker, between its customer and another customer, a market-maker, or a contrabroker. For this service the firm receives a stated commission or fee. This is an "agency transaction." *See* As Principal.

As Principal The role of a broker/dealer firm when it buys and sells for its own account. In a typical transaction, it buys from a market-maker or contrabroker and sells to a customer at a fair and reasonable markup; if it buys from a customer and sells to the market maker at a higher price, the trade is called a markdown. *See* As Agent.

Ask-Bid System A system used to place a market order. A market order is one the investor wants executed immediately at the best prevailing price. The market order to buy requires a purchase at the lowest offering (asked) price, and a market order to sell requires a sale at the highest (bid) price. The bid price is what the dealer is willing to pay for the stock, while the ask price is the price at which the dealer will sell to individual investors. The difference between the bid and ask prices is the spread. *See* Bid-and-Asked Quotations.

Assets   Everything of value that a company owns or has due: cash, buildings and machinery (fixed assets), and patents and good will (intangible assets). *See* Equity.

Authorized Stock   The maximum number of shares that the state secretary permits a corporation to issue.

Balance Sheet   A condensed statement showing the nature and amount of a company's assets, liabilities, and capital on a given date. It shows in dollar amounts what the company owns, what it owes, and the ownership interest (shareholders' equity).

Bar Chart   In technical analysis, a chart used to plot stock movements with darkened vertical bars indicating price ranges. Most charts are issued daily, weekly, or monthly.

Barter   To trade by exchange of commodities.

Bearer Bond   A bond that does not have the owner's name registered on the books of the issuing corporation and that is payable to the bearer.

Bear Market   A securities market characterized by declining prices. *See* Bull Market.

Bear Raiders   Groups of speculators who pool capital and sell short to drive prices down and who then buy to cover their short positions—thereby pocketing large profits. This practice was outlawed by the Securities Exchange Act of 1934.

Best-Efforts Offering   An offering of newly issued securities in which the investment banker acts merely as an agent of the corporation, promising only his "best efforts" in making the issue a success but not guaranteeing the corporation its money for any unsold portion. *See* All-or-None (AON) Offering.

Bid-and-Asked Quotation (or Quote)   The bid is the highest price anyone has declared that he/she wants to pay for a security at a given time; the asked is the lowest price anyone will accept at the same time.

Block   A large amount of securities, generally a minimum of either 10,000 shares or $200,000.

Blue Chip Stocks   Common stocks of well known companies with histories of profit growth and dividend payment, as well as quality management, products, and services. Blue chip stocks are usually high-priced and low-yielding. The term "blue chip" comes from the game of poker in which the blue chip holds the highest value.

Bond   A certificate representing creditorship in a coporation and issued by the corporation to raise capital. The company pays interest on a bond issue at specified dates and eventually redeems it at maturity, paying principal plus interest due.

Branch Office Manager (BOM)   The person charged with one or more of a member firm's branch offices. This person must meet certain requirements, such as passing a special exchange examination. Those who supervise the sales activities of three or more account executives must also pass the branch office manager examination.

Breakout   In technical analysis, the rise through a resistance level or the decline through a support level by the market price of a security.

Broker   An agent, often a member of a stock exchange firm or the head of a member firm, who handles the public's orders to buy and sell securities and commodities, for which service a commission is charged. *See* As Agent; As Principal.

Bull Market   A securities market characterized by rising prices. *See* Bear Market.

Buying Power   The dollar amount of securities a customer could purchase without depositing additional funds and continue to meet the initial margin requirements of Regulation T of the Federal Reserve.

Call Feature   (1) A feature of preferred stock through which it may be retired at the corporation's option by paying a price equal to or slightly higher than either the par or market value. (2) A bond feature by which all or part of an issue may be redeemed by the corporation before maturity and under certain specified conditions.

Capital Gain (Loss)   Profit (or loss) from the sale of a capital asset. Capital gains may be short-term (6 months or less) or long-term (more than 6 months). Capital losses are used to offset capital gains to establish a net position for tax purposes.

Cash Account   An account in a brokerage firm in which all transactions are settled on a cash basis.

Cash Cow   A colloquial term for any business that generates an ongoing cash flow. These businesses have well-known products and pay dividends reliably.

Cash Dividend   Any payment made to a corporation's shareholders in cash from current earnings or accumulated profits. Cash dividends are taxable as income.

Certificate of Deposit (CD)   A negotiable security issued by commercial banks against money deposited with them for a specified period of time. CDs vary in size according to the amount of the deposit and the maturity period, and they may be redeemed before maturity only by sale in a secondary market.

Charter   A document written by the founders of a corporation and filed with a state. The state approves the articles and then issues a certificate of incorporation. Together, the two documents become the charter and the corporation is recognized as a legal entity. The charter includes such information as the corporation's name, purpose, amount of shares, and the identity of the directors.

Clearance   (1) The delivery of securities and monies in completion of a trade. (2) The comparison and/or netting of trades prior to settlement.

Commission   A broker's fee for handling transactions for a client in an agency capacity.

Commission House Broker   A member of the NYSE executing orders in behalf of his or her own organization and its customers.

Commodity   A bulk good that is grown or mined, such as grains or precious metals. *See* Futures.

Common Stock   A unit of equity ownership in a corporation. Owners of this kind of stock exercise control over corporate affairs and enjoy any capital appreciation. They are paid dividends only after preferred stock. Their interest in the assets, in the event of liquidation, is junior to all others.

Conversion   (1) A bond feature by which the owner may exchange his or her bonds for a specified number of shares of stock. Interest paid on such bonds is lower than the usual interest rate for straight debt issues. (2) A feature of some preferred stock by which the owner is entitled to exchange preferred for common stock, usually of the same company, in accordance with the terms of the issue. (3) A feature of some mutual fund offerings allowing an investor to exchange shares for comparable value in another fund with different objectives handled by the same management group.

Convertible Bond   Bond that can be exchanged for a specified number of another security, usually shares, at a prestated price. Convertibility typically enhances the bond's marketability.

Convertible Preferred Stock   *See* Conversion (2).

Corporation   A business organization chartered by a state secretary as a recognized legal institution of and by itself and operated by an association of individuals, with the purpose of ensuring perpetuity and limited financial liability.

Credit Agreement A document containing the complete terms and arrangements by which financing will be conducted in a customer's account. It emphasizes when and how interest is charged for the lending service provided.

Crowd *See* Trading Crowd.

Cumulative Preferred Stock A preferred stock that accrues any omitted dividends as a claim against the company. This claim must be paid in full before any dividends may be paid on the company's common stock.

Current Market Value (1) According to Regulation T of the Federal Reserve Board, the latest closing price (or quotation, if no sale occurred). (2) According to NYSE rules, the up-to-the-minute last sale price of a security.

Current Ratio Current assets divided by current liabilities. Also known as working capital ratio.

Current Yield The annual dollar interest paid by a bond divided by its market price. It is the actual return rate, not the coupon rate. Example: Any bond carrying a 6% coupon and trading at 95 is said to offer a current yield of 6.3% ($60 coupon $\div$ $950 market price = 6.3%).

Customer's Agreement A document that explains the terms and conditions under which a brokerage firm consents to finance a customer's credit transaction. Also known as margin agreement or hypothecation agreement.

Cyclical Stock Any stock, such as housing industry-related stock, that tends to rise in price quickly when the economy turns up and fall quickly when the economy turns down.

Date of Record The date set by the corporate board of directors for the transfer agent to close the agency's books to further changes in registration of stock and to identify the recipients of a forthcoming distribution. Also known as record date. *See* Ex-Dividend Date.

Dealer   An individual or firm in the securities business acting as a principal rather than as an agent.

Debenture   An unsecured debt offering by a corporation, promising only the general assets as protection for creditors. Sometimes the so-called "general assets" consist of only goodwill and reputation.

Debit Balance   The balance owed by a customer in his or her account as reflected on the brokerage firm's ledger statement of settled transactions.

Debt/Equity Ratio   The ratio of long-term debt to shareholders' equity.

Debt Instrument   A bond or bond-like security—a non-equity.

Declaration Date   The day on which a corporation's board of directors announces a dividend.

Default   The failure of a corporation to pay principal and/or interest on outstanding bonds or dividends on its preferred stock.

Discount Bond   A bond that sells in the marketplace at a price below its face value.

Distribution   The sale of a large block of stock, through either an underwriting or an exchange distribution.

Diversification   (1) Spreading investments and contingent risks among different companies in different fields of endeavor. (2) Investing in the securities of one company that owns or has holdings in other companies. (3) Investing in a fund with a portfolio containing many securities.

Dividend Payout   The percentage of dividends distributed in terms of what is available out of current net income.

Dividends   Distributions to stockholders declared by the corporate board of directors.

Dividends Payable   A current liability showing the amount due to stockholders for dividends declared but not yet paid.

Dow-Jones Average A market average indicator consisting (individually) of (1) thirty industrial, (2) twenty transportation, and (3) fifteen public utility common stocks; the composite average includes these 65 stocks collectively.

Dow Theory A theory predicated on the belief that the rise or fall of stock prices is both a mirror and a forecaster of business activities.

Equity (1) The ownership interest in a company of holders of its common and preferred stock. (2) The excess of value of securities over the debit balance in a margin (general) account.

Escrow Assets in a third-party account to ensure the completion of a contract by all parties.

Ex-Dividend (Without Dividend) Date A date set by the Uniform Practice Committee or by the appropriate stock exchange, on which a given stock will begin trading in the marketplace without the value of a pending dividend included in the contract price. It is closely related to and dependent on the date of record. It is often represented as "X" in the stock listing tables in the newspapers.

Execution Synonym for a transaction or trade between a buyer and seller.

Expiration Date The date an option contract becomes void. The expiration date for listed stock options is the Saturday after the third Friday of the expiration month. All holders of options who wish to exercise must indicate their desire to do so by this date.

Farm Credit Bank Bank set up to deal with the specific financial needs of farmers and their businesses.

Federal Home Loan Banks (FHLB) A government-sponsored agency that finances the home-building industry with mortgage loans from monies raised on offerings of bond issues; interest on these bonds is free from state and local income tax.

Federal National Mortgage Association (FNMA) A publicly owned, government-sponsored corporation that purchases and sells mortgages insured by the Federal Housing Administration (FHA) or Farmers Home Administration (FHA); or guaranteed by the Veterans' Administration (VA). Interest on these bonds, called Fannie Maes, is fully taxable.

Fill-or-Kill (FOK) Order An order that requires the immdiate purchase or sale of a specified amount of stock, though not necessarily at one price. If the order cannot be filled immediately, it is automatically cancelled (killed).

Floor The securities trading area of an exchange. *See* Trading Post; Ring.

Floor Broker A person who works on the exchange floor executing the orders of public customers or other investors who do not have physical access to the area.

Floor Order Tickets Abbreviated forms of order tickets, used on the floor of the exchange for recording executions.

Flower Bond A type of treasury bond selling at a discount with a special privilege attached permitting redemption after the death of the owner at par value in satisfaction of federal estate taxes. These bonds were issued prior to April 1, 1971, and will be in circulation up to final maturity in 1998.

Fundamental Analysis A method for analyzing the prospects of a security through the observation of accepted accounting measures such as earnings, sales, assets, and so on. *See* Technical Analysis.

Futures Short for futures contract, which is an agreement to make or take delivery of a commodity at a specified future time and price. The contract is transferable and can therefore be traded like a security. Although futures contracts were once limited to commodities, they are now available on financial instruments, currencies, and indexes. Noncommodity futures contracts often differ from their predecessors in important respects; for example, "delivery" on an index is irrelevant.

Going Public A private company is "going public" when it first offers its shares to the investing public.

Good-til-Cancelled (GTC or Open) Order An order to buy or sell that remains valid until executed or cancelled by the customer. *See* Limit; Stop; Stop Limit.

Growth Company (Stock) A company (or its stock) that has made fast gains in earnings over the preceding few years and that is likely to keep on showing such signs of growth.

Immediate or Cancel (IOC) Order An order that requires immediate execution at a specified price of all or part of a specified amount of stock; the unexecuted portion has to be cancelled by the broker.

Individual Retirement Account (IRA) Under certain circumstances, individuals not enjoying a qualified retirement plan at their placeof employment may qualify to deduct from their federal taxable income an amount, as specified by the prevailing tax law, and set that amount aside for their retirement.

Indenture A written agreement between corporation and creditors containing the terms of a debt issue, such as rate of interest, means of payment, maturity date, terms of prior payment of principal, collateral, priorities of claims, trustee.

Investment Banker A broker/dealer organization that provides a service to industry through counsel, market making, and underwriting of securities.

Issue (Issuance) (1) Any of a company's class of securities. (2) The act of distributing securities.

Issued-and-Outstanding Stocks That portion of authorized stock distributed among investors by a corporation.

Joint Account An account including two or more people.

Junk Bond Any bond with a Moody's or Standard & Poor's credit rating of BB or lower. Such bonds, usually issued by companies without long track records, can produce high yields.

Keogh Plan Initiated under the provisions of the Self-Employed Individuals Tax Retirement Act of 1962, this term applies to programs that enable an individual to defer payment of any income taxes on either a percentage of annual earned income or $30,000 until the individual retires and begins to withdraw funds from this accumulated pool of capital.

Leverage   (1) In securities, increasing return without increasing investment. Buying stock on margin is an example. (2) In finance, the relationship of a firm's debt to its equity, as expressed in the debt-to-equity ratio. If the company earns a return on the borrowed money greater than the cost of the debt, it is successfully applying the principle of leverage.

Leveraged Buy-out   Taking over a controlling interest in a company using borrowed money.

Limit   The greatest price change permitted by the Chicago Mercantile Exchange in any particular commodity during the trading day.

Limited Trading Authorization   *See* Power of Attorney (2).

Limit Order   An order in which a customer sets a maximum price he or she is willing to pay as a buyer and a minimum price he or she is willing to accept as a seller. *See* Market Order; Stop Order.

Limit Price   A modification of an order to buy or sell. With a *sell* limit order, the customer is instructing the broker to make the sale at or above the limit price. With a *buy* limit order, the customer is instructing the broker to make the purchase at or below the limit price.

Liquidation   The voluntary or involuntary closing out of security positions.

Liquidity   (1) The ability of the market in a particular security to absorb a reasonable amount of trading at reasonable price changes. Liquidity is one of the most important characteristics of a good market. (2) The relative ease with which investors can convert their securities into cash.

Listed Stock   The stock of a company traded on a securities exchange and for which a listing application and registration statement have been filed with the SEC and the exchange itself.

Long Position   The ownership of securities.

Margin   (1) The amount of money or securities that an investor must deposit with a broker to secure a loan from the broker. Brokers may lend money to investors for use in trading securities. To procure such a loan, an investor must deposit cash with the broker. (The amount is prescribed by the Federal Reserve System in Regulation T.) The cash represents the equity, or margin, in the investor's account.

Margin Call   A demand on the customer to deposit money or securities with the broker when a purchase or short-sale is effected.

Margin (General) Account   An account in which a customer uses credit from a broker/dealer to take security positions.

Marketable Security   (1) A security that may be readily purchased or sold. (2) A U.S. government bond freely traded in the open market.

Market-Maker   (1) An options exchange member who trades for his or her own account and risk. This member is charged with the responsibility of trading so as to maintain a fair, orderly, and competitive market. He or she may not act as agent. (2) A firm actively making bids and offers in the OTC market.

Market Not Held Order   An order to buy or sell securities at the current market with the investor leaving the exact timing of its execution up to the floor broker. If the floor broker is holding a "market not held" buy order and the price could decline, he or she may wait to buy when a better price becomes available. There is no guarantee for the investor that a "market not held" order will be filled at a better price than if the order were not marked "not held."

Market Order   An order to be executed immediately at the best available price.

Market Price   (1) The last reported sale price for an exchange-traded security. (2) For over-the-counter securities, a consensus among market-makers.

Market Value   The price that would be paid for a security or other asset.

Maturity (Date)   The date on which a loan, bond, or debenture comes due; both principal and any accrued interest due must be paid.

Missing the Market   The failure by a member of the exchange to execute an order due to his or her negligence. The member is obliged to promptly reimburse the customer for any losses due to the mistake.

Money Market   The market for dealers who trade riskless, short-term securities: T-bills, certificates of deposits, banker's acceptances, and commercial paper.

Money Market Fund   Name for an open-ended investment company whose portfolio consists of money market securities.

Moody's Investors Service   One of the best-known bond rating agencies, owned by Dun & Bradstreet. *Moody's Investment Grade* assigns letter grades to bonds based on their predicted long-term yield (MIG1, MIG2, etc). Moody's also rates commercial paper, municipal short-term issues, and preferred and common stocks. Another publication is a six-volume annual, with weekly or semiweekly supplements, giving great detail on issuers and securities. Publications include *Moody's Bond Record* and *Moody's Bond Survey*. Moody's investment ratings are considered the norm for investment decisions by fiduciaries.

Mortgage-Backed Certificate (Security)   A security (1) that is issued by the Federal Home Loan Mortgage Corporation, the Federal National Mortgage Association, and the Government National Mortgage Association, and (2) that is backed by mortgages. Payments to investors are received out of the interest and principal of the underlying mortgages.

Municipal Bond (Security)   Issued by a state or local government, a debt obligation whose funds may either support a government's general financing needs or be spent on special projects. Many municipal bonds are free from federal tax on the accrued interest and also free from state and local taxes if issued in the state of residence.

Mutual Fund   An open-end investment company. A mutual fund offers the investor the benefits of portfolio diversification (that is, owning more different shares to provide greater safety and reduce volatility).

National Association of Securities Dealers (NASD) An association of broker/dealers in over-the-counter securities organized on a nonprofit, non-stock-issuing basis. Its general aim is to protect investors in the OTC market.

National Association of Securities Dealers Automated Quotation System (NASDAQ) A computerized quotations network by which NASD members can communicate bids and offers. *Level 1* Provides only the arithmetic mean of the bids and offers entered by members. *Level 2* Provides the individual bids and offers next to the name of the member entering the information. *Level 3* Available to NASD members only, enables the member to enter bids and offers and receive Level 2 service.

Net Asset Value (NAV) per Share (1) Net assets divided by the number of outstanding shares. (2) For an open-end investment company, often the net redemption price per share. (3) For a no-load, open-end investment company, both the net redemption price per share and the offering price per share.

Net Profit Margin The ratio of net profit divided by set sales.

New Issue (1) Any authorized but previously unissued security offered for sale by an issuer. (2) The resale of treasury shares.

Nominal Yield The annual interest rate payable on a bond, specified in the indenture and printed on the face of the certificate itself. Also known as coupon yield.

Normal Trading Unit The accepted unit of trading in a given marketplace: On the NYSE it is 100 shares (round lot) for stocks and $1,000 par value for bonds. In some relatively inactive stocks, the unit is 10 shares. For NASDAQ-traded securities it is 100 shares for stocks and $10,000 par value for bonds. *See* Odd Lots; Round Lots.

Nonpurpose Loan A loan involving securities as collateral that is arranged for any purpose other than to purchase, carry, or trade margin securities.

Not Held (NH) Order   An order that does not hold the executing member financially responsible for using his or her personal judgment in the execution price or time of a transaction.

Odd Lot   An amount of stock less than the normal trading unit. *See* Round Lot.

Offer   The price at which a person is ready to sell. *See* Bid-and-Asked Quotation (or Quote).

Offering Circular   (1) A publication that is prepared by the underwriters and that discloses basic information about an issue of securities to be offered in the primary market. (2) Sometimes used to describe a document used by dealers when selling large blocks of stock in the secondary market.

Office Order Tickets   Transaction order forms filled out in great detail at each sales office of member firms. *See* Floor Order Tickets.

Option   A contract wherein one party (the option writer) grants another party (buyer) the right to demand that the writer perform a certain act.

Order Department   A group that routes buy and sell instructions to the trading floors of the appropriate stock exchanges and executes orders in the OTC market for trading accounts of both firms and customers.

Over-the-Counter Market (OTC)   (1) A securities market, conducted mainly over the telephone, made up of dealers who may or may not be members of a securities exchange. Thousands of companies have insufficient shares outstanding, stockholders, or earnings to warrant listing on a national exchange. Securities of these companies are therefore traded in the over-the-counter market between dealers who act either as agents for their customers or as principals. The over-the-counter market is the principal market for U.S. government and municipal bonds and for stocks of banks and insurance companies.

Paper Loss/Profit   An unrealized loss or profit on a security still held. Paper losses and profits become actual when a security position is closed out by a purchase or sale.

Partnership   A type of business organization typified by two or more proprietors.

Pass-Through Security (P/T)   A debt security representing an interest in a pool of mortgages requiring monthly payments composed of interest on unpaid principal and a partial repayment of principal. Thus the payments are passed through the intermediaries, from the debtors to investors.

Par Value   The face or nominal value of a security. (1) A dollar amount assigned to a share of common stock by the corporation's charter. At one time, it reflected the value of the original investment behind each share, but today it has little significance except for bookkeeping purposes. Many corporations do not assign a par value to new issues. For preferred shares or bonds, par value has importance insofar as it signifies the dollar value on which the dividend/interest is figured and the amount to be repaid upon redemption. (2) Preferred dividends are usually expressed as a percentage of the stock's par value. (3) The interest on bonds is expressed as a percentage of the bond's par value.

Payment Date   The day a corporation makes payment of dividends to its previously determined holders of record.

Penny Stocks   Colloquial term for—but not limited to—low-priced, high-risk stocks that usually sell for less than $1 per share. These shares usually require a special margin maintenance requirement, and purchases are often limited to unsolicited orders.

Pink Sheets   A list of securities being traded by over-the-counter market makers, published every business day by the National Quotations Bureau. Equity securities are published separately on long pink sheets. Debt securities are published separately on long yellow sheets.

Point   (1) In stocks, $1. (2) In bonds, since a bond is quoted as a percentage of $1,000, a point equals $10. For example, a municipal security discounted at 3 1/2 points equals $35. It is quoted at 96 1/2 or $965 per $1,000. (3) In market averages, it means simply a point—a unit of measure.

Point and Figure (P&F) Chart   In technical analysis, a chart of price changes in a security. Upward price changes are plotted as *Xs*, and downward prices are plotted as *Os*. Time is *not* reflected on this type of chart.

Portfolio   Holdings of securities by an individual or institution. A portfolio may include preferred and common stocks, as well as bonds, of various enterprises.

Preferred Stock   Owners of this kind of stock are entitled to a fixed dividend to be paid regularly before dividends can be paid on common stock. In the event of liquidation, claims to assets are senior to those of holders of common stock but junior to those of bondholders. Holders of preferred stock normally do not have a voice in management.

Power of Attorney   (1) The legal right conferred by a person or institution upon another to act in the former's stead. (2) In the securities industry, a *limited power of attorney* given by a customer to a representative of a broker/dealer would normally give a registered representative trading discretion over the customer's account. The power is limited in that neither securities nor funds may be withdrawn from the account by the representative. (3) In the securities industry, an *unlimited power of attorney* given by a customer to a representative of a broker/dealer would normally give a registered representative full discretion over the conduct of the customer's account.

Preliminary Official Statement (POS)   Also known as the preliminary prospectus, the preliminary version or draft of an official statement, as issued by the underwriters or issuers of a security, and subject to change prior to the confirmation of offering prices or interest rates. It is the only form of communication allowed between a broker and prospective buyer before the effective date, usually to gauge the interest of prospective purchasers. Offers of sale are not accepted on the basis of a preliminary statement. A statement to that effect, printed in red, appears vertically on the face of the document. This caveat, required by the Securities Act of 1933, is what gives the document its nickname, "red herring."

Preliminary Prospectus *See* Preliminary Official Statement (POS).

Premium (1) The amount by which the price paid for a preferred security exceeds its face value. (2) The total price of an option, equal to the intrinsic value plus the time value premium. (3) The market price of a bond selling at a price above its face amount. For example, "trading at 101" means that, for $1,010, one could purchase a bond that would pay $1,000 principal at maturity. *See* Discount Bond.

Price-to-Earnings (P/E) Ratio A ratio used by some investors to gauge the relative value of a security in light of current market conditions. Ratio = Market price ÷ Earnings per share.

Price/Equity Ratio The ratio of the market price of a common share to the book value of a common share.

Principal Value The face value of an obligation that must be repaid at maturity and that is separate from interest. Often called simply "principal."

Private Placement The distribution of unregistered securities to a limited number of purchasers without the filing of a statement with the SEC. Such offerings generally require submission of an investment letter to the seller by all purchasers.

Proprietorship (Individual) A type of business structure consisting of one owner, who is personally responsible for all debt liabilities but who also can manage the business as he or she sees fit.

Pro Rata According to a certain rate, in proportion.

Prospectus A document that contains material information for an impending offer of securities (containing most of the information included in the registration statement) and that is used for solicitation purposes by the issuer and underwriters.

Proxy (1) A formal authorization (power of attorney) from a stockholder that empowers someone to vote in his or her behalf. (2) The person who is so authorized to vote on behalf of a stockholder.

Proxy Statement   Material information required by the SEC to be given to a corporation's stockholders as a prerequisite to solicitation of votes.

Public Offering (Distribution)   The offering of securities for sale by an issuer.

Put Option   A privilege giving its holder the right to demand acceptance of his or her delivery of 100 shares of stock at a fixed price any time within a specified lifetime.

Purchase and Sales (P&S) Department   The department in operations responsible for the first processing of a trade. Responsibilities include the recording of order executions, figuring monies due and payable as a result of trades, preparing customer confirmations, and making trade comparisons with other brokers.

Qualified Legal Opinion   A conditional affirmation of a security's legality, which is given before or after the security is sold. An unqualified legal opinion (called a *clean opinion*) is an unconditional affirmation of the legality of securities.

Quick Asset Ratio   *See* Acid Test Ratio.

Rate of Return   (1) In fixed income investment, *see* Current Yield. (2) In corporate financing, *see* Return on Equity.

Record Date   *See* Date of Record.

Redemption   (1) For bonds, the retirement of the securities by repayment of face value or above (that is, at a premium price) to their holders. (2) For mutual funds, the shareholder's privilege of converting his or her interest in the fund into cash— normally at net asset value.

Registered Bond   An outstanding bond whose owner's name is recorded on the books of the issuing corporation. Legal title may be transferred only when the bond is endorsed by the registered owner.

Registered Representative   *See* Account Executive.

Registered (Floor) Trader A member of the NYSE who buys and sells stocks for his or her own account and risk.

Registrar Often a trust company or bank, the registrar is charged with the responsibility of preventing the issuance of more stock than authorized by the company. It insures that the transfer agent issues exactly the same number of shares cancelled with each reregistration of certificates.

Registration Statement A document required to be filed with the SEC by the issuer of securities before a public offering may be attempted. The Securities Act of 1933 mandates that it contain all material and accurate facts. Such a statement is required also when affiliated persons intend offering sizable amounts of securities. The SEC examines the statement for a twenty-day period, seeking obvious omissions or misrepresentations of fact.

Regular Way Contract The most frequently used delivery contract. For stocks and corporate and municipal bonds, this type of contract calls for delivery on the fifth business day after the trade. For U.S. government bonds and options, delivery must be made on the first business day after the trade.

Regulation T A federal regulation that governs the lending of money by brokerage firms to its customers.

Repurchase Agreement (Repo) (1) A Federal Open Market Committee arrangement with a dealer in which it contracts to purchase a government or agency security at a fixed price, with provision for its resale at the same price at a rate of interest determined competitively. Used by dealers in government and municipal securities to reduce carrying costs. This transaction is not legal for nonexempt securities. (2) A method of financing inventory positions by sale to a nonbank institution with the agreement to buy the position back.

Resistance In technical analysis, an area above the current stock price where the stock is available in abundance and where selling is aggressive. This area is said to contain what chartists call a resistance level. For this reason, the stock's price may have trouble rising through the price. *See* Support.

Resistance Level   *See* Resistance.

Retirement of Debt Securities   The repayment of principal and accrued interest due to the holders of a bond issue.

Return on Equity   A corporation's net income divided by shareholder's equity.

Ring   The circular trading area in a commodity exchange. Also called the pit.

Round Lot   A unit of trading or a multiple thereof. On the NYSE, stocks are traded in round lots of 100 shares for active stocks and 10 shares for inactive ones. Bonds are traded in units of $1,000. *See* Normal Trading Unit; Odd Lot.

Savings Bond   Bond issued through the U.S. government at a discount and in face values from $50 to $10,000. The interest is exempt from state and local taxes, and federal tax until the bond is redeemed.

Secondary Market   (1) A term referring to the trading of securities not listed on an organized exchange. (2) A term used to describe the trading of securities other than a new issue.

Securities & Exchange Commission (SEC)   A government agency responsible for the supervision and regulation of the securities industry.

Sell Stop Order   A memorandum that becomes a market order to sell if and when someone trades a round lot at or below the memorandum price.

Settlement (Delivery) Date   The day on which certificates involved in a transaction are due at the purchaser's office.

Share   A stock certificate—a unit of measurement of the equity ownership of a corporation.

Shareholders' (Stockholders') Equity   The financial interest of the stockholders in the net assets of a company. It is the aggregate of the accounts of holders of preferred and common stock accounts, as depicted on a balance sheet.

Short Market Value The market value of security positions that a customer owes to a broker/dealer (short in the account).

Short Position (1) The number of shares in a given security sold short and not covered as of a particular date. (2) The total amount of stock sold short by all investors and not covered as of a particular date. (3) A term used to denote the writer of an option.

Short Sale The sale of a security that is not owned at the time of the trade, necessitating its purchase some time in the future to "cover" the sale. A short sale is made with the expectation that the stock value will decline, so that the sale will be eventually covered at a price lower than the original sale, thus realizing a profit.

Short-Stop (Limit) Order A memorandum that becomes a limit order to sell short when someone creates a round-lot transaction at or below the memorandum price (electing sale). The short sale may or may not be executed since the rules then require that it be sold at least one-eighth above the electing sale as well as high enough in value to satisfy the limit price.

Specialist A member of the NYSE with two essential functions: First, to maintain an orderly market, insofar as is reasonably practicable, in the stocks in which he or she is registered as a specialist. To do this, the specialist must buy and sell for his or her own account and risk, to a reasonable degree, when there is a temporary disparity between supply and demand. To equalize trends, the specialist must buy or sell counter to the direction of the market. Second, the specialist acts as a broker's broker, executing orders when another broker cannot afford the time. At all times the specialist must put the customer's interest before his own. All specialists are registered with the NYSE as regular, substitute, associate, or temporary.

Specialized Companies Investment companies that concentrate their investments in one industry, group of related industries, or a single geographic area of the world for the purpose of long-term capital growth.

Special Miscellaneous (Memorandum) Account (SMA)   An account defined under Regulation T used to record a customer's excess margin and buying power. Excess funds arise from sales proceeds, market value appreciation, dividends, or cash.

Standard & Poor's (S&P) Corporation   A source of investment services, most famous for its *Standard & Poor's Rating* of bonds and its composite index of 425 industrial, 20 transportation, and 55 public utility common stocks, called *Standard & Poor's Index*.

Stocks   Certificates representing ownership in a corporation and a claim on the firm's earnings and assets; they may pay dividends and can appreciate or decline in value. *See* Authorized Stock; Common Stock; Issued-and-Outstanding Stock; Preferred Stock; Treasury Stock.

Stop Limit Order   A memorandum that becomes a limit (as opposed to a market) order immediately after a transaction takes place at or through the indicated (memorandum) price.

Stop Loss Order   A customer's order to set the sell price of a stock below the market price, thus locking in profits or preventing further losses.

Stop Order   A memorandum that becomes a market order only if a transaction takes place at or through the price stated in the memorandum. Buy stop orders are placed above the market, and sell stop orders are placed below it. The sale that activates the memorandum is called the electing (activating or triggering) sale. *See* Market Order; Sell Stop Order.

Street Name   When securities have been bought on margin or when the customer wishes the security to be held by the broker/dealer, the securities are registered and held in the broker/dealer's own firm (or "street") name.

Subscription   An agreement to buy a new issue of securities.

The agreement specifies the *subscription price* (the price for shareholders before the securities are offered to the public). This right is called the subscription privilege or *subscription right*.

Support In technical analysis, an area below the current price of the stock where the stock is in short supply and where the buyers are aggressive. The stock's price is likely not to go lower than this level, which is called a *support level*. *See* Resistance.

Support Level *See* Support.

Sweetener A special feature in a securities offering, such as convertibility, that encourages the purchase of the security.

Technical Analysis An approach to market theory stating that previous price movements, properly interpreted, can indicate future price patterns.

Tennessee Valley Authority (TVA) A government-sponsored agency whose bonds are redeemable from the proceeds of the various power projects in the Tennessee River area. Interest payments on these bonds are fully taxable to investors.

Ticker (Tape) A trade-by-trade report in chronological order of trades executed, giving prices and volumes. Separate tapes exist for various markets. The mechanism used to be mechanical, but it is now some sort of electronic display.

Trade Date The date a trade was entered into, as opposed to settlement date.

Trading Authorization The legal right conferred by one person or institution on another to effect the purchase and/or sale of securities in the former's account.

Trading Crowd Members of an exchange involved in the purchase and sale of a particular issue. They gather at the specialist's position.

Trading Floor The location of any organized exchange where buyers and sellers meet to transact business.

Trading on the Equity The situation that exists when the rate of return a company earns in its business is higher than the cost it pays for the money it borrows, that is, the rate of return is greater than the rate of interest paid on borrowed funds.

Trading Post Twenty-three locations on the floor of the NYSE that were seven-foot-high, horseshoe-shaped structures with an outside circumference of from 26 to 31 feet. The one exception is a table-like structure, Post 30, in the garage, where most inactive preferred stocks are traded in multiples of 10 shares. The posts have been replaced by a round structure with a lot of electronics display.

Transfer Agent An agent of a corportion responsible for the registration of shareowner's names on the company records and the proper re-registration of new owners when a transfer of stock occurs.

Treasury Bill A federal bearer obligation issued in denominations ranging from $10,000 to $1 million with maturity dates usually of three months to a year. A T-bill is fully marketable at a discount from face value (which determines the interest rate).

Treasury Stock Shares of stock reacquired by a corportion through purchase, and occasionally by donation, that are treated as authorized-but-unissued stock for purposes of calculating dividends, voting, or earnings.

Trend Movement, up or down, in a security's market price or in the market itself, for a period of six months or more.

Two-Dollar Broker A member of the New York Stock Exchange who executes orders in any security for any organization, in return for a brokerage fee. The fee, which is negotiable, is actually larger than $2 per trade. These brokers are also known as independent brokers or agents.

Underwriter Also known as an "investment banker" or "distributor," a middleman between an issuing corporation and the public. The underwriter usually forms an underwriting group, called a syndicate, to limit risk and commitment of capital. He or she may also contract with selling groups to help distribute the issue—for a concession. In the distribution of mutual funds, the underwriter may also be known as a "sponsor," "distributor," or even "wholesaler." Investment bankers also offer other services, such as advice and counsel on the raising and investment of capital.

Underwriting Agreement   The contract between the investment banker and the corporation, containing the final terms and prices of the issue. It is signed either on the evening before or early in the morning of the public offering date (effective date).

Uniform Gifts to Minors Act   A simplified law that enables minors to own property or securities in a beneficial fashion without need of trust instruments or other legal documents. Someone of legal age must serve as custodian for the minor's assets. In the securities industry, the term describes securities bought and sold under the provisions of this law.

United States Government Securities   Debt issues of the U.S. government (Treasury Department), backed by the government's unlimited power of taxation, such as Treasury bills, notes, bonds, and Series EE and Series HH bonds. *See* Marketable Securities Savings Bond.

Vertical Line Charting   A method of technical analysis in which the high and low for the period (usually a day) are shown as a vertical line on the chart, with the closing price shown as a small horizontal line.

Warrant   An inducement attached to new securities in distribution giving purchasers a long-term (usually a five- to ten-year) privilege of subscribing to one or more shares of stock reserved for them by the corporation from its unissued or treasury stock reserve. *See* Subscription Right.

Watered Stock   A corporation's issuance of additional shares without increasing its capital. Also called diluting the shares.

Wire House   Any large exchange member firms with many branch offices.

Yield (Rate of Return)   The percentage return on an investor's money in terms of current prices. It is the annual dividend/interest per share or bond, divided by the current market price of that security.

Yield-to-Maturity   The calculation of an average rate of return on a bond (with a maturity over one year) if it is held to its maturity date and if all cash flows are reinvested at the same rate of interest. It includes an adjustment for any premium paid or discount received. It is a calculation used to compare relative values of bonds.

Zero-Coupon Discount Security   A debt security that offers no payments of interest—only payment of full face value at maturity—but that is issued at a deep discount from face value.

Index